Lecture Notes in Economics and Mathematical Systems

542

Springer
Berlin
Heidelberg
New York
Hong Kong
London
Milan
Paris
Tokyo

Jörg Lingens

Union Wage Bargaining and Economic Growth

Springer

Author

Dr. Jörg Lingens
University of Regensburg
Economics Department
Universitätsstr. 31
93053 Regensburg
Germany

Cataloging-in-Publication Number: 2004106460

ISSN 0075-8442
ISBN 3-540-21522-0 Springer-Verlag Berlin Heidelberg New York

Springer-Verlag is a part of Springer Science+Business Media

springeronline.com

Typesetting: Camera ready by author
Cover design: *Erich Kirchner*, Heidelberg

Printed on acid-free paper 55/3142/du 5 4 3 2 1 0

To Julia

Preface

Writing a book is not possible without the generous input of many people. It is a pleasure to have the opportunity to thank at least some of these people.

Prof. Dr. Jochen Michaelis, the supervisor of my dissertation, taught me how to do economic analysis and initiated my interest in labour market issues. Discussions with him have always been enlightening and have greatly improved the analysis in this book. Moreover, he always encouraged me when I experienced a slump in my motivation. He never lost his calmness and good temper, not even in situations when my need for discussion must have been bothering him. Thanks for that Jochen.

I'm indebted to Prof. Dr. Peter Weise for taking over the job as the second referee of my thesis. He gave very valuable comments and sacrificed his christmas holiday to write the referee report as fast as possible. I also want to thank Prof. Stefan Voigt and Prof. Dr. Reinhold Kosfeld, the other two members of the dissertation committee, for the discussion during the defence of the thesis.

Thanks goes to my colleagues at the economics department of the University of Kassel, especially Christina E. Bannier (née Metz) and Martin Debus who never lost their patience with me. Enumerable times I burst into their offices to discuss my ideas and thoughts with them. Nevertheless, they were cheerful, giving fruitful comments and helpful suggestions. Besides discussing economics with them, they also had always time for a nice chat or a good laugh. Thank you both for the good times!

A very special thanks goes to my friend Spiros Andreopoulos. Spiros was the one who opened my eyes to see what economics is really about. He was also the one who inspired me to do research after finishing university. Eventually, this research resulted in the book you are holding in your hands.

Last, but definitely not least, I want to thank the people at home. My parents, Wilhelm and Edith Lingens, who made it possible for me to begin my academic studies, which were a necessary condition for getting the chance of writing the thesis. And my partner Julia Welteke for her encouragement, support and patience.

All these people have been crucial factors in finishing this thesis, however, all shortcomings and errors are solely my responsibility.

Regensburg,
April 2004

Jörg Lingens

Contents

List of Figures

Part I

Introduction

Introduction

There seems to be consensus among economists that growth is the important macroeconomic variable. It determines the evolution of the consumption possibilities of an economy and hence, the evolution of the welfare of an economy. Furthermore, it is well-known that even small deviations from a long run growth path have huge welfare implications. To put it in the words of Barro and Sala-i-Martin (1995): "Economic growth is the part of macroeconomics that really matters".

At least since the emergence of the endogenous growth theory, there exists a vast literature on the sources of economic growth and it seems that the determinants of economic growth are quite well understood, not only from a theoretical but also an empirical point of view (see, e.g., the textbooks by Barro and Sala-i-Martin (1995), Grossman and Helpman (1991) or Aghion and Howitt (1999)). It is important that countries invest resources in some way so that capital (in the form of machines or human capital) is accumulated or that R&D is performed.[1]

Something which is a bit puzzling at first glance is that although we observe substantial unemployment, the labour market in the majority of growth models is assumed to be perfectly competitive and hence, there will always be full-employment. So with these models we are not able to analyse growth and unemployment simultaneously. This "classic" dichotomy is by and large justified by two arguments:

1. The first intuition when thinking about growth and unemployment is that unemployment only has level effects. The long run path is shifted downwards, but the form of the path is not affected.
2. Unemployment is a short-run, disequilibrium phenomenon and hence, it does not need to be considered when analysing growth.

[1] Note that these effects are questioned recently (see, e.g., the "scale effect" literature, beginning with Jones (1995)) and that it is less clear whether there is a one to one relationship between these investments and the rate of growth.

The first intuitive argument clearly seems to be false, because in growth models the labour market plays an important role in the allocation of resources to some kind of investment and to the production of consumption goods. But with this, every distortion in the labour market will alter the resource allocation and hence, influences the rate of growth.

The second argument is not quite convincing either. It is true that as long as we assume unemployment to be caused by business cycle fluctuations, it is not that important for long-run growth. But it seems that, at least in continental europe, unemployment is more an equilibrium, long-run than a business cycle phenomenon. This is also reflected in the data on structural unemployment rates in core europe (see, OECD Economic Outlook (2002)):[2]

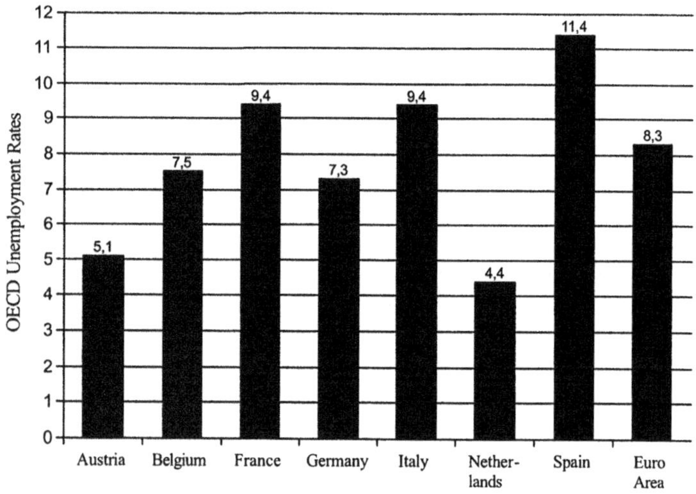

Fig. 1.1. The structural rate of unemployment for selected OECD Countries. Source: OECD Economic Outlook (2002).

Figure 1.1 depicts the structural unemployment rate for some continental european countries and the euro area as a whole. What can be easily seen is that core europe suffers from serious equilibrium unemployment. Hence,

[2] Note that the OECD defines the structural unemployment rate as the Non-accelerating Inflation Rate of Unemployment (NAIRU). The idea is that when there is no wage pressure from the labour market (causing accelerating inflation), it is in its long-run equilibrium. The NAIRU is quite similar to the natural rate concept by Phelps (1968). For more information on the estimation techniques, see "http://www.oecd.org/htm/M00009000/M00009783.htm#Table23new"

we cannot neglect imperfect labour markets (and therewith unemployment) when analysing growth models, because long-run unemployment exists and matters.

When analysing growth and unemployment, we need a model in which both are endogenously determined. This begs the question which labour market model should one employ.

Without doubt, one of the first and prominent candidates is the search theoretic approach, put forward by, e.g., Pissarides (2000). The general idea is that workers and employers have to search for each other and that no instantaneous matching is possible. The amount of employment is determined via a matching function which could be interpreted as a production function for matches with vacancies and unemployed as the factors of production. With these search frictions, steady state unemployment will occur in the economy.

There exist two main strands of argumentation in terms of the way growth and unemployment could be interrelated in these search models. The first argument states that higher productivity (caused, e.g., by a higher rate of technological progress) will cause the unemployment rate to decline. Thus, there would be a positive relation between growth and unemployment (this effect is usually described as "capitalisation effect", see Pissarides (2000)). The argument for this positive relation goes as follows: Before firms can hire workers, they must invest some resources today to find a new worker. The revenues of the filled vacancy will occur in the future. So with optimal firm behaviour the marginal costs of filling a job must be equal to the discounted marginal revenues of a filled job. The crucial point is that the effective discount rate is a negative function of the rate of productivity growth. Therefore, a higher rate of productivity growth leads to a lower discount rate. With this firms will invest more resources to find workers. So c.p. there will be more matches in the economy and therewith a lower rate of unemployment.

The view that a higher rate of growth will increase employment was challenged in a paper by Aghion and Howitt (1994) (see, also the textbook version in Aghion and Howitt (1999) ch.4). They argue that this capitalisation effect is only valid as long as productivity growth is spread evenly over all firms, which is typically not the case. In reality, only some firms adopt new technologies that allow them to produce with a higher productivity whereas other firms do not adopt these technologies and decline. So technological progress will destroy old jobs and create new ones. Thus, in addition to the capitalisation effect, we have to take a creative destruction effect into account. The ultimate effect of growth on unemployment is ambiguous.

The main drawback of these models that combine unemployment, caused by costly search and economic growth is that only one direction of causality is analysed namely that from growth to unemployment. Both, the Pissarides (2000) as well as the Aghion and Howitt (1994) model only analyse the effect of higher growth on the rate of unemployment. This is for sure a very important question, but we think the reversed causality deserve more attention.

We think that we urgently need to know whether unemployment has, besides the negative resource effect today, a long-run impact. This is important, e.g., to judge economic policies aiming to reduce unemployment. Depending on the impact of unemployment on the rate of growth these policies might yield a "double" dividend in making the economy more efficient, in a static as well as in a dynamic sense or they may have a negative impact on the rate of growth. Hence, it is important to know the long-run impact of labour market imperfections.

Therefore, we will focus on the impact of unemployment on the rate of economic growth. We will offer a common basis and a coherent framework to analyse this important question. We have chosen union wage bargaining as the institutional explanation for equilibrium unemployment. This choice has not been made on an arbitrary basis. There are many good reasons for focusing on union wage bargaining, but we think the following two are the most important. Firstly, union wage bargaining is the common way of wage determination in continental europe. This point is very nicely depicted in

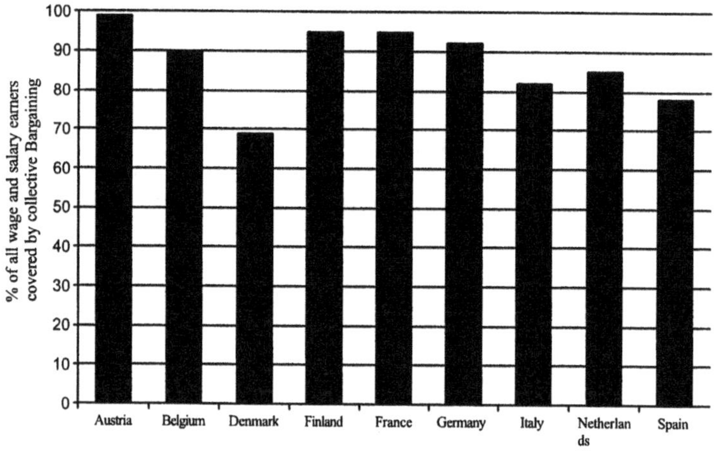

Fig. 1.2. Union Wage Coverage. Source: CESIfo DICE Database.

figure 1.2 where the percentage of all wage/salary earners is shown who are covered by collective wage agreements.[3] The coverage rates for continental europe reach from around 70% up to 99% (with the exception of Denmark). Thus, at least when analysing the situation in core europe we have to take union wage bargaining into account.

[3] Note, that these do not need to be members in a labour union.

The second reason for focusing on collective bargaining is the following. The majority of (endogenous) growth models assume that firms in the economy will in some way or another invest resources in the accumulation of capital or in R&D. The incentive for firms to do so is usually that these activities generate rents (e.g., monopoly rents) which firms can appropriate. But we also know that unions are institutions that try to get parts of these rents via the wage bargain. As Groot (1996) puts it, there will be a struggle for rents when firms and unions bargain the wage.

Hence, there will be a natural economic mechanism how unemployment caused by union wage bargaining distorts the allocation of resources. So the relation between equilibrium unemployment in the collective bargaining case and economic growth seems to be more obvious than the idea that this is the case for other causes of unemployment, e.g., efficiency wage considerations.

When analysing collective bargaining, we firstly have to analyse the game theoretic foundations of the solution of a bargaining problem. Since we consider bargaining in growth models, special attention has to be paid in which way the dynamic modifies the solution and the solution concept of a bargaining problem, respectively.

This is done in the first chapter of this work. As our first step we analyse the Nash bargaining solution, because this approach is the most commonly used in the literature (see, e.g., Booth (1995)). The main drawback of this solution is that it is axiomatic, i.e., a solution to a bargaining problem is found by narrowing the set of all possible solutions by imposing assumptions a rational solution should fulfil. As such, it does not rest on proper game theoretic grounds.

In a next step we analyse an alternating offers game which is a game theoretic approach to bargaining. We derive the solution of this game and show that it converges with the Nash bargaining solution when we define bargaining power as the relative rate of time preference of the two bargaining parties. A crucial point in this respect is that the alternating offers game assumes a stationary environment, hence, an environment that does not change during the bargain. Also, if we want to apply the Nash solution in growth models, an environment that is inherently dynamic, we have to show that the solution of an alternating offers game in a dynamic situation also converges with the Nash solution. This is eventually done in a third step in which a dynamic alternating offers game is analysed. It will be shown that also in this case the solution converges with the Nash solution as long as the dynamic evolution of the environment affects both bargaining partners in the same way. This is the case when analysing the balanced growth path of endogenous growth models. Thus we can use the Nash solution as a shortcut for the extensive form game.

The next part deals with the impact of union wage bargaining on the accumulation of capital. Capital accumulation plays a central role in the explanation of the increase in production possibilities, i.e., economic growth (see, e.g., Barro and Sala-i-Martin (1995) where it is shown that at average up to 50% of the rate of growth of GDP could be explained by increases in the stock of capital). Moreover the first "modern" growth model, the Solow-Swan model, analysed the effects of capital accumulation. Hence, it seems to be a natural first step to integrate collective bargaining into these kinds of models.

Firstly, we analyse the impact of union wage bargaining on the investment behaviour of firms, because capital accumulation is done via investment. The main idea is that the union wage policy is time inconsistent. At some point in time the union will want to set a low wage to encourage the firm to invest a lot, because a higher stock of capital in the next period implies c.p. higher wages and hence, higher utility for the union. The problem is that once investment is done, the union wants to extract some of the quasi-rents by setting a higher wage. But this will be anticipated by the firm and it will invest less than without union wage bargaining. This point is shown in a simple two period model. Then a more general model with an infinite horizon is analysed. This model allows us to take, e.g., reputational mechanism into account which could alleviate the time inconsistency problem.

Secondly, we present a model in which union wage bargaining is introduced into a standard Solow growth model and into a Diamond type model. The Solow model is an infinite horizon model and the Diamond model is an OLG model. Although both models with perfect labour markets generate quite the same results, the results differ when introducing union wage bargaining. In the Solow model, the union will set a low wage that either guarantees full employment or a wage which is so high, savings will be too low to ensure the existence of a steady state. In this case, the capital stock is run down to zero. Which "equilibrium" will be realised depends on the rate of time preference of unions. The economic intuition is that the union faces an intertemporal trade-off: a larger share of the pie today and smaller pies in the future or a smaller share today and larger pies in the future. If the rate of time preference exceeds a certain threshold, the union will not care so much about smaller pies in the future and will set a wage that is too high and vice versa. So in the presented model there will only exist a steady state with full employment.

This effect is not present in the Diamond model in which there will also exist a steady state with unemployment. The intuition in this case is that the union does not maximise utility over an infinite horizon, but that the union only bargains the wage for one generation and hence, faces an inherently static problem. The result is that the stock of capital in the unionised economy is lower than in the one with perfect labour markets. This is because the union causes unemployment which implies that the marginal product of capital and hence, the rate of interest will decline. But this discourages savings and so the capital stock declines.

The last chapter of the part is devoted to the analysis of a so-called AK model, i.e., a model in which only the accumulation of capital ensures endogenous growth. This is because a learning-by-doing spill-over is assumed which guarantees that the economy does not face declining marginal products of capital (at least at the aggregate level). This model is a simple version of a model put forward by Daveri and Tabellini (2000). It is very close to the basic Diamond model, but in this case the steady state stock of capital and the rate of growth decline.

The second important determinant of economic growth is the increase in total factor productivity (see again Barro and Sala-i-Martin (1995)). It is usually assumed that the increase in total factor productivity is caused by the investment of resources into R&D. So to analyse the impact of collective bargaining on the evolution of factor productivity we must integrate imperfect labour markets into a growth model with endogenous research and development. This is done in the following three parts.

The first deals with the effect of collective bargaining in a model with creative destruction which is a modified version of Lingens (2003). The idea is that a monopolist sells an intermediate good to the consumption good sector and that innovators perform R&D hoping to become the new monopolist. So there will be creative destruction in the intermediate good sector. Growth is due to the fact that the newly innovated intermediate good is more efficient than the old one. The impact of union wage bargaining in this model is that depending on the production function in the intermediate sector, the amount of resources employed in the research sector and the rate of growth can increase, decrease or be unchanged. The intuition for this unorthodox result is that when we assume high-skilled labour to be employed in the intermediate and in the research sector, the rationing of low-skilled labour caused by the union will dampen high-skilled demand in both sectors of the economy. Hence, the effect of union wage bargaining on the rate of growth depends on the asymmetry of this decrease, and this is driven by the elasticity of substitution between high-skilled and low-skilled labour in the intermediate sector.

In the next step we integrate collective bargaining into a model with expanding product varieties (see, e.g., Grossman and Helpman (1991)). This is the competing explanation for the increase in factor productivity. In contrast to the model with creative destruction, this model assumes that the number of existing product varieties increases via R&D. But with this the division of labour will be deeper in the economy. Hence, the economy can produce a larger amount of consumption goods with an unchanged primary resource base. The legitimation as to why we analyse collective bargaining in this kind of model is twofold. First, we want to check whether the result derived in the creative destruction model is robust to changes in the assumption about how R&D affects the economy. Second, the model with expanding product varieties has the appealing features that it is relatively easy to handle and that it is a general equilibrium model. This allows us to discuss the effects of economic policies such as the employment and growth effects of taxation and of tax reforms.

The last issue discussed within the model of expanding product variety is the effect of simultaneous wage bargaining. In this case we assume that low-skilled labour is employed in the intermediate as well as the research sector. With this we are able to allow for simultaneous union wage bargaining in both sectors of the economy. The interesting point is that the impact of collective bargaining on the rate of growth is no longer ambiguous, but that the rate of growth will decline compared to the model with perfectly competitive labour markets. The reason why this result stands in stark contrast to the results of the R&D models before is the following: Unemployment occurs not only in the intermediate as before but also in the research sector. Moreover, high-skilled labour is only employed in the research sector. With this, union wage bargaining does not have the possible (indirect) effect of shifting resources to the research sector. Thus, the effect of the union is very sensitive to the assumption where the union bargains the wage (which is trivial) but also to the assumption in which sector high-skilled labour, which is not covered by the union, is employed.

The last part analyses the impact of union wage bargaining in economies in which dual labour markets exist, i.e., one labour market that is perfectly competitive and another where the wage is bargained by the union (see, e.g., Saint-Paul (1996) or Bulow and Summers (1988)). The merit of this assumption is that it is a common fact that we find "good" and "bad" jobs in an economy and thus, these models take an important real world observation into account. The interesting point in these models is that the impact of collective bargaining on unemployment is quite indirect. Union members who are unemployed could move into the competitive sector of the economy and find a job, but they do not do so, because (to some extend) they would rather queue for the higher paid union jobs. Hence, we observe "wait unemployment" (see, e.g., Burda (1988)).[4] The growth effects of this wait unemployment are that the resources employed in R&D decline, because the high-tech sector is assumed to be the one in which the union bargains the wage. Hence, the rate of growth will decline. This point is shown in an OLG model based on Quang and Vousden (1999) and in an infinite horizon model based on Groot (2001).

[4] The notion of wait unemployment is also stressed by the empirical observation that primary sector workers seldom take up secondary sector jobs instead of becoming unemployed (see, e.g., Clark and Summers (1979)).

Part II

Bargaining Theory

1

Static Bargaining Models

1.1 The Nash Bargaining Solution

The Nash solution to bargaining is widely used in applied work especially in the literature on wage bargaining between a firm and a union (see, e.g., Oswald (1985), Booth (1996) or Layard et al. (1991)). In this section we will show the rationale behind the Nash bargaining solution (NBS in the following). The NBS was put forward in a paper by John Nash (1950) in which he uses an axiomatic approach to find a solution to bargaining situations. Axiomatic means that he does not look at the bargain itself, i.e., the procedure of offer and counteroffer, but only determines the outcome by imposing properties (axioms) a solution should fulfil. As such, this solution to a bargaining problem does not rest on proper game theoretic grounds, but only looks at the set of possible outcomes and gradually narrows the set by excluding all solutions that do not fulfil these axioms. Another important point is that only non zero sum bargains are considered, i.e., a solution must be mutually beneficial to the bargaining partners.

1.1.1 The General Idea

Let us assume, that two players are involved in a bargaining situation. Denoting $\mathbf{x}$ as a possible agreement and $U_i(\mathbf{x})$ as the utility player i gets from an agreement $\mathbf{x}$. Furthermore Ω denotes the set of all possible utility pairs the two bargainers could get. When there is no agreement, we assume for simplicity that the utility both bargainers get is zero. The number of possible agreements (i.e., the elements of Ω) is infinite. The question is now how to find a "rational" solution. This is done by assuming certain properties a solution should meet. Nash states four axioms (see, e.g., Gravelle and Rees (1992)) a solution should fulfil:

1. Pareto efficiency: An agreement between the two bargainers should be efficient in the sense, that no other possible agreement $(U_1(\mathbf{x}); U_2(\mathbf{x})) \in \Omega$

exists for which both agents would be better off. Hence, pareto inefficient agreements are not taken into account as a candidate for a rational solution to the problem.

2. Linear Invariance: Assume that the utility representation is transformed linearly. Hence, let $V_i(.)$ be the transformed utility function of player i, then it must hold that $V_i(.) = \alpha + \beta \cdot U_i(.)$. An agreement $\mathbf{x}$, which should be a rational solution to a bargaining situation must be invariant against changes of the utility representation. If this would not be the case, the solution of an (otherwise identical) situation would depend on how utility is measured, but this does not seem to be a plausible assumption.
3. Symmetry: The solution of a symmetric bargaining situation (i.e., a situation in which the utility from disagreement is the same for both players and the set Ω is symmetric around the ID line in $U_i - U_j$-space) will be symmetric, too. So the solution is on the ID line. The rationale behind this axiom is that all asymmetries of the players should be incorporated into the bargaining structure and so it is consequent that in a situation in which there are no asymmetries between players the rational solution should also be symmetric (see, e.g., Osborne and Rubinstein (1994)).
4. Invariance of irrelevant alternatives: Take two possible bargaining situations with identical disagreement payoffs. Let us denote the set of possible agreements of the two situations as Ω_1 and Ω_2, respectively. Furthermore assume that the set of possible agreements of the second situation is completely contained in the set of possible agreements of the first situation, thus, $\Omega_2 \subset \Omega_1$. If an agreement $(U_i(\mathbf{x}^*); U_j(\mathbf{x}^*))$ is a solution to the first bargaining situation and is contained in Ω_2, then it should also be a solution to the second. This axiom seems very plausible. When a certain agreement is the solution to a bargaining situation, why should it not be the solution to a related bargaining situation where the only difference is that in the second situation some irrelevant alternatives (i.e., alternatives that will not be chosen) are not contained in the set of possible agreements? The problem is in a real bargaining situations irrelevant alternatives might influence the process of bargaining and this obviously affects the outcome, but (and this is the main problem of this axiomatic approach) this process is not modelled here.

A rational solution should fulfil these four axioms. Now consider the so called Nash product:

$$NP = (U_1 - D_1) \cdot (U_2 - D_2), \tag{1.1}$$

where $(D_1; D_2)$ is the utility bargainer one and two, respectively, get in case of no agreement (usually $(D_1; D_2)$ are called the disagreement payoffs). We have assumed these being zero. It can be shown that the utility pair $(U_1^*; U_2^*) \in \Omega$ that maximises the Nash product is the only solution that fulfils the four axioms.[1] So the maximiser of the Nash product is the rational solution to a bargaining problem.

Beside this "plain" NBS, there is also another variant, called the asymmetric NBS, which is a generalisation of the "plain" solution. Because it is very often employed in the literature on wage bargaining, we also want to shed some light on this solution. In the standard NBS, the rational solution depends only on the set of possible utilities, Ω, and on the disagreement payoffs. But in real bargaining situations certain attributes of the bargainers also (which are usually labelled as bargaining power) determine the outcome of a bargaining situation. To catch the impact of bargaining power on the solution, the asymmetric Nash product is used:

$$NP = (U_1 - D_1)^{\gamma} \cdot (U_2 - D_2)^{1-\gamma}, \tag{1.2}$$

where the parameter γ catches the notion of bargaining power. The utility pair, which maximises the asymmetric Nash product is the solution to a bargaining situation. As before this solution fulfils all stated axioms except symmetry (for a more formal representation see, e.g., Muthoo (1999)). This is straightforward, because in the asymmetric case not all the differences between the players are incorporated into the bargaining structure (i.e., Ω). So even when the set of possible utility pairs is symmetric and the disagreement payoffs are identical between the bargaining partners, the solution needs not to be symmetric, because, e.g., one bargainer's bargaining ability is better. Only when γ is 1/2 the solution given by the asymmetric NBS is also symmetric, hence the "plain" NBS and the asymmetric NBS coincide, when $\gamma = 1/2$.

1.1.2 An Application to Wage Negotiations

For a very simple application of the NBS, consider a situation in which a firm bargains with a union over the wage. Assume for the moment that employment in the firm is exogenous. The "physical" outcome of the bargain is the wage. For the utility representation we assume the following union utility function:

$$U = w \cdot \bar{L}, \tag{1.3}$$

where w is the wage and $\bar{L}$ is the exogenously given level of employment. The utility of the firm is given by the profit function:

$$\Pi = P \cdot X - w \cdot \bar{L}, \tag{1.4}$$

where P is the price of the product and X is the amount produced. Applying the asymmetric NBS (and assuming the disagreement payoffs to be zero), we get for the Nash product:

[1] In this section, we only want to give an overview over the NBS and the intuition behind it. Formal proofs are omitted, but these can be found in most textbooks on bargaining, e.g., Muthoo (1999) or Osborne and Rubinstein (1994). A nice geometrical proof can be found in the original paper (Nash (1950)).

$$NP = (U)^{\gamma} \cdot (\Pi)^{1-\gamma} = (w \cdot \bar{L})^{\gamma} \cdot (P \cdot X - w \cdot \bar{L})^{1-\gamma}. \tag{1.5}$$

Maximising this with respect to the wage, we get for the bargained wage:[2]

$$w^U = \gamma \cdot \frac{P \cdot X}{\bar{L}}. \tag{1.6}$$

So the negotiated wage will be a part of the per worker revenue. This part (and thus, the wage) will be the higher, the higher is, e.g., the bargaining power of the union. In the case of $\gamma = 0$ (when the firm can fix the wage unilaterally) the wage will be zero. In the case of the symmetric solution ($\gamma = 1/2$), the revenue will be split equally.

When we consider an economy in which employment is determined by the labour demand function of the firm, we can proceed as above. However we also have to take into account, that $L(w)$, hence, employment is a function of the bargained wage (to see such an application in detail see, e.g., Layard et al. (1991)).

1.2 The Rubinstein Solution

The NBS is a convenient method of solving such a complex problem of determining the outcome of some bargaining situations. We get an easy formula (the Nash product) which must be maximised to get a solution to a bargaining problem. Furthermore this solution fulfils axioms, which seem to be clear and straightforward. Although it seems very natural to apply the NBS to various kinds of bargaining situations, the mechanical application is sometimes problematic (see, e.g., Binmore et al. (1986) or Manzini (1999)). The main drawback of the NBS is that the bargaining process itself is not explicitly modelled. So when applying the NBS one has to be very careful in specifying parameters. For example in a concrete bargaining situation the question arises which are the disagreement points of the two players? Is it the payoff they get when they perpetually disagree or is it the payoff of temporary disagreement? What does the notion of bargaining power (see the asymmetric NBS) exactly mean and how can it be specified? To tackle these problems, one has to look at concrete bargaining situations and derive equilibria using the tools of game theory.

1.2.1 The General Idea

One of the most influential game theoretic models which presents a solution to bargaining problems is the alternating offers game by Rubinstein (Rubinstein

[2] Note, that we could also have maximised with respect to the union's utility function subject to the constraint that $\Pi = X \cdot P - U$. Plugging this result into equation (1.3) and solving for the wage would yield the same result.

(1982)). In this game two players bargain over the partition of a cake (which is the synonym for the gain both players can get from cooperation) using the alternating offers procedure. This means that at some point in time t player i makes an offer to player j on how to partition the cake. Player j can accept the offer (in this case the game ends) or he can reject the offer. In case of rejection, it is player j's turn to make an offer at time $t + \Delta$ (hence, Δ is the time between offer and counteroffer). Player i has the opportunity to accept or reject the counteroffer. In case of rejection it is again his turn to make an offer at $t + 2\Delta$. This procedure goes on until both players reach an agreement. If they perpetually disagree, both get the disagreement payoff (which we assume for simplicity to be zero).

An important assumption of the game is, that a delay between offer and counteroffer exists. This delay may be infinitesimally small, but must not be zero. The friction in the bargaining process drives the solution, because both players have positive rates of time preference which means that any delay in finding the solution is costly. A player whose turn it is to accept or reject an offer has to take into account that in case of rejection he might get a bigger piece of the cake when it is his turn to make an offer, but because of the friction he has to discount the (potentially) bigger piece of the cake. A very similar situation arises when a player has to make an offer. In this case the player has to take into account that his offer might be rejected and he has to wait 2Δ time periods until it is again his turn to make an offer. So both players (independently of the situation they are in) have a strong incentive to find an early agreement, because any delay "hurts" both players in terms of foregone utility.

Let us assume a bargaining game in which two players (1 and 2) bargain over the partition of a cake. As before there is a set of possible (physical) agreements. A possible agreement is denoted by $\mathbf{x}$. The utility of player i from an agreement is $U_i(x_i)$ and the set of all possible utility pairs is Ω. Furthermore we define the set of present value utility pairs as Ω^t (see Muthoo (1999)). The present value utility of a player i of an agreement at time t is $PVU_i = \rho_i^t \cdot U_i(x_i)$, where ρ_i is a measure of the rate of time preference of player i. Moreover, we define the pareto frontier of the set Ω. The elements of this pareto frontier are pareto efficient agreements which are in Ω. So a utility pair $(U_1(x_1); U_2(x_2))$ which is an element of Ω is also an element of the pareto frontier when there does not exist any other utility pair (which is element of Ω) that leaves both players better off. We assume that the pareto frontier can be depicted by the graph of a concave function and we call this function ϕ. This implies that for all elements of the pareto frontier it holds true that $U_2(x_2) = \phi(U_1(x_1))$.

When we want to solve for the solution of the bargain we have to determine the subgame perfect equilibrium of the bargaining game of alternating offers. Assume the existence of a x_1^* (this is an offer of player 1 when it is his turn to pose an offer) and a x_2^* (this is the offer of player 2) for which the following holds: $U_2(x_1^*) = \rho_2^{\Delta} \cdot U_2(x_2^*)$ and $U_1(x_2^*) = \rho_1^{\Delta} \cdot U_1(x_1^*)$. Assume furthermore that these utility pairs are elements of the pareto frontier. It can be shown that these agreements are subgame perfect equilibria. Therefore, x_1^* is the subgame perfect equilibrium of a bargaining game in which player 1 starts making an offer and x_2^* the equilibrium of a game in which 2 starts making an offer.

Let us assume that we are at some point in time t where it is player 1's turn to make an offer. He knows that any offer x_1 being equal or exceeding x_1^* will be accepted by player 2 (player 2 will accept any offer x for which holds that $U_2(x) \geq \rho_2^\Delta \cdot U_2(x_2^*)$, so given the assumption above, player 2 will accept x_1^*). Obviously offering a x_1 that exceeds x_1^* is not optimal for player 1, because he could lower his offer without fearing rejection of player 2. So offering more than x_1^* does not pay for player 1. But what happens when he offers less than x_1^*? In this case player 2 will reject the offer. Then the maximum player 1 can get is $\rho_1^\Delta \cdot U_1(x_2^*)$ (the maximum player 2 is willing to offer to him when he wants 1 to accept) or $\rho_1^{\Delta \cdot 2} U_1(x_1^*)$ (which is the maximum amount player 1 can get, when it is again his turn of making an offer). Both payoffs are smaller than $U_1(x_1^*)$, so it is optimal for player 1 to offer x_1^* every time when it is his turn to make an offer. In the case when it is 1's turn to respond to an offer, it is optimal for him to accept any offer x_2 for which holds that $U_1(x_2) \geq \rho_1^\Delta U_1(x_1^*)$, because this is the discounted maximum amount he can get when it is his turn to make an offer. So offering x_1^* every time, when it his turn to make an offer and always accepting every offer, which is bigger than x_2^* (or equal) is the equilibrium strategy of player 1.

Applying similar arguments one can show that it is Player 2's equilibrium strategy to offer always x_2^* and accepting any offer that is bigger than x_1^* (or equal). Thus, we get two relations that must be fulfilled in a subgame perfect equilibrium:

$$U_1(x_1^*) = \phi^{-1}(\rho_2^\Delta \cdot U_2(x_2^*)), \tag{1.7}$$

$$U_2(x_2^*) = \phi(\rho_1^\Delta \cdot U_1(x_1^*)). \tag{1.8}$$

These two equations determine a subgame perfect equilibrium of the (general) alternating offers bargaining game.[3] One can also show that the subgame perfect equilibrium that is given by the described strategy is the only subgame perfect equilibrium of the bargaining game (see, e.g., Muthoo (1999) or Shaked and Sutton (1984)).[4]

The equilibrium solution of the bargaining game has some interesting properties. One property is that it is stationary, i.e., every time a player i has to make an offer, he will always offer x_i. This is due to the fact that the game

---

[3] A unique solution to the above given system of equations exists, because the function, that depicts the pareto frontier is strictly decreasing (this is a result of the definition of the pareto frontier).

[4] The idea is to prove that the set of subgame perfect equilibria consists of only one element and this is done by showing that the supremum and the infimum of the set are identical.

does not change as we move along the game tree (see Manzini (1998)). The set of possible agreements is the same and the discount rate of the players is time constant (i.e., when a player discounts from time 1 to 0, it is essentially the same, as discounting from time 2 to 1, so discounting between two arbitrary points in time is the same).[5]

Another interesting property is that the equilibrium offer of player i is immediately accepted by the other player. Hence, there is immediate agreement in the bargaining game. Two players meet, the player, whose turn it is to make an offer, makes the equilibrium offer which is accepted by the other player and the game ends.

1.2.2 An Application to Wage Negotiations

Let us consider again the above given example of wage bargaining to demonstrate how the Rubinstein solution is derived. As above we assume for simplicity that employment is exogenous. As we have seen, a subgame perfect equilibrium, which is the solution to the bargaining game, can be derived using the equilibrium strategy which states that a player will make such an offer that the other is indifferent between acceptance and rejection. So in our wage bargaining example the following two equations must hold:

$$\Pi(w^U) = \rho_F^{\Delta} \cdot \Pi(w^F), \tag{1.9}$$

$$U(w^F) = \rho_U^{\Delta} \cdot U(w^U), \tag{1.10}$$

where w^U and w^F is the wage offer of the union and the firm respectively and ρ_i is the rate of time preference of the union ($i = U$) and the firm ($i = F$). Using the definition of the firm's profit and the union's utility function, we can solve these two equations for the wage the union will offer when it is the union's turn to make a wage offer, w^U, and the wage the firm will offer, w^F. This yields:

$$w^U = \frac{P \cdot X}{\bar{L}} \cdot \frac{(1 - \rho_F^{\Delta})}{(1 - \rho_U^{\Delta} \cdot \rho_F^{\Delta})}, \tag{1.11}$$

$$w^F = \rho_U^{\Delta} \cdot \frac{P \cdot X}{\bar{L}} \cdot \frac{(1 - \rho_F^{\Delta})}{(1 - \rho_U^{\Delta} \cdot \rho_F^{\Delta})}. \tag{1.12}$$

So the wage that will be the solution to the bargaining problem will be a part of the average revenue per worker (this is due to the fact, that we assumed employment to be exogenous). This fraction of the average revenue (independently whose turn it is to make an offer) depends on the relation of the rates of time preference of the two players. This is intuitively clear. The higher the

[5] This might be a problem, especially in changing environments. In the next section we show how to cope with these modifications in a bargaining model in which the environment changes over time.

rate of time preference of one player, the more costly it is for him to reject an offer and wait another round until it is his turn to make an offer. Hence, the more eager he will be to accept an offer. This point can be made very clear when we look at the extreme case in which one player's rate of time preference is infinitely high. In this case waiting for the next round is not a rational option, because the gain this player can achieve is worthless. Since the other player knows this (this is a very crucial point; in this bargaining game, the players know exactly the preferences of each other, hence, we have common knowledge), he will offer literally nothing to the other player and he will accept.[6] So the rate of time preference of a player captures (in some way) his bargaining power.

Another interesting point is that the wage the union will offer is strictly higher than the wage the firm will offer (even when the rates of time preference of the firm and the union are identical). So the utility of the union will be higher when it is its turn to make an offer and the profit of the firm will be lower in this case compared to a situation, where it is the firm that makes an offer. So we can conclude that the bargaining game exhibits a first mover advantage, i.e., the player who is first in making an offer can gain a bigger piece of the pie than he could if he were the responder. This property of the Rubinstein solution is due to the assumed friction in the bargaining process (delay between offer and counteroffer). The player whose turn it is to make an offer is in a better situation than the responder, because if the responder rejects the offer he has to wait some time until he can make the counteroffer, but during this time utility is lost. So the player beginning the game needs only to offer a smaller part of the gain to make the other player indifferent between acceptance and rejection.

1.3 Rubinstein vs Nash

In the last two sections we saw two inherently different methods of solving bargaining problems. On the one hand we have the NBS where the solution was found by stating axioms that the solution should posses. So the solution was stated without proper analysis of the bargaining process. On the other hand we have the Rubinstein solution where the solution was derived using game theoretic tools from the bargaining process itself.

Although the two solution methods are structurally different, the solutions seem to have similarities. These become very obvious, when concentrating on the solution of the wage bargaining examples. The NBS states that the wage is some part of the average per-worker revenue, where the part a bargainer gets depends on some exogenously defined bargaining power. The Rubinstein

[6] Notions of fairness or reciprocity (see Fehr and Gaechter (1998)) are not taken into account. Both players are fully rational and both will accept any offer that makes them slightly better off than rejecting the offer.

solution also states that the wage is some part of the average revenue, but in this case the part a player gets depends on the relation of the rate of time preference of the players. The only structural difference between these two solutions is, that in the Rubinstein case it is important who is the first to make an offer whereas this is irrelevant in the NBS.

But this unpleasant first mover advantage vanishes, when assuming that the friction of the bargaining process is infinitesimally small, hence, the time between offer and counteroffer approaches zero.[7] So when we take the limit of equations (1.11) and (1.12) as Δ approaches zero we get:

$$\lim_{\Delta \to 0} = w^U = w^F = \frac{\log(\rho_F)}{\log(\rho_F) + \log(\rho_U)} \cdot \frac{P \cdot X}{\bar{L}}. \tag{1.13}$$

We see that in the limit both wages which were derived from the Rubinstein approach (the wage the union will offer and the wage the firm will offer) converge to a common wage that will be offered irrespectively of whose turn it is to make an offer. This is the result of the vanishing first mover advantage.

This limiting Rubinstein solution is equal to the asymmetric NBS when we interpret the wage bargaining parameter γ in the NBS as the relation of the rates of time preference of the two players. So when $\gamma = \frac{\log(\rho_F)}{\log(\rho_F)+\log(\rho_U)}$, we can interpret the NBS as the limiting solution of a Rubinstein game.[8]

This result does not only hold in the demonstrated special case, but also in the general alternating offers game (see, e.g., Binmore (1987) or Muthoo (1999)). Often this result is also used as a legitimation for the usage of the simple NBS, because it is interpreted as the limiting solution of a (not explicitly modelled) strategic game.

In the next section we will see that the NBS solution does not only depict the limiting solution of the static alternating offers game, but can also (making some restrictions) depict the limiting solution of a dynamic alternating offers game.

[7] This friction can be infinitesimally small, but must not vanish, because in this case no solution would be found.

[8] Another important point is how to identify the disagreement points of the Nash bargaining solution when no game theoretic game is modelled. When looking at the literature, e.g., Muthoo (1999), it is shown that the point of perpetual disagreement in the Rubinstein game (the so called impasse point) should be identified as the disagreement point of the Nash solution.

2

Dynamic Wage Bargaining

In the preceding section we have analysed solution methods to bargaining problems. A crucial point for the application of the NBS as well as for the Rubinstein solution was that the bargain takes place in stationary (or steady state) situations. When describing the general idea of the Rubinstein solution, we have said that in an equilibrium, a player whose turn it is to make an offer will always make the same offer. This was due to the fact that the alternating offers procedures (which is inherent dynamic) occurs in a stationary environment. So the subgame beginning at some point in time t is essentially the same as the subgame beginning at any other point in time. Neither the utility function of the players, nor the (physical) size of the cake changes. The only thing that changes is the discounted value of an agreement and this is what drives the solution.

Since we will analyse the effects of union wage bargaining on the growth rate of an economy in what follows, the question begs whether we can also apply the NBS in dynamic models.

When analysing bargaining problems in dynamic models, we have to take into account, that the environment, in which the bargain takes place changes. E.g., in an endogenous growth model the size of the gain might change during the bargain. So when analysing bargaining situations in non-stationary environments, we cannot simply use the Rubinstein solution (or the NBS when we assume, that the time between offer and counteroffer approaches zero) to determine the outcome of such a bargaining game. What we need is a more general approach which takes changes in the environment into account. This is done in a paper by Coles and Muthoo (2003) in which a generalised Rubinstein alternating offers procedure is used to determine the equilibrium outcome of a non-stationary bargaining game. We present the general idea of this model and give some legitimation as to why we can use the NBS even in non-stationary environments.

2.1 The General Idea

Consider two players bargaining over the partition of some gain according to the alternating offers procedure. This means that when bargaining begins at time t, at times $t + n \cdot \Delta$ player i makes an offer to player j, which he can accept (the bargain ends in this case) or reject. In case of rejection, it is player j's turn to make a counteroffer (and so on). Δ is, as above, the time between offer and counteroffer (this is the friction in the bargaining process) and n is an element of $\mathbb{N}$. If n is zero or even, it is player 1's turn to make an offer; if it is odd, it is 2's turn to make an offer. The set of available utility pairs at time t is denoted by $\Omega(t)$.[1] Moreover the pareto frontier of the set $\Omega(t)$ is the combination of utility pairs for which holds that it is not possible to make both players better off. We assume that the pareto frontier can be depicted using a function $\phi(.)$. Hence, along the pareto frontier the following functional relation holds: $U_2 = \phi(U_1, t)$, where U_i is the utility of player i. It is assumed, that the pareto frontier is concave (this follows from the definition of the frontier), shrinking over time (this ensures that there is an incentive for both players to find a solution) and that the pareto frontier evolves smoothly through time (so that the time derivative exists).

To determine an equilibrium, assume that at some arbitrary point in time t there exists a utility pair for player j (who is the responder to an offer) for which holds that $U_j^*(t) = U_j^*(t + \Delta)$. By using the arguments given in the static Rubinstein game (mutually indifference) it can be shown that for any point in time t where it is player i's turn to make an offer, $U_j^*(t)$ is the equilibrium offer (for an intuitive proof, see the appendix of this section). So the sequence of equilibrium offers (which is the equilibrium sequence of the non-stationary bargaining game) fulfils two requirements:

$$U_j(t) = U_j(t + \Delta), \tag{2.1}$$

$$U_j(t) = \phi(U_i(t), t). \tag{2.2}$$

Now let us focus on subgames where it is player 1's turn to make an offer. Given the two requirements in equations (2.1) and (2.2) an equilibrium sequence must fulfil, we know that the equilibrium sequence of player 1's offers $\{U_1^*(t)\}$ must satisfy the following equation:

$$\phi(U_1^*(t), t) = \phi(U_1^*(t + 2 \cdot \Delta), t + \Delta). \tag{2.3}$$

This recursive equation states that in an equilibrium, the utility player 2 can get today from accepting the equilibrium offer must be equal to the utility he can get when it is his turn to make an offer. This latter utility is determined by what utility player 1 can get if it is again his turn to make an offer (taking into account, that the pareto frontier might change from t to $t + \Delta$).

[1] So this general solution to an alternating offers game can also be applied to the specific Rubinstein model.

Any sequence of offers that hurts this equality cannot be an equilibrium. The argument behind this equation is essentially the same as the equilibrium arguments of the static Rubinstein game. The only difference is that it explicitly takes changes of the pareto frontier (e.g., due to changes in the bargaining environment) into account.

In the following we want to concentrate on the equilibrium sequence in bargaining games in which the time between offer and counteroffer approaches zero, hence $\lim_{\Delta \to 0}$. Consider a first-order Taylor expansion of the recursive equation (2.3) around t (the time when it is player 1's first turn to make an offer) and $U_1^*(t)$[2]:

$$\begin{aligned}\phi(U_1^*(t+2\cdot\Delta), t+\Delta) = \phi(U_1^*(t), t) + (U_1^*(t+2\cdot\Delta) - U_1^*(t)) \cdot \phi_U(U_1^*(t), t) \\ +(t+\Delta-t)\cdot\phi_t(U_1^*(t), t) + R,\end{aligned} \tag{2.4}$$

where R is the remainder term and ϕ_U and ϕ_t is the derivative of the pareto frontier with respect to utility and time, respectively. Using (2.3) and rearranging, equation (2.4) gives:

$$\frac{U_1^*(t+2\cdot\Delta) - U_1^*(t)}{2\cdot\Delta} = -\frac{1}{2}\cdot\frac{\phi_t(U_1^*(t), t)}{\phi_U(U_1^*(t), t)} + \frac{R}{2\cdot\Delta}. \tag{2.5}$$

In the limit, as the time between offer and counteroffer approaches zero, the remainder term will vanish and equation (2.4) determines a differential equation which describes how the equilibrium utility of player 1 changes as time goes by. Thus, the solution of this differential equation determines the equilibrium sequence of a non-stationary bargaining game in the limit as Δ approaches zero.

Assume that $U_1^{**}(t)$ is the solution to the differential equation (it is actually the solution to the differential equation, with respect to the boundary condition, that any $U_1(t)$ must be in $[0, \phi^{-1}(0,t)]$). It can be shown that this solution exists and is unique (this is done in the paper of Coles and Muthoo (2003) (see Lemma 1 and 2)).[3]

When we want to interpret the solution of the differential equation as being the solution to a non-stationary alternating offers bargaining game, it must be shown that a subgame perfect equilibrium sequence U_1^* which satisfies equation (2.3), converges to the solution of the differential equation as Δ approaches zero. This is also shown in Coles and Muthoo (2003). The basic

[2] This gives an equation for a hyperplane which is the approximation to the three dimensional function $\phi(.,.)$.

[3] The intuition behind the uniqueness proof is that it is assumed that two solution trajectories exist and to show that the distance between these two trajectories does not approach zero in the limit as t goes to infinity. But the boundary condition (and the condition of the shrinking pareto frontier) requires that all solutions of the differential equation approach to the origin. Hence, the assumption that two solution trajectories exits is contradicted.

(technical) intuition as to why these sequences converge as the bargaining friction vanishes is that if they would not, there would exist some small Δ for which both trajectories would diverge as t goes to infinity. This would again violate the boundary condition. So we can state that the solution to the following differential equation:

$$\frac{dU_1^*(t)}{dt} = -\frac{1}{2} \cdot \frac{\phi_U(U_1^*(t), t)}{\phi_t(U_1^*(t), t)}, \tag{2.6}$$

is the subgame perfect equilibrium of an alternating offers game (which satisfies the above given assumptions) in a non-stationary environment.

First of all let us give a geometric interpretation of the equilibrium trajectory. Remember that only pareto efficient offers were considered, hence:

$$U_2^*(t) = \phi(U_1^*(t), t). \tag{2.7}$$

Differentiating equation (2.7) with respect to time yields:

$$\frac{dU_2^*(t)}{dt} = \phi_U(U_1^*(t), t) \cdot \frac{dU_1^*(t)}{dt} + \phi_t(U_1^*(t), t). \tag{2.8}$$

By using equation (2.6), we get the following relation:

$$\frac{\frac{dU_2^*(t)}{dt}}{\frac{dU_1^*(t)}{dt}} = -\phi_U(U_1^*(t), t). \tag{2.9}$$

This equation states that marginal utility along the pareto frontier (at the equilibrium outcome, this is the rhs) must be equal to the ratio of utility loss[4] of the two agents due to a delay (this is the lhs). The geometric interpretation of equation (2.9) is that in an equilibrium the slope of the pareto frontier must be equal to the slope of a trajectory.

Now let us turn to the relation between the NBS and the limiting solution of the non-stationary alternating offers game. The NBS solution of the bargaining situation (where we assume, that the utility of perpetual disagreement is zero to both players) is given by the maximand of the following Nash product:

$$NP = (U_1(t)) \cdot (U_2(t)). \tag{2.10}$$

The maximisation of the Nash product subject to the pareto frontier gives the following relation:

$$\frac{U_2(t)}{U_1(t)} = -\phi_U(U_1, t). \tag{2.11}$$

In geometrical terms, the NBS states that the slope of the pareto frontier at some point must be equal to the slope of a ray from the origin to that point.

[4] Note that the slope $\phi_U(.,.)$ is negative. This is due to the definition of the pareto frontier.

When comparing this geometrical interpretation with the interpretation of equation (2.9), we can conclude that if the trajectory is a straight line (and ends in the origin, which is true given the boundary condition) the NBS and the solution of the non stationary bargaining game are identical. This is because in this case, the solution trajectory is a ray through the origin.

It can be shown (see Coles and Muthoo (2003)) that this will only be the case when the slope of the pareto frontier at the solution of the differential equation (2.6) is constant through time. With this the slope of the trajectory is constant, hence, it must be a ray. Furthermore it can be shown that when the pareto frontier shrinks homothetically the NBS and the bargaining solution given by the solution of the differential equation coincide for all points in time (for a formal proof see Coles and Muthoo (2003)). The (technical) intuition behind this property is that when the pareto frontier shrinks homothetically, points of the pareto frontier at various points in time that lie on any ray through the origin are associated with the same slope of the frontier. Hence, along a ray through the origin, the slope of the pareto frontier does not change and the constancy of this slope is the requirement for both solutions to be identical. Economically this homothetical shrinkage means that the evolution of time affects the situation of both players in the same way. This implies, e.g., that the rate of growth along a balanced growth path has no asymmetric affects to both players.

For standard endogenous growth models it will be the case that time will affect both players in the same way. Therefore, we can apply the NBS as a proxy for the limiting solution of the non-stationary alternating offers game. So we will use the "shortcut" NBS in the following chapters in dynamic models without leaving sound game theoretic grounds.

2.2 Appendix

In this Appendix we give intuitive proof as to why the offer $U_j^*(t) = U_j^*(t+\Delta)$ is a subgame perfect equilibrium. Consider a game where it is player 1 who is first to make an offer at time t. Assume utility pairs which are elements of the pareto frontier and for which the following holds:

$$U_2^*(t) = U_2^*(t+\Delta), \tag{A1}$$

$$U_1^*(t+\Delta) = U_1^*(t+2\cdot\Delta). \tag{A2}$$

It can be shown that $U_2^*(t)$ is the equilibrium offer of player 1 at time t (similar arguments hold true for $U_1^*(t+\Delta)$ with reversed roles for player 1 and 2). Player 2's optimal strategy is to accept any offer in which $U_2(t) \geq U_2(t+\Delta)$. Now let us assume that player 1 would deviate from the offer $U_2^*(t)$, given player 2's strategy. If player 1 offered $U_2(t) > U_2^*(t)$, player 2 would accept this offer. However, it is not optimal for player 1, because he could lower his offer without fearing the rejection of player 2. If player 1 offered $U_2(t) < U_2^*(t)$

player 2 would reject the offer and the maximum utility player 1 could obtain in this case would be $Max[U_1^*(t+\Delta), \phi^{-1}(U_2^*(t+2\cdot\Delta), t+2\cdot\Delta)]$. Each is smaller than $\phi^{-1}(U_2^*(t), t)$. So a deviation from the proposed offer is not profitable. As such, it will be the equilibrium offer. Using similar arguments we can show, that it is optimal for player 2 to offer $U_1^*(t+\Delta)$, whenever it is his turn to make an offer. Equation (2.3) follows from the combination of equations (A1) and (A2).

Part III

Unions and Capital

3

Unions and Investment

One of the most important sources of economic growth is the accumulation of capital. By investing the amount of resources that are saved in an economy, it is possible to produce a bigger amount tomorrow. Thus, the question which way will investment change when integrating imperfect labour markets is the first natural step to analyse the impact of union wage bargaining on the rate of growth.

Therefore in the following section we will analyse the impact of union wage bargaining on the investment behaviour in the economy. The first work that analysed the effect of unions on investment is a paper by Grout (1984). In this paper a union and a firm bargain over the wage and employment, and the firm decides how much to invest. The result is that without legally binding wage contracts, the labour market imperfection will cause investment to decline. The economic intuition for this result is the following: The union has an incentive to exploit the quasi-rents generated by the investment of the firm. So when there are no binding wage contracts the union cannot commit to a low wage path and the firm will invest less, because it knows that it will be exploited by the union.

In the following we will analyse this hold-up problem in more detail. First, we demonstrate the basic idea in the two period case which is based on the textbook model in Heijdra and Ploeg (2002). Then we present a generalised model with an infinite horizon, based on Ploeg (1987). The only difference to the Grout (1984) model is that we consider a right-to-manage framework, i.e., that the union and the firm bargain the wage and the firm chooses employment unilaterally.

3.1 Unions and Investment–The Two Period Case

Consider an economy that exists for two periods. At the beginning of period t_1 there is a given stock of capital. Firms produce output using labour and capital. For simplicity, the production function is assumed to be Cobb-Douglas. In period t_1 firms can also invest with the consequence that they have a bigger stock of capital in period t_2. Since it is assumed that the installation of new investment is costly, firms have to balance the additional gain from investing (namely higher profits tomorrow) and the cost of additional investment. Furthermore, firms can choose how many workers they wish to employ in t_1 and t_2. The goal of the firm is to maximise the present value of the stream of profits today and tomorrow. Profits in the two periods are given by:

$$\Pi_1 = L_1^{\alpha} \cdot K_1^{1-\alpha} - w_1 \cdot L_1 - I_1 \cdot (1 + b \cdot I_1), \tag{3.1}$$

$$\Pi_2 = L_2^{\alpha} \cdot (K_1 + I_1)^{1-\alpha} - w_2 \cdot L_2, \tag{3.2}$$

where L_1 and L_2 is employment in period t_1 and in period t_2, respectively. K_1 is the predetermined stock of capital; w_1 and w_2 are the wages in the two periods and the term $I_1 \cdot (1 + b \cdot I_1)$ indicates the installation costs (which are quadratic in our example). Using equations (3.1) and (3.2) we can determine employment in period t_1 and t_2 and investment which will maximise the present value of the profit stream. This present value is given by:

$$\Pi = \Pi_1 + \frac{1}{1+\rho} \cdot \Pi_2, \tag{3.3}$$

where ρ is the rate of time preference. Substituting equations (3.1) and (3.2) into equation (3.3) and maximising the latter equation gives three first order conditions for the three choice variables of the firm:

$$\frac{\partial \Pi}{\partial I_1} = \frac{1-\alpha}{1+\rho} \cdot L_2^{\alpha} \cdot (K_1 + I_1)^{-\alpha} - (1 + 2 \cdot b \cdot I_1) = 0, \tag{3.4}$$

$$\frac{\partial \Pi}{\partial L_1} = \alpha \cdot L_1^{\alpha-1} \cdot K_1^{1-\alpha} - w_1 = 0, \tag{3.5}$$

$$\frac{\partial \Pi}{\partial L_2} = \alpha \cdot L_2^{\alpha-1} \cdot (K_1 + I_1)^{1-\alpha} - w_2 = 0. \tag{3.6}$$

The interpretation of these conditions is straightforward. Firms will demand labour (independently of the time period) until the marginal product of labour in terms of additional production equals the marginal costs, which is the wage. Firms will invest until the discounted marginal value of capital (this is the gain of additional investment) will be equal to the marginal (installation) costs. Note, the optimal amount of investment is a function of employment in the second period. When employment is high, investment will be high, too. The marginal product of capital will increase when employment increases. Thus, investment will be more profitable (remember that the installation costs are exogenously given) and so firms will invest more. Using the first order conditions we get the following:

$$L_1 = \left(\frac{\alpha}{w_1}\right)^{\varepsilon} \cdot K_1, \tag{3.7}$$

$$L_2 = \left(\frac{\alpha}{w_2}\right)^{\varepsilon} \cdot (K_1 + I_1), \tag{3.8}$$

$$I_1 = \frac{q-1}{2 \cdot b}, \tag{3.9}$$

where $\varepsilon \equiv \frac{1}{1-\alpha}$ and $q \equiv \frac{(1-\alpha)\cdot L_2^{\alpha}\cdot(K_1+I_1)^{-\alpha}}{1+\rho}$, so q is the relation between the marginal productivity of capital and the rate of time preference of firms. If q equals one, investment will be zero. In this case the value of investment will be equal to the marginal costs. As such, q could be interpreted as Tobin's marginal q (see, e.g., Caballero (1999)). Using equations (3.7), (3.8) and (3.9), one could determine equilibrium employment in both periods and equilibrium investment as a function of the wages in the two periods, the initial stock of capital and the two parameters. Assuming further that the whole stock of labour, $\bar{L}$, would be supplied inelastically, the wages in the two periods would be fixed and the model would be solved.

Since we want to discuss the effect of union wage bargaining on investment in such a model, we have to consider the wage to be endogenous in the two periods. Assuming that all workers are members of a monopoly union, the union unilaterally sets the wage in every period as to maximise the present value of the utility stream of a representative worker. After the union has set the wage, the firm will choose employment. So the firm has the right-to-manage and contracts must be on the labour demand curve. The instantaneous utility function (i.e., utility in every period) is given by[1]:

$$V_i = \frac{L_i}{N} \cdot \log(w_i) + (1 - \frac{L_i}{N}) \cdot \log(B), \tag{3.10}$$

where B is the unemployment benefit a union member gets when unemployed and N is the stock of labour and $i \in [1,2]$.[2]

The union does not want to maximise instantaneous utility, but the present value utility stream of the instantaneous utilities in the two periods. So the overall utility function is given by:

$$\Psi = V_1 + \frac{1}{1+\rho} \cdot V_2. \tag{3.11}$$

The union chooses w_1 and w_2 (subject to the labour demand functions given by equations (3.7) and (3.8)) to maximise equation (3.11). With this we get

[1] For an overview over potential specifications of union utility functions, see e.g. the surveys of Oswald (1985), Booth (1995) or Pencavel (1994).

[2] This utility function and a function where the union would maximise utility of all its members would yield the same result, because membership is exogenous to the union.

the following two first order conditions for the wage the union will set in the two periods:

$$\frac{\partial \Psi}{\partial w_1} = \frac{L_1}{N} \cdot \frac{1}{w_1} + \left(\frac{1}{N} \cdot \log(w_1) - \frac{1}{N} \cdot log(B)\right) \cdot \frac{\partial L_1}{\partial w_1} = 0, \tag{3.12}$$

$$\frac{\partial \Psi}{\partial w_2} = \frac{L_2}{N} \cdot \frac{1}{w_2} + \left(\frac{1}{N} \cdot \log(w_2) - \frac{1}{N} \cdot log(B)\right) \cdot \left(\frac{\partial L_2}{\partial w_2} + \frac{\partial L_2}{\partial I_1} \cdot \frac{\partial I_1}{\partial q} \cdot \frac{\partial q}{\partial w_2}\right) = 0. \tag{3.13}$$

The economic intuition for the first first order condition is straightforward. For the optimal wage in period t_1 the following must hold: the marginal utility gain from a higher wage must exactly outweigh the marginal utility loss of a higher wage. The marginal gain is given by the wage increase and this has the direct effect that instantaneous utility will increase. The utility loss is indirect. When the wage increases, employment will decline (remember that all contracts must be on the labour demand schedule). However, this employment decrease will result in lower expected utility of the union members. The optimal wage demand will balance both effects.

The economic intuition for the second first order condition is more subtle. When the union raises the second period wage there will again be the direct utility gain (and the marginal utility is the same as in the first period). The negative effect is the employment decrease caused by the wage increase. But moreover there is a second negative effect of a wage hike on employment. With a higher wage, q will be lower. This can be seen easiest, when substituting $(K_1 + I_1)$ in q by the relation in equation (3.7). With this $q \equiv \frac{1-\alpha}{1+\rho} \cdot \left(\frac{\alpha}{w_2}\right)^{\alpha \cdot \varepsilon}$. But with a lower q, investment and therewith the stock of capital in period t_2 will be lower, too. Firms will invest less, when the wage in the second period increases, because with a higher anticipated wage, employment will decrease. This lowers c.p. the marginal product of capital. With unchanged installation costs, the optimal amount of investment declines.

So a wage hike in period t_2 has two negative employment effects. On the one hand there is the standard effect that we move upwards *on* a given labour demand curve *and* that the labour demand curve *itself* is shifted inwards, because the stock of capital decreases.

Using equations (3.7) and (3.9) we can determine the indirect employment effect of lower investment caused by a wage hike. This is given by:

$$\varpi = -\frac{\partial L_2}{\partial I_1} \cdot \frac{\partial I_1}{\partial q} \cdot \frac{\partial q}{\partial w_2} \cdot \frac{w_2}{L_2} = \left(\frac{\alpha}{w_2}\right)^{\varepsilon \cdot (\alpha+1)} \cdot \frac{K_1 \cdot \varepsilon \cdot \alpha}{2 \cdot b} \cdot \left(\frac{1-\alpha}{1+\rho}\right) \cdot \frac{w_2}{L_2} > 0. \tag{3.14}$$

Manipulating equations (3.12) and (3.13) gives the equilibrium wages the union will set:

$$\log(w_1^*) = \log(B) + \frac{1}{\varepsilon}, \tag{3.15}$$

$$\log(w_2^*) = \log(B) + \frac{1}{\varepsilon + \varpi}, \tag{3.16}$$

The equilibrium wages the union will set in both periods[3] are mark-ups over the unemployment benefit. These mark-ups depend on the wage elasticity of the labour demand curves. When the curves are steep, the wage the union will set is high, because in this case a wage increase is not punished so hard by an employment decrease. The interesting point is that the wage, the union will set in period t_2 is *lower* than the wage it sets in period t_1. This is because the labour demand curve in the second period is more elastic, since the second period wage also determines the level of investment. So the union will want to set a low wage to encourage the firm to invest a lot.

The problem of this strategy (when there are no legally binding long term contracts) is that it is time inconsistent. In period t_1 it is optimal for the union to announce to set a very low wage, because in this case investment is stimulated and the union will gain from the additional stock of capital, too. Once investment is done, the firm has tied its hands. In this situation the firm is a "sitting duck" for the union and it is no longer optimal to set a low wage, but to set a very high wage to get a large share of the benefit of higher investment.

However the firm knows that the union has the incentive to deviate from the announced low wage. Hence, it will not believe the union and anticipates that after the investment is completed, the union will set the same wage as in period one. The only credible equilibrium in this model is that the firm expects the wage in the second period to be the same as in the first period. So $\log(w_2) = \log(B) + \frac{1}{\varepsilon}$. In a credible equilibrium the wage is higher than announced and investment will be lower. In an economy with union wage bargaining and without legally binding contracts, investment will be too low.

Note that with legally binding contracts investment would be higher than without, but that even with legally binding wage contracts, investment will be lower than in the competitive economy. This is because the wage will be higher than in the competitive economy as long as $\frac{1}{\varpi+\varepsilon}$ is not equal to one.

3.2 Unions and Investment–The Infinite Horizon Case

In the preceding section we have analysed the effects of union wage bargaining on investment in a simple two-period model. We have seen that the wage strategy of the union in this framework is time inconsistent and that without legally binding wage contracts, investment will be too low.

[3] Note that w_2 is not really the equilibrium wage, because ϖ is an endogenous variable and depends on w_2. But this is not relevant for the point we will make.

In this section the model is generalised (following Ploeg (1987)) in two respects. The most important point is that an infinite horizon economy is analysed. This allows us to discuss points such as reputation and the like. The second point is that we work with general functional forms. We will also see that in this more general model the union's wage strategy is time inconsistent. But in this infinite horizon economy, the union has the chance to build up reputation. This is obviously impossible in two stage games and in all other finite horizon games, because the union has the incentive to cheat at the last stage of the game. But the firm knows this (by backward induction) and so the union cannot credibly commit to a wage path.[4]

Consider the following model. The firm wants to maximise the present value of profits which is given by the following function:

$$\Pi = \int_0^{\infty} e^{-\rho \cdot t} \cdot (f(K, L) - w \cdot L - p_i \cdot i - \chi(i)) \, dt. \tag{3.17}$$

So the firm produces output using capital, K, and labour, L.[5] The firm can buy investment goods, i, in every period and the price of these goods is p_i. In addition to buying investment goods, they have to be installed and the installation costs of the investment are given by the function $\chi(i)$.[6] This function is over-linearly increasing in investment, hence $\chi'(i)$ as well as $\chi''(i)$ are positive. The capital accumulation equation is given by:

$$\dot{K} = i - \delta \cdot K. \tag{3.18}$$

The dot over K indicates the first derivative with respect to time and δ is the rate of depreciation.

The choice variables of the firm are labour input and investment. Maximising equation (3.17) with respect to labour gives the following first order condition for the present value profit maximising labour input:[7]

$$\frac{\partial \Pi}{\partial L} = e^{-\rho \cdot t} \cdot \left(\frac{\partial f(K, L)}{\partial L} - w \right) = 0. \tag{3.19}$$

Equation (3.19) shows that, as in the standard static neoclassical models, in the optimum additional output produced by labour must be equal to the wage.

The determination of the optimal level of investment is a bit more complex, since the investment decision today affects, via the accumulation of capital,

[4] The arguments in this union-firm game are quite similar to ones put forward in the time inconsistency of monetary policy literature, e.g. Walsh (1998).

[5] We assume again that the output of a firm is the numéraire in the economy and hence, the price can be normalised to one.

[6] These costs do not only reflect installation costs, but also, e.g., internal adjustment costs which are caused by the investment.

[7] We can apply standard static optimisation methods, because the choice of L has no intertemporal consequences.

all future output levels. We can solve for the optimal amount of investment using intertemporal optimisation. The current value Hamiltonian associated with this problem is given by the following equation:

$$\mathcal{H} = f(K,L) - w \cdot L - p_i \cdot i - \chi(i) + \lambda(t) \cdot (i - \delta \cdot K), \tag{3.20}$$

where $\lambda(t)$ is the costate variable and can be interpreted as the shadow value of additional investment. The choice variable of this problem is i and the state variable is K. The first order conditions of this problem are the following:

$$\frac{\partial \mathcal{H}}{\partial i} = -p_i - \chi(i) + \lambda = 0, \tag{3.21}$$

$$-\frac{\partial \mathcal{H}}{\partial K} = -\frac{\partial f(K,L)}{\partial K} + \delta \cdot \lambda = \dot{\lambda} - \rho \cdot \lambda. \tag{3.22}$$

Furthermore the transversality condition, which states that the value of the stock of capital (measured by the shadow value) must be zero as time approaches infinity, must be fulfilled.

The first order condition (3.21) states that the marginal value of investment given by the shadow value must be equal to marginal costs. Moreover this equation gives the optimal level of investment as an implicit function of the difference between the shadow value and the price of an investment good. When the shadow value exceeds the price of the investment good, taking the internal adjustment costs into account, investment will be positive.[8]

The second first order condition shows the evolution of the shadow value of capital as a function of the marginal productivity of capital. The economic interpretation of equation (3.22) is that the shadow price of investment is driven by the difference between marginal productivity of capital and marginal costs which consist of the rate of time preference and depreciation. A noteworthy point is that when there are no internal adjustment costs, the shadow price of investment will be equal to the price of the investment good. Thus, in this case we would again have the standard neoclassical optimality conditions for investment, namely that the marginal productivity must be equal to marginal costs and investment will close the gap between the optimal stock of capital and the actual one (see, e.g., Sala-i-Martin (1991)).

The stock of capital will be constant in a steady state. Hence, investment will be just sufficient to match the capital loss due to depreciation. In this case we can determine the equilibrium stock of capital using a phase plane. This is shown in figure 3.1 where the two zero motion lines of the shadow price of capital and the capital stock are depicted.

Because we want to analyse the effects of union wage setting on the investment decision of the firm, we have to analyse the wage setting process of

[8] We can also relate this result to Tobin's "q" theory. We can define Tobin's marginal "q" as the relation between the shadow value of investment and the purchasing price of investment. When this ratio exceeds one, there will be investment (see, e.g., Hayashi (1982)).

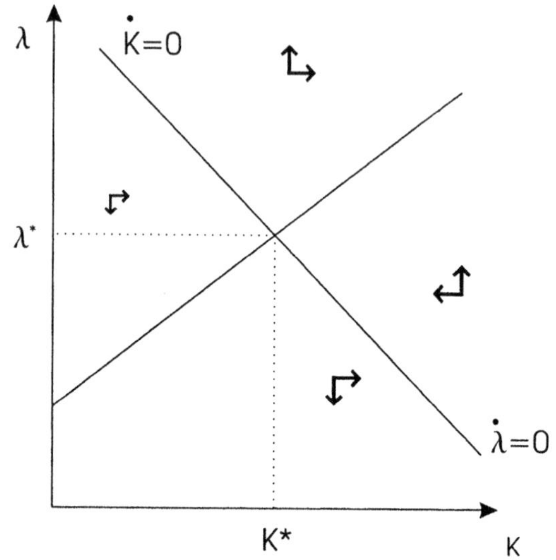

Fig. 3.1. The Equilibrium Stock of Capital

the labour union. The union maximises the present value of the time path of an instantaneous utility function. The utility function is the following:

$$U = \int_0^\infty e^{-\rho \cdot t} \cdot (L \cdot U(w) + (N - L) \cdot U(B))\, dt, \tag{3.23}$$

where N is again the total labour force and B is the unemployment benefit. Because the union monopolizes labour supply, it will set a wage that maximises its utility function. By increasing the wage, the union has to take two things into account. First, only contracts on the labour demand curve are feasible, as such a higher wage is associated with lower employment (this is what we will call the static constraint) and second, the wage bargain indirectly influences capital accumulation (which is the intertemporal constraint). By plugging the (static) labour demand function into the utility function, we get the Hamiltonian for the union's problem as:

$$\begin{aligned} \mathcal{H} = L(K,w) \cdot (U(w) - U(B)) + N \cdot U(B) + \mu \cdot (i(\lambda - q) - \delta \cdot K) + \\ \vartheta \cdot ((r + \delta) \cdot \lambda - \frac{\partial f(K,L)}{\partial K}), \end{aligned} \tag{3.24}$$

where μ is the shadow value of investment of the union and ϑ is the shadow value that the union attaches to the shadow price of investment of firms. So the union takes into account that wage demands affect the shadow price of investment and thereby the steady state stock of capital. This in turn affects employment.

The first order conditions of this problem read:

$$\frac{\partial \mathcal{H}}{\partial w} = \frac{\partial L(w,K)}{\partial w} \cdot (U(w) - U(B)) + L \cdot U'(w) \\ -\vartheta \cdot f_{KL}(K,L) \cdot \frac{\partial L(w,K)}{\partial w} = 0, \tag{3.25}$$

$$-\frac{\partial \mathcal{H}}{\partial K} = -\frac{\partial L(w,K)}{\partial K} \cdot (U(w) - U(B)) + \mu \cdot \delta = \dot{\mu} - \rho \cdot \mu, \tag{3.26}$$

$$-\frac{\partial \mathcal{H}}{\partial \lambda} = \mu \cdot \frac{\partial i(p_i - \lambda)}{\partial \lambda} + \vartheta \cdot \delta = \dot{\vartheta}, \tag{3.27}$$

where f_{KL} is the derivative of the marginal product of capital with respect to L. The first first order condition reveals that in the optimum the marginal revenue of a wage increase must be equal to the marginal costs. These marginal costs consist of a direct effect via the static constraint and an indirect one via the effect on capital accumulation. This can be seen very easily by rewriting equation (3.25) as:

$$L \cdot U'(w) = \underbrace{-\frac{\partial L(w,K)}{\partial w} \cdot (U(w) - U(B))}_{direct \quad loss} + \underbrace{\vartheta \cdot f_{KL}(K,L) \cdot \frac{\partial L(w,K)}{\partial w}}_{indirect \quad loss}, \tag{3.28}$$

where the lhs of equation (3.28) depicts the marginal gain of a wage increase and the rhs the marginal loss.

Focusing on steady states, equations (3.26) and (3.27) change to:

$$\mu = \frac{1}{\delta + \rho} \cdot \left(\frac{\partial L(w,K)}{\partial K} \cdot (U(w) - U(B) \right) > 0, \tag{3.29}$$

$$\vartheta = -\frac{1}{\delta} \cdot \left(\mu \cdot \frac{\partial i(p_i - \lambda)}{\partial \lambda} \right) < 0. \tag{3.30}$$

Equations (3.29) and (3.30) show that the steady state shadow value of the stock of capital is positive and that the shadow value the union attaches to the shadow price of investment is negative. The economic intuition for these properties is the following. With a higher stock of capital, labour demand of firms increases. Hence, with an outward shift of the labour demand curve, the union can reach a higher indifference curve. So the union values capital at a positive rate, which is in a steady state given by μ. Given the same arguments, the union's value of the shadow value of investment is negative, because when the shadow price of investment increases, investment and hence the stock of capital will decrease (see equation (3.21)). This implies that ϑ will be negative in a steady state. Equation (3.25) implicitly depicts that the wage of the union is a mark-up over the unemployment benefit, where the mark-up is a function of the direct and indirect loss of a wage hike.[9] So employment in the unionised

[9] This can be seen easiest, when assuming a situation with an isoelatic labour demand function and risk neutral individuals.

economy is lower than in the competitive. With this the zero motion line of λ in figure 3.1 shifts inwards, implying that the steady state stock of capital declines.

What we want to show is that in this generalised version the wage strategy of the union is also time inconsistent.

A strategy is said to be time inconsistent when the optimal path of an action changes over time (see, e.g., Blanchard and Fischer (1989)). In our model this means that the wage the union would like to set for some time t at time 0 differs from the wage for t the union would like to set at time $s > 0$. It can be shown that the wage strategy of the union is time inconsistent, when applying arguments put forward by Turnovsky (2000). The idea is that at the beginning of the planing horizon the union treats ϑ as an additional policy parameter. On this basis it will announce a wage path. From that time on ϑ will approach its (negative) steady state value. If the union has at some point in time the chance to reoptimise its wage path, ϑ will be again policy parameter and the union will choose a higher wage than announced. The economic intuition is the same as in the simple two period case.

An additional feature of this model compared to the simple two-period case is that reputation can be implemented, because the game between the firm and the union is repeated infinitely. Assume that the firm trusts the union when it has not cheated for some time. If the union cheats in such a situation the firm will punish the union by not believing the wage announcement for a certain amount of time and hence, by lowering the level of investment (see, Ploeg (1987)). So when the union deviates from the announced wage path it has to balance the gains from higher wages to the future losses of the punishment. It is clear that the union will be more reluctant to deviate from its wage path when the rate of time preference is low and the punishment, e.g., the length of the punishment period is high.

Summarising, we can say that the wage strategy of the union in the infinite horizon case without legally binding wage contracts is time inconsistent. So steady state investment and the stock of capital will be too low. This is the same rationale as in the two period case. In addition to this effect, reputation has been considered. This implies that the punishment of the firm makes the union more reluctant to deviate from the wage strategy. Therefore, with reputation, the outcome will be somewhere between the case with binding wage contracts and the simple two period case.

4

Unions in a Solow Type Growth Model

In the preceding section we have analysed the effect of union wage bargaining in a model with endogenous investment and adjustment costs. With this model we have shown that the wage strategy of the union is time inconsistent and that investment and hence, the stock of capital will be lower than in the economy with competitive labour markets.

In this section we will consider a standard neoclassical growth model with infinitely lived agents in which a union sets the wage and thereby rations labour. The model is based on a paper by Kemp and Van Long (1987) and is one of the first attempts to integrate imperfect labour markets into a standard growth model. One of the main results of the paper is that as long as the union is not too impatient (the rate of time preference is not too high) it will choose the same wage path (and hence, the same employment path) as would be realised with a perfectly competitive labour market. In this case the same steady state is reached as in the non-union case. If on the other hand the union is very impatient no steady state is reached. This is because the wage the union will set is so high that savings which are only done by capital owners will decline and will be too low. As a consequence the per capita capital stock will decline until all capital is eventually exhausted. So there are only two polar cases. Either there will be a steady state without unemployment (in this case the union will refrain its wage setting power) or the union will set a wage exceeding the competitive outcome with the result of a collapsing stock of capital.

In what follows we will present the model of Kemp and Van Long (1987) and we will analyse the results of the model with general functional forms of the production function. Then we will apply a CES production function as a concrete example technology. Moreover we will discuss an interesting extension of the model put forward by Palokangas (1989). He analyses union wage bargaining in an economy very similar to that of Kemp and Van Long with one difference; he assumes a concave-convex production technology with no constant returns to scale and a slightly different savings function. The interesting result of the Palokangas (1989) model is that there might exist a medium case in which there will be unemployment in a steady state.

4.1 The Model of Kemp and Van Long (1987)

4.1.1 The General Case

Consider an economy in which output is produced using labour and capital. It is assumed that the production function exhibits constant returns to scale (CRS) and thus, is linear homogenous. The production function is given by the following equation[1]:

$$Y = F(K, L), \tag{4.1}$$

which is in per worker terms:

$$y = F(z), \tag{4.2}$$

where Y is output, K is capital, L is labour, y is output per worker, $\frac{Y}{L}$, and z is the capital to labour ratio, $\frac{K}{L}$. Furthermore assume that N denotes population, which grows at an exogenously given rate of n. k is the capital to population ratio, $\frac{K}{N}$. If there is full employment in the economy, z will be equal to k; in general $z \geq k$ holds.

The evolution of the economy is driven by the accumulation of capital. To keep things as simple as possible it is assumed that capitalists only get capital income and workers only get wage income and that only capitalists save. Since the rental rate of capital is equal to its marginal product and as savings must be equal to investment (note that a closed economy is considered), the following equation must hold:

$$\dot{K} = s \cdot \underbrace{K \cdot F_K}_{Capital \quad Income}, \tag{4.3}$$

where a subscript denotes the first derivative of the function with respect to the variable, a dot over a variable indicates the first derivative with respect to time and s is the exogenous savings rate. With equation (4.3) the equation of motion of the per capita capital stock is given by:

$$\dot{k} = s \cdot k \cdot f'(z) - n \cdot k. \tag{4.4}$$

With $z = k$ (which is the economy with competitive labour markets) equation (4.4) is the equilibrium equation of the standard growth model of the Solow and Swan type (see, e.g., the textbook of Barro and Sala-i-Martin (1995) or Jones (2002)). Imposing the steady state condition (constance of per capita

[1] Time subscripts have been omitted when it is not confusing, i.e., when the variables refer to the same period of time t.

variables), equation (4.4) would give the equilibrium values of the per capita stock of capital (and hence, of the equilibrium per capita production).

However in the case of an imperfect labour market, employment and population do not need to be identical since some members of the population are unemployed and hence, (besides k) there is an additional endogenous variable z which must be determined to solve the model with the non-walrasian labour market.

We assume that labour in the economy is represented by a trade union which has the power to set the wage unilaterally. Firms have the right to set employment according to the labour demand curve. Furthermore we assume that the union will set the wage path so as to maximise the present value of the wage bill. The wage bill at some time t is given by:

$$L \cdot F_L(K, L), \tag{4.5}$$

with $F(K, L) = L \cdot f(\frac{K}{L})$, $F_L(K, L)$ can be written as $f(z) - f'(z) \cdot k$. So the wage bill is given by:

$$N \cdot \frac{k}{z} \cdot (f(z) - f'(z) \cdot L) = N \cdot k \cdot b(z), \tag{4.6}$$

with the function $b(z)$ given as $\frac{f(z)}{z} - f'(z)$. Using equation (4.6), the utility function of the union is given by:

$$U = \int_0^{\infty} e^{-\rho \cdot t} \cdot N \cdot k \cdot b(z) \cdot dt. \tag{4.7}$$

Instead of assuming that the union chooses a wage path that maximises (4.7), we assume for simplicity that the union chooses the optimal z path. Whether the union chooses the wage path or the employment path is irrelevant for the result of the model. By choosing a wage path, the union indirectly chooses an employment path since the wage and employment are interrelated via the labour demand function. The assumption is only to simplify the exposition.

The constraints the union faces in its optimal choice are on the one hand the (static) resource constraint that employment, L, cannot exceed population, N, and the (dynamic) constraint that changes in z also change the rate of capital accumulation (which also determines the time path of the wage bill). So the constraints read:

$$z \geq k, \tag{4.8}$$

$$\dot{k} = s \cdot k \cdot f'(z) - n \cdot k. \tag{4.9}$$

The maximisation problem the union faces can be solved using intertemporal optimisation (see, e.g., Dixit (1990)). The (current value) Hamiltonian of the above given problem is:

$$\mathcal{H}(z, k, \mu) = N \cdot k \cdot b(z) + \mu \cdot (s \cdot f'(z) - n \cdot k), \tag{4.10}$$

where z is the control variable, k the state variable and μ the costate variable of this problem. The costate variable μ depicts the marginal value of additional per capita capital stock to the union. The Lagrangian of this problem (which is needed because of the static resource constraint) is given by:

$$\mathcal{L} = \mathcal{H} + \lambda \cdot (z - k). \tag{4.11}$$

The first order conditions for the optimal path of z are given by the following equations (see, e.g., Kamien and Schwartz (1991)):

$$\frac{\partial \mathcal{L}}{\partial z} = -N \cdot \frac{k}{z^2} \cdot (f(z) - z \cdot f'(z) + z^2 \cdot f''(z)) + \mu \cdot s \cdot k \cdot f''(z) + \lambda = 0, \tag{4.12}$$

$$\dot{\mu} = \rho\mu - N \cdot \left(\frac{1}{z}\right) \cdot (f(z) - z \cdot f'(z)) - \mu \cdot (s \cdot f'(z) - n) + \lambda. \tag{4.13}$$

Let us define the share of output that capitalists will get (for various capital to labour ratios) as $\theta(z) = \frac{z \cdot f'(z)}{f(z)}$. Moreover define the elasticity of substitution between labour and capital as $\sigma = \frac{d(k)/k}{d(\frac{w}{r})/\frac{w}{r}}$. Since factors of production are paid their marginal product, the following must hold $w = f(z) - z \cdot f'(z)$ and $r = f'(z)$. Moreover $\frac{d(\frac{w}{r})}{dz} = -\frac{f''(z) \cdot f(z)}{(f'(z))^2}$. Plugging this into the definition of the elasticity of substitution we get: $\sigma = -\frac{f'(z) \cdot (f(z) - z \cdot f(z))}{z \cdot f(z) \cdot f''(z)}$. Using all this, (4.12) modifies to:

$$-N \cdot k \cdot f''(z) \cdot \left(1 - \frac{\sigma}{\theta}\right) + \mu \cdot s \cdot k \cdot f''(z) + \lambda = 0. \tag{4.14}$$

Equation (4.14) reveals an interesting property of the model. As long as σ exceeds θ (or σ exceeds one) it is optimal for the union to set a wage path that guarantees $k = z$. Therefore, the union will do nothing and will set the competitive wage path. The economic intuition for this property is that as long as σ exceeds one, the share of output devoted to labour is a declining function of L. Hence, when the union rations labour by setting a wage above the competitive level, labour's share in output will decrease. In such a situation a union that wishes to maximise the wage bill will do nothing.

With the first order conditions at hand we are able to analyse the model. Consider first the case where the resource constraint is not binding (hence, $z \leq k$). In this case the optimal path of z satisfies the following equation:

$$\frac{\partial \mathcal{H}}{\partial z} = N \cdot (-k) \cdot f''(z) \cdot \left(1 - \frac{\sigma}{\theta}\right) + \mu \cdot s \cdot k \cdot f''(z) = 0. \tag{4.15}$$

Assuming that $\frac{\sigma}{\theta}$ is an increasing function in z (which is true as long as the share of output devoted to capital will decrease as K increases, which is, e.g., the case when the production function is CES and σ is smaller than one) there will be an equilibrium path $z^*(\mu)$ that maximises the wage bill given the intertemporal constraint. The above analysis rests on the assumption that the resource constraint is not binding. If it is binding ($k > z^*(\mu)$) the union will choose the capital to labour path that is nearest to the optimal path without resource constraint. Hence, the union will choose the maximum of the set $[k, z^*(\mu)]$.

We can analyse the steady state of the economy geometrically using a phase diagram that shows combinations of k and μ which ensure zero motion of these variables. When using a phase diagram it is important to know for which combinations of k and μ the resource constraint will bind. The condition for which the constraint begins to bind is given by (see equation (4.14)):

$$N \cdot \left(1 - \frac{\sigma}{\theta}\right) - \mu \cdot s = 0. \tag{4.16}$$

If this condition holds the union will be indifferent between rationing labour and refraining to do so, because the marginal utility of rationing labour (the first term on the left hand side) will be exactly offset by a decline of marginal utility as savings will decline. Figure (4.1) shows that the binding constraint

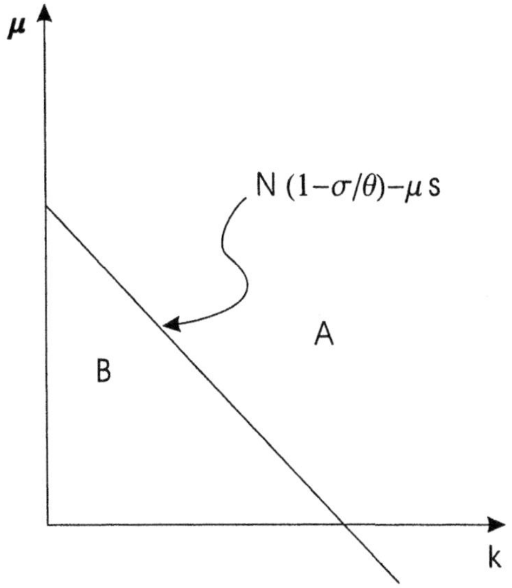

Fig. 4.1. The binding Constraint

divides the μ-k space into two regions. In region A the union will always choose the competitive wage path and hence, will do nothing. In this region the larger share of the pie today will not outweigh the loss of pie in the future. In region B it is advantageous for the union to set a wage exceeding the competitive outcome.

For comparative static analysis we need the two zero motion loci. Define $\bar{z}$ as the capital labour ratio for which the per capita capital stock is constant. Moreover define $\bar{\mu}$ as the shadow value for which $z = \bar{z}$. The zero motion line for the per capita capital stock is in this case a horizontal line in region B at $\bar{\mu}$. If in region B the shadow value is equal to $\bar{\mu}$, the capital labour ratio will be $\bar{z}$ which ensures the zero motion of the per capita capital stock independently of the values of k. When reaching the binding constraint z will be equal to k. In this case the per capita capital stock that ensures zero motion will be $k = \bar{z}$. Since k is independent of μ in this case, the zero motion locus will be a vertical line in Region A. The zero motion locus of k is shown in figure (4.2). Figure (4.2) shows that when the per capita capital stock is to the right (left)

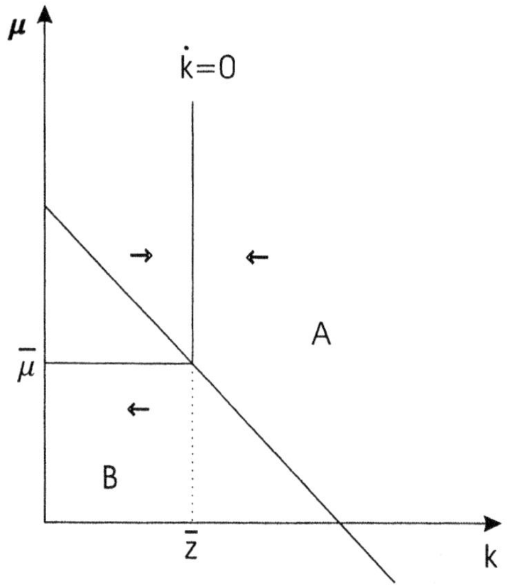

Fig. 4.2. Zero Motion of k

of $\bar{z}$ or the shadow value will be below (above) $\bar{\mu}$ the per capita capital stock will decline (increase).

The zero motion locus for the shadow price of savings μ can be derived using equation (4.13). Again we have to discriminate the analysis for region A from that of region B. Equation (4.13) reveals that the condition $\dot{\mu} = 0$ is independent of k. Hence, the zero motion locus in that region is a horizontal line. An interesting question is whether this zero motion line exists, hence, whether there exist some μ for which the motion of μ is zero when the resource constraint is not binding? To analyse this point define the following function:

$$F(\mu) = \rho \cdot \mu - N \cdot \left(\frac{1}{z}\right) \cdot (f(z) - z \cdot f'(z)) - \mu \cdot (s \cdot f'(z) - n). \tag{4.17}$$

Equation (4.17) shows the function that governs the evolution of μ when the resource constraint is not binding. The question of whether the zero motion line in region B exists boils down to the question of whether $F(\mu) = 0$ has a solution.

A nice way to analyse this is to look at the properties of the function $F(\mu)$. First of all let us turn to the interception of $F(\mu)$ with the ordinate, hence, we turn to the analysis of $F(0)$. Equation (4.17) depicts that when μ is zero, the sign of $F(0)$ is determined by $-N \cdot (\frac{1}{z}) \cdot (f(z) - z \cdot f'(z))$. As we have assumed a linear homogenous production function with two inputs, the production elasticity of z must be smaller than one, implying that $f(z) - z \cdot f'(z)$ must be positive. From this reasoning it follows that $F(0)$ is smaller than zero. Since we know that $F(0) < 0$ we only need to show that the slope of $F(\mu)$ is strictly positive, to guarantee that there exist some positive μ for which $\dot{\mu}$ is zero.

$$\begin{aligned} \frac{dF(\mu)}{d\mu} &= \rho - N \cdot z'(\mu) \cdot \left(\frac{f'(z) \cdot z - f(z)}{z^2} + f''(z)\right) \\ &\quad - s \cdot (z'(\mu) \cdot \mu \cdot f''(z) + f'(z)) - n. \end{aligned} \tag{4.18}$$

Remember that $z'(\mu)$ is negative. The economic intuition for this point is that with a high shadow value of savings the union will be reluctant to set a high wage. Hence, employment will be high and z will be low as μ increases. So all parts of the sum determining the sign of the slope of $F(\mu)$ are negative except for ρ.[2] Hence, we can distinguish two cases for the existence of the zero motion locus of μ in region B. When the rate of time preference of the labour union is high enough, the first derivative will be positive and there exists some μ for which $F(\mu)$ is zero. On the other hand when the rate of time preference is very low there will be no μ for which the function $F(.)$ will be zero (hence, in such a case the zero motion locus does not exist in Region B, see Kemp and Van Long (1987)). A very interesting point follows from this analysis. Since both, the zero motion loci of k and of μ are horizontal lines in region B, the model will not exhibit a steady state in region B.[3] But this implies that no steady state with unemployment exists in the economy.

When the constraint begins to bind, z will be equal to k and so in region A the zero motion line is a function of k, therefore $F(\mu)$ is a function of k. Equation (4.13) describes the evolution of μ. When the resource constraint is binding, by equation (4.12) the following holds:

$$\lambda = -k \cdot \mu \cdot s \cdot f''(k) + N \cdot \frac{1}{k} \cdot (f(k) - z \cdot f'(k) + k^2 \cdot f''(k)). \tag{4.19}$$

[2] Remember that $f''(z)$ is assumed to be negative and that, by the assumption of the production elasticity of z being smaller than one, $f'(z) \cdot z - f(z)$ is negative, too.

[3] We desist from considering the knife edge case in which $F(\mu)$ will be zero when $\mu = \bar{\mu}$. In this case the two zero motion loci would be one line.

Plugging this into equation (4.13) we get the equation of motion for the shadow price of savings in case of the binding resource base as:

$$\dot{\mu} = \rho \cdot \mu - \mu(s \cdot f(k) - n) + \frac{N}{k} \cdot k^2 \cdot f''(k) - \mu \cdot s \cdot k \cdot f''(k). \tag{4.20}$$

Hence, when the resource constraint binds and μ should not change over time, the following condition must hold:

$$\mu = -\frac{\frac{N}{k} \cdot k^2 \cdot f''(k)}{\rho - s \cdot f'(k) - n - s \cdot k \cdot f''(k)}. \tag{4.21}$$

Using equation (4.21) we can conclude that a steady state in region A exists as long as μ given by equation (4.21) at $k = \bar{z}$ will be bigger than $\bar{\mu}$. Hence, a steady state in region A exists as long as the following equation holds:

$$\bar{\mu} < -\frac{\frac{N}{\bar{z}} \cdot \bar{z}^2 \cdot f''(\bar{z})}{\rho - s \cdot f'(\bar{z}) - n - s \cdot \bar{z} \cdot f''(\bar{z})}. \tag{4.22}$$

This equation will be satisfied when the rate of time preference of the union ρ will be low enough. So when the rate of time preference is very high the condition given by equation (4.22) will not be satisfied and the steady state of the economy will not be in region A.

Moreover, both zero motion loci are parallel in region B. So it follows that when the rate of time preference of the union is very high, the economy will not reach a steady state. The union will set a wage that is so high that savings (done by the capitalists) are so low that the per capita stock of capital will steadily decline. Thus, the capital stock of the economy will be exhausted in the very long run. This point is depicted in figure 4.3. Figure 4.3 very nicely illustrates the point that no interception between the two zero motion loci exist and hence, the economy will not reach a steady state. The economic intuition behind this property is the following. When setting the wage the union faces a trade-off: higher wages today will increase the share of output the union will get. However, savings will decline and therefore the absolute amount of output in the future will decline, too. When the rate of time preference of the union is high, the union will pose more weight on the current gains of higher wages than on the future losses. So the wage path, the union will set is too high to keep the per capita capital stock in balance, with the result that the capital stock will eventually be exhausted.

Now assume that the rate of time preference of unions is low enough to guarantee a steady state in region A (but high enough so that the zero motion locus of μ exists in region B).[4] Figure 4.4 depicts such a situation. The interesting point in this case is that the economy will converge to a steady

[4] We only consider this case although the economic intuition for the case where the rate of time preference is so low that the zero motion locus of μ only exists in region A (see Kemp and Van Long (1987)) is similar to the reasoning in the text.

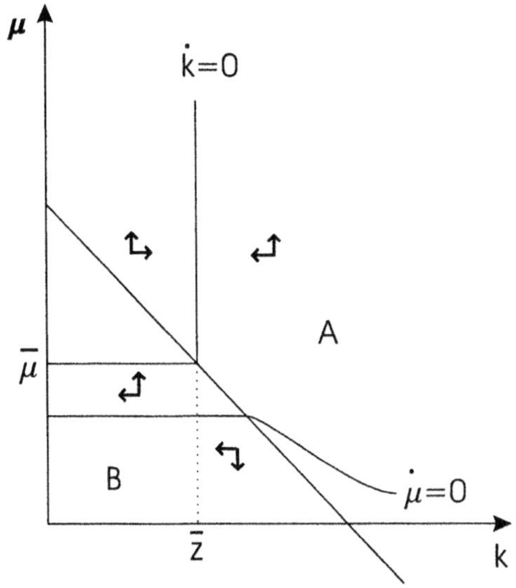

Fig. 4.3. Phase Plane for high ρ

state in which the union will set the same wage path as the one that would be realised in the competitive economy. So when the rate of time preference is very low, the future loss of production opportunities is so high that the union is reluctant to set a wage other than the competitive one. The unionised economy will not differ from the perfectly competitive one. All comparative static results that hold for the usual neoclassical growth model (e.g., the effects of a higher propensity to save) will also hold in the growth model with union wage bargaining. The economy with the unionised labour market mimics the economy with perfect labour markets (when the rate of time preference is low enough).

4.1.2 The CES Case

Consider the model of the preceding section with a concrete production function, namely a CES production function. This function is given by (see, e.g., Coto-Millán (1999)):

$$Y = \left(\psi \cdot L^{-\kappa} + (1-\psi) \cdot K^{-\kappa}\right)^{-\frac{1}{\kappa}}, \tag{4.23}$$

where ψ is an indicator of the division of output between capital and labour and κ is a parameter depicting the substitutability between the two inputs.

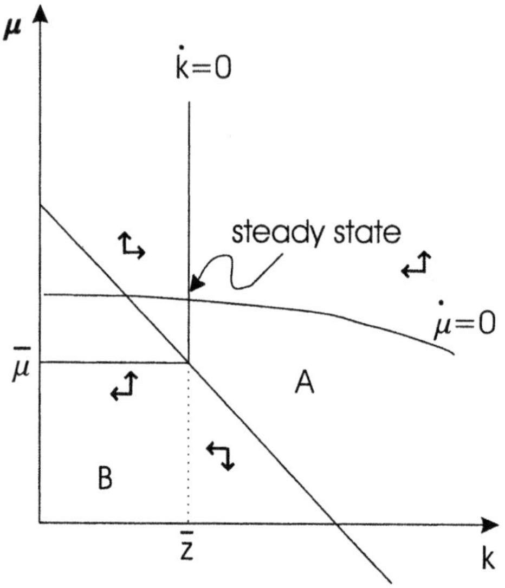

Fig. 4.4. Phase Plane for low ρ

We want to assume that the share of output is a decreasing function in L.[5] With profit maximising firms, labour's share in output is given by:

$$\frac{\frac{\partial Y}{\partial L} \cdot L}{Y} = \frac{1}{1 + \frac{1-\psi}{\psi} \cdot \left(\frac{K}{L}\right)^{-\kappa}}. \tag{4.24}$$

From equation (4.24) it is easy to see that labour's share in output is a declining function in L, as long as κ is positive which implies that the elasticity of substitution between labour and capital is smaller than one.[6]

Capitalists' income is given by:

$$K \cdot \frac{\partial Y}{\partial K} = Y^{1+\kappa} \cdot K^{-\kappa} \cdot (1 - \psi). \tag{4.25}$$

The evolution of the per capita capital stock is given by:

$$\frac{\dot{k}}{k} = \frac{\dot{K}}{K} - n, \tag{4.26}$$

[5] As was already noted, when we do not assume this, the union will be reluctant to set a wage exceeding the competitive one, because in such a case labour's share in output would decline

[6] With the labour and capital demand equations that could be derived using equation (4.23) it is easy to verify that the elasticity of substitution is given by $\sigma = \frac{1}{\kappa+1}$.

where n is the (exogenously given) population growth rate. Since we assume that only capitalists save with an exogenous marginal savings rate s, the evolution of the capital stock modifies to:

$$\dot{k} = k \cdot s \cdot (1 - \psi) \cdot Y^{1+\kappa} \cdot K^{-\kappa-1} - n \cdot k. \tag{4.27}$$

Note that when the wage bill increases (due to unionised labour market) savings will decline and as such, investment will decline.

As in the analysis in the preceding section, we assume that the union wants to maximise the present value of the entire wage bill.[7] The union sets the wage unilaterally, but firms have the right to manage, so only points on the labour demand curve are feasible. Union's utility function is given by:

$$U = \int_0^{\infty} e^{-\rho \cdot t} \cdot w \cdot L. \tag{4.28}$$

When plugging the labour demand curve $w = Y^{1+\kappa} \cdot \psi \cdot L^{-1-\kappa}$ into equation (4.28), we get union's utility as a function of L and K, hence:

$$U = \int_0^{\infty} e^{-\rho \cdot t} \cdot Y^{1+\kappa} \cdot \psi \cdot L^{-\kappa}. \tag{4.29}$$

For expository reasons, we assume that the union directly chooses the employment path L that maximises equation (4.29). This is only a short cut in the argumentation, because by setting a wage path the union indirectly sets the employment path. The intertemporal control problem the union has to solve, gives the following present value Hamiltonian and the first order conditions appertaining to the Hamiltonian[8]:

$$\mathcal{H} = Y^{1+\kappa} \cdot \psi \cdot L^{-\kappa} + \mu \cdot (k \cdot s \cdot (1 - \psi) \cdot Y^{1+\kappa} \cdot K^{-\kappa-1} - n \cdot k), \tag{4.30}$$

$$\frac{\partial \mathcal{H}}{\partial L} = Y^{1+\kappa} \cdot L^{-1-\kappa} \cdot \zeta + \mu \cdot s \cdot (1+\kappa) \cdot Y^{\kappa} \cdot K^{-1-\kappa} \cdot (1+\psi) \cdot k \cdot \left(\frac{\partial Y}{\partial L}\right) = 0, \tag{4.31}$$

$$\begin{aligned} \frac{\partial \mathcal{H}}{\partial k} = (1+\kappa) \cdot Y \cdot \frac{\partial Y}{\partial k} \cdot \psi \cdot L^{-\kappa} - \mu \cdot k^{-\kappa} \cdot s \cdot (1-\psi) \cdot \left(\frac{Y}{N}\right)^{1+\kappa} \cdot \\ \left(\kappa \cdot k^{-1} \cdot + (1+\kappa) \cdot Y^{-1} \cdot \frac{\partial Y}{\partial k}\right) - n \cdot \mu = \rho \cdot \mu - \dot{\mu}, \end{aligned} \tag{4.32}$$

[7] This is the easiest union utility function one could imagine. We have done this to keep the model as simple as possible. We could have also assumed more sophisticated functions with, e.g., unemployment benefit and so on. This would not change the main results. The crucial point is that the union has an infinite planning horizon.

[8] Besides this intertemporal constraint, the union faces also the static constraint, that employment cannot exceed population (resource constraint). We will consider this constraint later.

where $\zeta \equiv -\kappa \cdot \psi + (1+\kappa) \cdot \psi \cdot \eta$ and η denotes the production elasticity of labour.

Manipulating (4.31) gives the optimal employment path the union will set (as a function of the shadow value of savings and the per capita capital stock) as:

$$L^* = \left(-\mu \cdot s \cdot (1+\kappa) \cdot (1+\psi) \cdot k^{-\kappa} \cdot \left(\frac{1}{N}\right)^{1+\kappa} \right)^{-\frac{1}{\kappa}} \cdot \left(\frac{\eta}{\zeta}\right). \tag{4.33}$$

Equation (4.33) reveals that the employment path the union will set, will be the higher (and hence, the lower will be the wage path), the higher is μ. Hence, if the union values capital accumulation very high, it will not want to set a wage that is too high, because this would dampen savings.

A higher stock of capital has also positive employment effects, because labour demand is shifted outward and the union can reach a higher indifference curve with a higher wage and higher employment.[9]

Equation (4.33) also determines the function that divides the μ-k plane into region A and B. All combinations of μ and k for which the optimal L given by the equation equals or exceeds N will form region A. In this region the resource constraint is binding. All other combinations form region B, for which the optimal L the union wants to set is lower than N and hence, in this case the resource constraint is not binding.

Using equations (4.27) and (4.32), the steady state values of k and μ could be determined (if they exist). With these values, optimal employment is eventually determined. As was already analysed in the general case, the zero motion lines of μ and k will only intercept in region A. Hence, the optimal employment path the union would like to set (given by equation (4.33)) exceeds N. Because of the resource constraint this choice is not feasible and so the union will set the highest employment path possible. Given the resource constraint, this is N. Hence, the union will set the competitive wage path and will not use its monopoly power.

4.2 The Palokangas Model (1989)

In the last section we have analysed the effects of union wage setting in a dynamic economy, i.e., in a neoclassical growth model. The result of this model was that when the union is not too impatient, it will not use its wage setting

[9] The change in the stock of capital also has second round effects, because the production elasticity of labour changes. The production elasticity will decline when the stock of capital increases. So the change in the stock of capital has countervailing employment effects. To keep the model tractable we suppress the second round effects and assume that the first round effects always dominate the second round ones.

power and the full employment path will be realised. A main drawback of the model is that it is somewhat contradicted by the observations we make in reality. On the one hand it is a common observation that (at least a part) of unemployment in western europe is caused by union wage bargaining (see, e.g., Layard et al. (1990)). On the other hand we cannot observe that the capital stock is run down to zero. When we look at the evolution of the capital stock in some OECD countries (as done in figure 4.5), the graphs nicely depict that the capital to labour ratio is increasing over time for all countries, even in countries in which union coverage is very high (as, e.g., Germany) and which suffer from high unemployment rates. So it seems that in reality we

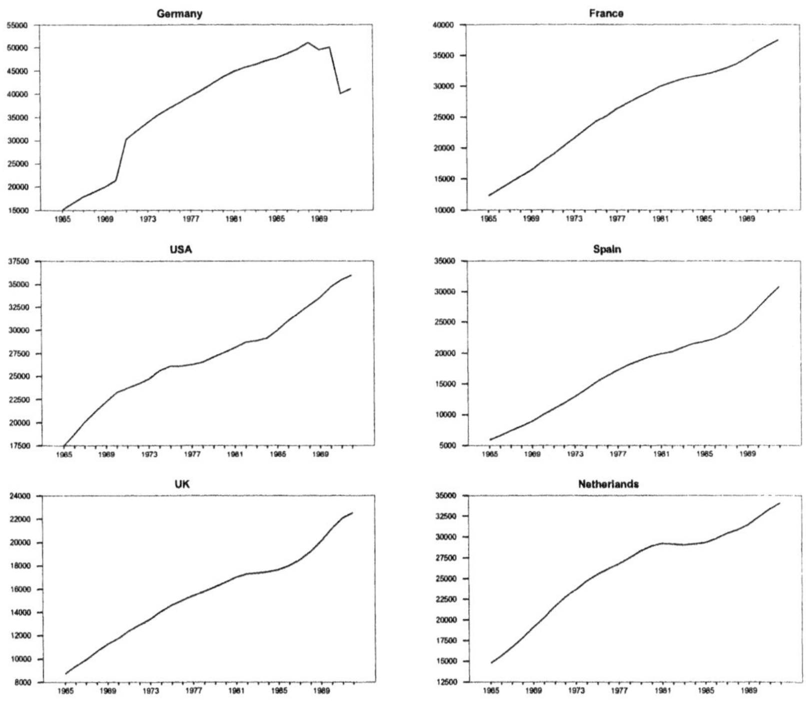

Fig. 4.5. The capital to labour ratio in six OECD countries. Source: The Penn World Tables, Mark 5.6.

have an intermediate case in which the union will set a wage exceeding the competitive one (and hence, the economies experience unemployment), but that the wage is not so high to run down the stock of capital to zero. This intermediate case is analysed in a model by Palokangas (1989) which is basically a variety of the model of Kemp and Van Long (1987). The modifications are that on the one hand the production function is more sophisticated. Instead of using a constant returns to scale function as done in the preceding section, a convex-concave production function is applied. The economic legitimation for this alteration of the used production function is that for latter stages of development a convex technology may be a good proxy, but if we want to analyse the whole process of development, convex-concave technologies might better reflect reality. On the other hand, the savings function of capitalists differs from that of the basic model.

Consider the following production function:

$$Y = f(x) \cdot g(K), \tag{4.34}$$

where x is the labour to capital ratio, $\frac{L}{K}$, (in the terms of the Kemp and Van Long (1987) model $x = z^{-1}$) and $f(.)$ is a constant returns to scale function with the usual properties that the first derivative is positive and the second is negative. The function $g(K)$ depicts the concavity-convexity property of the production function. Palokangas (1989) assumes the following form for $g(K)$:

$$g(K) = \begin{cases} K^q & K \geq k \\ k^{q-e} \cdot K^e & K < k, \end{cases} \tag{4.35}$$

where e exceeds one and $0 < q < 1$. The threshold k is an exogenously given constant. Equation (4.35) shows that as long as the capital stock is smaller than the threshold k, the production function has increasing returns to scale, because the elasticity of $g(k)$ with respect to K exceeds one. The opposite is true, when the capital stock exceeds (or is equal to) the threshold k. In this case the production function is characterised by decreasing returns to scale.

Labour income (the wage bill) is given by:

$$\frac{\partial Y}{\partial L} \cdot L = \frac{L}{K} \cdot f'(x) \cdot g(K). \tag{4.36}$$

We assume that by setting a wage which exceeds the competitive one (i.e., by rationing labour), the union can increase the wage bill. Taking the derivative of (4.36) with respect to L, one can easily see that we implicitly assume that the wage elasticity of the labour demand curve, $E(x)$, is smaller than one (as equation (4.37) reveals):

$$\frac{\partial \frac{\partial Y}{\partial L} \cdot L}{\partial L} = \frac{g(K)}{K} \cdot (1 - E(x)), \tag{4.37}$$

where $E(x) \equiv -\frac{x \cdot f''(x)}{f'(x)}$. The residual between production and the part that labour receives is the capitalists' income which is given by $Y - \frac{\partial Y}{\partial L} \cdot L = (f(x) - x \cdot f'(x)) \cdot g(K)$. As in the preceding model it is assumed that only capitalists save.[10] The assumed savings function is different than the usual "constant fraction of income"-type. The savings function is given by:

[10] As before this is a crucial assumption.

$$S = a \cdot \left(\underbrace{s \cdot (f(x) - x \cdot f'(x)) \cdot g(K)}_{capilatists \quad income} - K \right). \tag{4.38}$$

As such, savings are a constant fraction of income (where s is the savings rate) minus the stock of capital times an adjustment parameter a. The economic rationale for such a savings function rests on the assumption of life cycle consumption and live cycle savings. Assume that marginal utility of consumption as well as savings declines. Thus, when aggregate wealth of the capitalists (which is the stock of capital) is very high (the savings rate in the past has been very high) the marginal utility of additional savings is low. Therefore, a higher stock of aggregate wealth lowers savings.[11]

Again we assume that the union can unilaterally set the wage. The aim of the union is to maximise the present value of the stream of wage bills over an infinite horizon. Taking into account that the union can only choose points on the labour demand curve, union's utility reads:

$$U = \int_0^\infty e^{-\rho \cdot t} \cdot x \cdot f'(x) \cdot g(K) \cdot dt. \tag{4.39}$$

The union chooses the wage path that maximises (4.39). Hence, the union indirectly sets L or x to maximise utility. By choosing the optimal path of x the union again faces a static and a dynamic optimisation problem. Firstly, the union has to take the dynamic constraint that any change in x changes savings into account and secondly the union cannot choose a x that exceeds $\frac{N}{K}$ (where N is the exogenous and time constant stock of population).

Assume for the moment that the static resource constraint is not binding. In this case the union can choose x only taking the dynamic restriction of the evolution of the capital stock into account. The current value Hamiltonian for this problem is the following (remember that $\dot{K}$ must equal S):

$$\mathcal{H} = x \cdot f'(x) \cdot g(K) + \mu \cdot (a \cdot s \cdot (f(x) - x \cdot f'(x)) \cdot g(K) - K), \tag{4.40}$$

where x is the control variable and K and μ are the state and the costate variable, respectively.

The first order conditions of this problem are given by:

[11] Besides this economic rationale there is also a theoretical motivation for this assumption. Because it is assumed that population growth is zero, there must be the possibility that the equation of motion of capital can be zero (only in this case a steady state exists). So a savings function which can be zero is needed to ensure the existence of the steady state.

$$\frac{\partial \mathcal{H}}{\partial x} = x \cdot f''(x) + f'(x) \cdot g(K) - \mu \cdot a \cdot s \cdot x \cdot f''(x) \cdot g(K) = 0, \tag{4.41}$$

$$\begin{aligned} \frac{\partial \mathcal{H}}{\partial K} &= x \cdot f'(x) \cdot g'(K) + \mu \cdot p \cdot a \cdot s \cdot \\ (f(x) - x \cdot f'(x)) \cdot g'(K) - \mu \cdot a &= \rho \cdot \mu - \dot{\mu}, \end{aligned} \tag{4.42}$$

$$\frac{\partial \mathcal{H}}{\partial \mu} = a \cdot (s \cdot (f(x) - x \cdot f'(x)) \cdot g(K) - K) = \dot{K}. \tag{4.43}$$

Assuming $g(K) \neq 0$, equation (4.41) reveals that the optimal path of x is only a function of the shadow value of savings μ, hence $x^*(\mu)$. The optimal path of x will be the higher, the higher is μ. Using the definition of $E(x)$ and plugging this into (4.41) gives (after some straightforward manipulations):

$$\mu = \left(-\frac{1}{E(x)} + 1\right) \cdot \left(\frac{1}{a \cdot s}\right). \tag{4.44}$$

With the assumption that $E(x) > 1$, equation (4.44) discloses that the shadow value of savings is always positive. Using equation (4.41) we can also derive $\frac{d\mu}{dx}$, which is given by:

$$\frac{d\mu}{dx} = \frac{1}{E(x)^2 \cdot a \cdot s} \cdot E'(x). \tag{4.45}$$

With $E'(x)$ being positive, (this follows from the assumption that the Hamiltonian is concave in x (see Palokangas (1989)) the first derivative of x^* with respect to μ is positive. The economic intuition for this property is the following. If the union values savings a lot, it will be reluctant to set a high wage as this would cause savings to decline.

To determine the optimal path of x in the economy, we need to know the evolution of μ. This is give by (4.42) which is a function of K which in turn is given by (4.43). Because we want to concentrate on steady states[12] we only determine the steady state values of μ and K. Since we have no explicit functional forms, we use the phase diagram to do comparative statics on the state and the costate variable. An important point is that as before the μ-K-plane is divided into two regions. The first region (let us call it again B) is the region in which the resource constraint will not bind, because with all combinations of K and μ in that region, the union will find it optimal to set x smaller than $\frac{N}{K}$. On the other hand region A consists of combinations of μ and K for which the union will find it optimal to set a labour to capital path which is bigger than $\frac{N}{K}$, hence in this region the resource constraint is binding. The border line that separates the two regions is given by: $x^*(\mu) = \frac{N}{K}$. This curve will be downward sloping in the μ-K-space. The intuition is the following: Take some μ_0 and K_0 for which the union would set $x(\mu_0)$ equal to $\frac{N}{K_0}$. Now

[12] Remember that in this model a steady state implies that the economy will not grow at all, because the rate of population growth is zero.

consider that μ_0 increases to μ_1. In this case the union is reluctant to set a high wage and would set $x(\mu_1)$ bigger than $\frac{N}{K_0}$. So K_0 must decrease to K_1 to keep the demands of the union just in line with the resource constraint, hence, $x(\mu_1) = \frac{N}{K_1}$. With this the borderline between the two regions must be downward sloping.

First of all consider region B, where the resource constraint does not bind. To determine possible steady states in region B, we have to analyse the zero motion loci for capital and for the shadow value of savings. With equation (4.42) we can determine the slope of the zero motion locus of μ for the case that the constraint is not binding (hence, $x = x^*(\mu)$). The zero motion locus is given by:

$$0 = \underbrace{(\rho + a) \cdot \mu - (x \cdot f'(x) + \mu \cdot s \cdot a(f(x) - x \cdot f'(x))) \cdot g'(K)}_{J}. \tag{4.46}$$

With equation (4.46) the slope of the zero motion locus of μ is given by:

$$\frac{d\mu}{dK}|_{\dot{\mu}=0} = -\frac{\frac{\partial J}{\partial \mu}}{\frac{\partial J}{\partial K}}. \tag{4.47}$$

The numerator of equation (4.47) is:

$$\frac{\partial J}{\partial K} = -\left(x \cdot f'(x) + s \cdot a \cdot \mu \cdot \underbrace{(f(x) - x \cdot f'(x))}_{Y - w \cdot L > 0} \right) \cdot g''(K). \tag{4.48}$$

The sign of the numerator of equation (4.47) is determined by the sign of $g''(K)$ and this is given by equation (4.35) as:

$$g''(K) = \begin{cases} q \cdot (q-1) \cdot K^{q-2} < 0 & K \geq k \\ e \cdot (e-1) \cdot k^{q-e} K^{e-2} > 0 & K < k. \end{cases} \tag{4.49}$$

The denominator of equation (4.47) is given by the following equation:

$$\begin{aligned} \frac{\partial J}{\partial \mu} &= (\rho + a) - s \cdot a \cdot g'(K) \cdot (f(x) - x \cdot f'(x)) - \\ &\{x' \cdot f' + x' \cdot x \cdot f'' + s \cdot a \cdot \mu \cdot (-x \cdot x' \cdot f'')\} \cdot g'(K). \end{aligned} \tag{4.50}$$

Equation (4.50) can be simplified by noting that the term in curly brackets is zero when the union sets the optimal x. Manipulating the term in curly brackets and using the definition of $E(x)$ gives: $x' \cdot f' \cdot (-1 + E(x) - s \cdot a \cdot \mu \cdot E(x))$, where the term inside the parentheses is zero by equation (4.41). With this simplification and the condition given in equation (4.46), the denominator modifies to:

$$\frac{\partial J}{\partial \mu} = \frac{x}{\mu} \cdot g'(K) \cdot f'(x). \tag{4.51}$$

With (4.51) it is obvious that the denominator is positive. Hence, the slope of the zero motion locus of μ is positive as long as K is smaller than the threshold k and negative when K exceeds the threshold. To the north of the zero motion line, $\dot{\mu}$ is positive and below the zero motion line negative.[13]

The zero motion locus of K in region B can be derived using the same methods as applied before. The zero motion line of K is given by:

$$0 = \underbrace{a \cdot (s \cdot (f(x) - x \cdot f'(x)) \cdot g(K) - K)}_{T}. \tag{4.52}$$

Using equation (4.52), the slope of the zero motion locus is given by :

$$\frac{d\mu}{dK}|_{\dot{K}=0} = -\frac{\frac{\partial T}{\partial \mu}}{\frac{\partial T}{\partial K}}. \tag{4.53}$$

Using straightforward algebra, this modifies to:

$$\frac{d\mu}{dK}|_{\dot{K}=0} = -\frac{a \cdot \left(\frac{g'(K) \cdot K}{g(K)} - 1\right)}{a \cdot s \cdot (-f''(x) \cdot x) \cdot g(K)}. \tag{4.54}$$

Equation (4.54) reveals that the slope of the zero motion line of K is determined by the sign of the elasticity of $g(K)$ with respect to K. With equation (4.35) this elasticity is given by:

$$\frac{g'(K) \cdot K}{g(K)} = \begin{cases} q < 1 & K \geq k \\ e > 1 & K < k. \end{cases} \tag{4.55}$$

So when K is smaller than the threshold k, the slope of the zero motion locus of K is negative and vice versa. To the north of the zero motion locus of K, $\dot{K}$ is positive, whereas $\dot{K}$ is negative for points below the zero motion line.

Now we turn to region A. Let us assume that the borderline of the two regions (which is negatively sloped) intercepts the zero motion line of K in the part where the slope of the zero motion locus is positive. The zero motion locus of K in region A is no longer a function of μ (see, equation (4.43) with $x = \frac{N}{K}$). Hence, the zero motion line is a vertical line in region A. The slope of the zero motion locus of μ in region A is basically the same as that in region B (see, Palokangas (1989)).[14]

All properties of the dynamic system can be depicted in a phase diagram which is shown in figure 4.6. In the case shown by figure 4.6 the two zero

[13] Another more technical point is that the zero motion line of μ is discontinuous at the threshold k (this is because g(K) is also discontinuous at this point). The limit of μ is bigger when K approaches k from the left than when K approaches from the right. See, Palokangas (1989) for this point.

[14] We do not want to go into detail about the properties of the functions in region A, because we want to concentrate on the more interesting case in which there are steady states with unemployment.

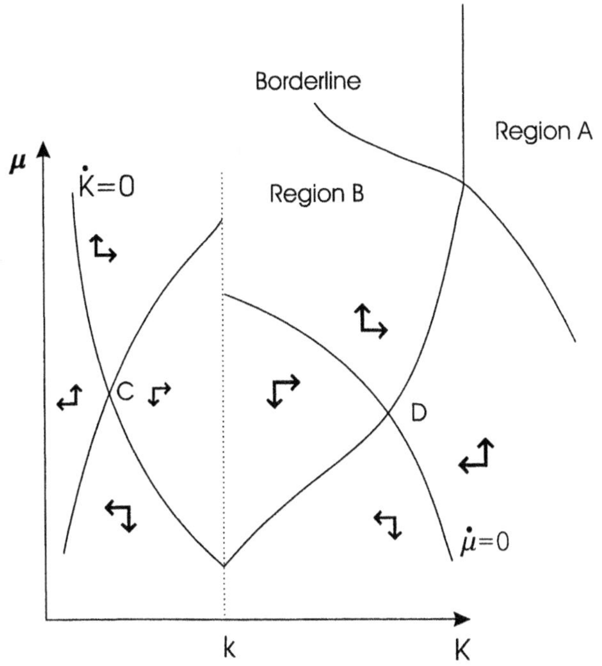

Fig. 4.6. The Phase Plane of the Palokangas (1989) Model

motion lines intercept two times and both interceptions are in region B (thus, in a situation in which there is unemployment). So the model generates two steady states (in points C and D). The steady state in C is not stable whereas the steady state with the higher capital stock (point D) is saddle path stable.

If the capital stock in the economy is lower than the capital stock given by the steady state in C, the union will set a high wage so that the capital stock runs down to zero and will be finally completely exhausted. The economic intuition for this property is that in the case of a low stock of capital, the utility gain for the union by setting a high wage (the impact effect) will be much higher than the future utility losses due to the lower stock of capital. When the stock of capital is not too low, the union will be reluctant to bargain a wage that is too high for capital accumulation.

When the stable steady state is reached, the union will set exactly the employment path that ensures capital accumulation to be zero. The wage which the union sets in this case will exceed the competitive wage and there will be unemployment.

In the Kemp and Van Long (1987) model it was shown that the rate of time preference of unions is a crucial parameter for the question whether the economy reaches a steady state with full employment or whether no steady state exists at all. In the Palokangas (1989) model this question boils down to whether there will be a steady state with full employment or with unemployment.

Consider the case shown in figure 4.6. What will happen to the zero motion lines if the rate of time preference decreases? First of all note that the zero motion line of K will be unchanged (see equation (4.43)). Only the zero motion line of the shadow value of savings will be affected (see equation (4.42)). If ρ decreases (the union will be more patient) the zero motion line of μ will be shifted upwards.[15] If this upward shift is large enough (hence, the union gets very patient) the interception of the two zero motion lines will be in region A. Very patient unions will not use their monopoly power and will set a wage path that guarantees full employment. The economic intuition is the same as in the Kemp and Van Long (1987) model. If the union is very patient it will value the utility loss in the future due to lower savings a lot and so it will be reluctant to set a wage that exceeds the competitive outcome. If the union is very impatient the value of this utility loss is low and so there will exist a steady state with unemployment.

An interesting question in this regard is whether the existence of a steady state with unemployment is caused by the assumption of the convex-concave production function or the different savings function. In a related paper, Kemp and Van Long (1990) show that steady states with unemployment will even exist with a CRS production function if capitalists save optimally (hence, a Ramsey type of model is analysed). So only a change in the savings function generates intermediate cases in which there exist steady states with unemployment.[16]

[15] This is true because $\dot{\mu}$ increases as μ increases and it decreases as ρ decreases. Hence, μ can be higher (given K) without hurting the zero motion relation.

[16] In the model in which savings are not fixed but an optimal decision of capitalists, it is important that the union can bind itself to the wage path it sets/announces. If this was not be the case, the same time inconsistency problem described in the section on union wage bargaining and investment would arise.

5

Unions in a Diamond Type Growth Model

In the preceding chapter the effect of union wage setting on the economy was analysed in a dynamic framework of the Solow (1956) type. These models were characterised by infinitely lived agents and a union that chose an intertemporal optimal wage path. The alternative modelling strategy to the infinite horizon case is to apply an overlapping generations model (OLG). The first paper to employ this structure in a neoclassical model was the Diamond (1965) model, so these kind of models are often referred to as Diamond type models.

In the next section we analyse a standard OLG model with capital accumulation in which the wage is determined in a bargain between unions and firms. The reason for this generalisation of the union effects in neoclassical models is twofold. First of all it is a robustness check whether the impact of union wage bargaining differs depending on the structure of modelling. Secondly the OLG models offer new insights and results. The most interesting point is that steady state unemployment even exists in models with a very simple structure (i.e., CRS production function). The reason for this difference compared to the result of the Solow model is that in the OLG model the union only covers one generation of young. As such, the wage setting problem has no intertemporal dimension, but is inherently static (see, e.g., Devereux and Lockwood (1991)). So the union in the OLG model does not face an intertemporal trade-off since it does not care about the next generation of young. With this it is always optimal to raise the wage above the competitive level.

We will analyse the impact of union wage bargaining on the steady state stock of capital in an OLG model using a (slightly) modified version of the Bräuninger (2000) model.

5.1 The Basic Model

The structure of the economy is very simple. Assume that firms in the economy produce according to the following production function (in which Y_t is output at time t, K_t is capital at t and L_t is employment at t):

$$Y_t = K_t^{\alpha} \cdot L_t^{1-\alpha}. \tag{5.1}$$

The labour demand and the capital demand function of firms are given by profit maximisation:

$$\frac{w_t}{P_t} = (1-\alpha) \cdot L_t^{-\alpha} \cdot K_t^{\alpha}, \tag{5.2}$$

$$\frac{r_t}{P_t} = \alpha \cdot K_t^{\alpha-1} \cdot L_t^{1-\alpha}, \tag{5.3}$$

where r_t and w_t is the rate of interest at t and the wage, respectively and P_t is the price of output. Because we assume that all firms produce one homogenous good[1] we treat Y as the numéraire and can set the price equal to one.

The economy is inhabited by young and old individuals. The young work and save and the old get capital income and consume. The number of young individuals is N (which is time constant) and they supply inelastically one unit of labour to the firms. Thus, equilibrium employment is given by N. To determine the steady state stock of capital in the economy, we only have to determine the evolution of the rate of capital accumulation (see equation (5.1)).[2] Because we assume a closed economy, capital accumulation has to be financed by the savings of the young. Utility of the young can be represented by the following CES function:

$$U_t^{young} = \left((C_t^{young})^{-\rho} + (C_{t+1}^{old})^{-\rho}\right)^{-\frac{1}{\rho}}. \tag{5.4}$$

The young at time t care about their consumption today (C_t^{young}) and their consumption when they are old (C_{t+1}^{old}). The parameter ρ indicates the substitutability of consumption today against consumption tomorrow. The budget constraint faced by the young when choosing their consumption path is that the present value of their income must be equal to the present value of consumption. As the wage is the only source of primary income, the budget restriction of the young (using equation (5.2)) reads:

$$(1-\alpha) \cdot Y_t = C_t^{young} + C_{t+1}^{old} \cdot \frac{1}{1+r_t}. \tag{5.5}$$

To solve the maximisation problem of the young we can use the following Lagrangian function:

$$\mathcal{L} = \left((C_t^{young})^{-\rho} + (C_{t+1}^{old})^{-\rho}\right)^{-\frac{1}{\rho}} + \lambda \cdot \left((1-\alpha) \cdot Y_t - C_t^{young} - C_{t+1}^{old} \cdot \frac{1}{1+r_t}\right). \tag{5.6}$$

[1] Hence, we assume perfect competition in contrast to Bräuninger (2000) in which there is monopolistic competition.

[2] In section 6 we also analyse an AK model with a very similar structure.

With this we get the following first order conditions for the maximum of equation (5.4) subject to the budget constraint (5.5):

$$\left((C_t^{young})^{-\rho} + (C_{t+1}^{old})^{-\rho}\right)^{-\frac{1}{\rho}-1} \cdot (C_t^{young})^{-\rho-1} - \lambda = 0, \tag{5.7}$$

$$\left((C_t^{young})^{-\rho} + (C_{t+1}^{old})^{-\rho}\right)^{-\frac{1}{\rho}-1} \cdot (C_{t+1}^{old})^{-\rho-1} - \frac{\lambda}{1+r_t} = 0, \tag{5.8}$$

$$(1-\alpha) \cdot Y_t = C_t^{young} + C_{t+1}^{old} \cdot \frac{1}{1+r_t}. \tag{5.9}$$

With these first order conditions, consumption of the young at time t is given by:

$$C_t^{young} = \underbrace{(1-\alpha) \cdot Y_t}_{wage \quad income} \cdot \frac{1}{1+(1+r_t)^{\frac{\rho}{\rho+1}}}. \tag{5.10}$$

Because savings of the young are given by their income minus their consumption and the young finance next period's stock of capital (remember that the old have no bequest motive and consume their stock of capital), we get the following equation for the evolution of the stock of capital:

$$K_{t+1} - K_t = (1-\alpha) \cdot Y_t \cdot \left(1 - \frac{1}{1+(1+r_t)^{\frac{\rho}{\rho+1}}}\right) - K_t. \tag{5.11}$$

Keeping in mind that the whole labour force is full employed, hence, $L_t = N$ and plugging in the production function for Y_t and the capital demand function for the rate of interest, equation (5.11) constitutes a first-order difference equation in the stock of capital:

$$K_{t+1} - K_t = (1-\alpha) \cdot (N^{1-\alpha} \cdot K_t^{\alpha}) \cdot \left(1 - \frac{1}{1+(1+\alpha \cdot K_t^{\alpha-1} \cdot N^{1-\alpha})^{\frac{\rho}{\rho+1}}}\right) - Kt. \tag{5.12}$$

We could impose steady state conditions on equation (5.12) ($K_{t+1} = K_t = K$) and could determine the steady state stock of capital in the economy.[3] The steady state stock of capital is apparently a function of the income of the young and of the rate of interest. The steady state stock of capital will be high, when the income of the young and the rate of interest is high.

5.2 Union Wage Bargaining

In the last section we have determined the steady state of the economy when labour markets were perfectly competitive. In this section we will integrate union wage bargaining into the economy and we will analyse the effects on the

[3] In an economy with no population growth, the assumption of a steady state obviously implies that the economy will not grow at all!

steady state capital stock. We assume that the wage of the young is bargained every period by a labour union and that the union only covers one generation of young. When the young turn old after one period the union splits up and the then young form a new union. The advantage of this assumption is that the union only faces a static problem and it can treat the stock of capital as being fixed during the bargain.

The union wants to maximise the income of its members, M, where the number of members is exogenous to the union. The utility function takes the following explicit form:

$$U(i) = w(i)_t \cdot L(i)_t + (M(i) - L(i)_t) \cdot AI_t, \tag{5.13}$$

where the index i indicates firm-level variables. So we assume that a union and a firm bargain the wage at the firm-level. This implies that all macroeconomic effects are assumed constant during the bargain. AI_t is the alternative income of the union members that do not get a job in firm i. They might find a job somewhere else in the economy and get a wage or might become unemployed and receive unemployment benefit. The crucial point is that the alternative income is exogenous to the firm-level union.

The bargained wage is determined by maximising the following Nash product:

$$\Omega = (U(i) - \bar{U}(i))^{\gamma} \cdot (\Pi(i) - \bar{\Pi}(i))^{1-\gamma}, \tag{5.14}$$

where γ is bargaining power of unions, $\Pi(i)$ is the profit of firm i and $\bar{U}(i)$ and $\bar{\Pi}(i)$ is the utility of the union and the profit of the firm respectively, when both parties do not reach an agreement. When both parties fail to reach an agreement, we assume that all union members get the alternative income and that the profit of the firm in such a case will be $-r \cdot K_t(i)$. So we assume that the firm has installed the stock of capital in advance of the bargain and has committed itself.[4] Solving the bargaining problem subject to the labour demand function we get the following bargained wage in firm i (see the Appendix to this section):

$$w(i)_t = \phi \cdot AI_t, \tag{5.15}$$

where $\phi \equiv \left(\frac{1}{1-\frac{\gamma \cdot \alpha^2}{1-\alpha+\alpha \cdot \gamma}}\right)$. The bargained wage at the firm-level is a mark-up over the alternative income of union members. This mark-up is a function of the bargaining power of unions and the wage elasticity of the labour demand function.

To simplify the exposition we assume that the alternative income is a weighted average of the wage and the unemployment benefit. The weights are

[4] Implicitly we assume that the firm is not able to sell the capital goods when the bargain fails. Hence, there is no secondary market for capital goods or the costs of deinstallation are prohibitively high.

the employment and the unemployment rate, respectively. So the alternative income is given by:

$$AI_t = (1-u)\cdot w + u \cdot B, \tag{5.16}$$

where u is the unemployment rate $u = \frac{N-L_t}{N}$.[5]

Assuming symmetry over bargaining units $w(i)_t = w_t$, we get the bargained wage in the economy as:

$$w_t = \frac{\phi \cdot u}{1-\phi+u\cdot\phi}\cdot B, \tag{5.17}$$

The wage at the aggregate level is a mark-up over the unemployment benefit. The mark-up is not only a function of the bargaining power and the labour demand elasticity, but also of the unemployment rate. This is because a high unemployment rate decreases the alternative income and makes being unemployment more costly for the union members. So the union is cautious not to bargain a wage that is too high.

We assume that the unemployment benefit is a constant fraction of the wage, hence, $\frac{B}{w_t} = b$. With this, the unemployment rate in the economy is solely determined by equation (5.17) and is given by:

$$u = \frac{\phi - 1}{\phi\cdot(1-b)}. \tag{5.18}$$

The unemployment rate in the economy will increase when the replacement ratio b increases and the mark-up ϕ increases (e.g., caused by higher union bargaining power).

To determine the effects of the union on the steady state stock of capital, we again have to determine the savings of the young. We assume the same utility function as in the basic model, but in the economy with union wage bargaining, savings will be the sum of savings done by the employed and the unemployed. With this, savings in the economy are given by:

$$S_t = \left(1 - \frac{1}{1+(1+r_t)^{\frac{\rho}{\rho+1}}}\right)\cdot\left(w_t\cdot L_t + (N-L_t)\cdot B\right). \tag{5.19}$$

Using the labour demand equation (remember that wage contracts will be on the labour demand curve) and the definition of unemployment rate, the savings equation reads after some manipulation:

$$S_t = \left(\frac{1}{1+(1+r_t)^{\frac{\rho}{\rho+1}}}\right)\cdot\left((1-\alpha)\cdot N^{1-\alpha}\cdot K_t^{\alpha}\cdot(1-u)^{1-\alpha} + u\cdot N\cdot B\right). \tag{5.20}$$

[5] We could also have specified the alternative income in a more sophisticated way as, e.g., done in Bräuninger (2000) or Layard and Nickell (1990) but this is not important for the point we want to make.

Substituting the rate of interest by the capital demand equation (5.3) and using equation (5.20), the evolution of the stock of capital in the unionised economy reads:

$$K_{t+1} - K_t = \left(1 - \frac{1}{1 + (1 + \alpha \cdot K_t^{\alpha-1} \cdot N^{1-\alpha} \cdot (1-u))^{\frac{\rho}{\rho+1}}}\right) \cdot \\ \left((1-\alpha) \cdot N^{1-\alpha} \cdot K_t^{\alpha} \cdot (1-u)^{1-\alpha} + u \cdot N \cdot B\right) - K_t. \tag{5.21}$$

With equation (5.21) at hands we can analyse the effects of the union on the steady state rate of capital.

The primary effect of the union is that labour is rationed and thus, there is unemployment and the wage exceeds the competitive outcome. So the union has the direct effect on capital accumulation that the income of the young will change and therefore, savings will change. On the one hand less young are employed which dampens income. On the other hand those who are employed receive a higher wage. Despite of these countervailing effects, the aggregate income of the young (employed and unemployed) will decline as long as the unemployment benefit is low enough.[6] This can be easily shown by differentiating equation (5.20) with respect to u which gives:

$$\frac{\partial S_t}{\partial u}|_{r_t = fix} = \left(\frac{1}{1 + (1 + r_t)^{\frac{\rho}{\rho+1}}}\right) \cdot \left(-(1-\alpha)^2 \cdot N^{1-\alpha} \cdot K_t^{\alpha} \cdot (1-u)^{-\alpha} + N \cdot B\right) \tag{5.22}$$

Equation (5.22) depicts that as long as the relation $B < (1-\alpha)^2 \cdot N^{-\alpha} \cdot K_t^{\alpha} \cdot (1-u)^{-\alpha}$ holds, savings will decline when the union bargains the wage. We assume this condition to hold.

Besides this direct effect on the income of the young, the union also indirectly affects the capital accumulation in the economy by altering the rate of interest. As capital is the only asset in the economy, the rate of interest will be determined by the marginal productivity of capital. But if there is unemployment in the economy, the marginal product of capital will decline and with this the rate of interest will decline, too (see, e.g., Daveri and Tabellini (2000)). As such, also this indirect effect dampens savings in the economy.[7]

These union effects can be shown geometrically using the phase diagram of equations (5.12) and (5.21). Figure 5.1 depicts that in the case of the union bargaining the wage, the steady state stock of capital K_U^* will be lower than the one with competitive labour markets K^*. The shift of the difference equation to the left is due to the fact that for every given stock of capital savings and hence, investment will be lower (at least with our assumption that the unemployment benefit is not too high).

---

[6] A main drawback is that this is only a partial equilibrium model, where the unemployment benefit is exogenous.

[7] This will obviously only be the case for certain values of the intertemporal elasticity of substitution (given by the utility function).

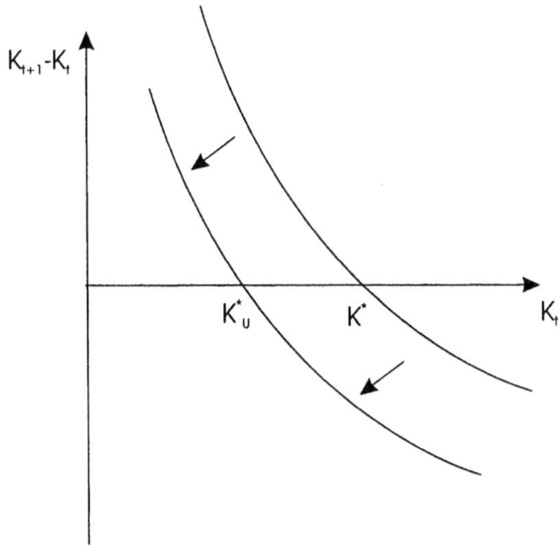

Fig. 5.1. Phase Diagram of the OLG Model

Summarising we can state that the union wage bargaining causes the steady state stock of capital to decline. Besides the steady state effects, the union will dampen the rate of economic growth during the transition to the new steady state.[8]

An interesting point of the OLG model in comparison to the models with infinitely lived agents is first of all that even in a simple model with a CRS production technology a steady state with unemployment exists. This result stands in contrast to that of the Kemp and Van Long (1987) model which said that only a steady state with full employment exists. The source of these different results is that in the OLG case the union only considers the current gain of the higher wage, because it only exists for one period whereas in the infinite horizon model the union also took the future losses into account. Another interesting point is that in both, the more sophisticated infinite horizon model as well as in the OLG model the labour market imperfection will result in a lower steady state stock of capital. This is due to the fact that in both models the union lowers the "saveable" income and alters the incentive to save.

[8] The union will also have impact on the rate of growth when production is linear in capital (i.e. in AK models). This will be analysed in the next chapter within a similar framework.

5.3 Appendix

Plugging in for the utility function and the profit function, and taking logs of equation (5.14) we get:

$$\log(\Omega) = \gamma \cdot \log(L(i)_t \cdot (w(i)_t - AI_t)) + (1-\gamma) \cdot (\alpha \cdot Y_t). \tag{A1}$$

Maximising equation (A1) with respect to the wage and keeping in mind that employment is (via the labour demand equation) a function of the wage, we get the following:

$$\gamma \cdot \frac{\frac{\partial L(i)_t}{\partial w(i)_t} \cdot (w(i)_t - AI_t) + L(i)_t}{L(i)_t \cdot (w(i)_t - AI_t)} + (1-\gamma) \cdot \frac{\frac{\partial Y(i)_t}{\partial L(i)_t} \cdot \frac{\partial L(i)_t}{\partial w(i)_t}}{\alpha \cdot Y(i)_t} = 0. \tag{A2}$$

Manipulation of (A2) gives the bargained wage as:

$$w(i)_t = \left(\frac{1}{1 - \frac{\gamma \cdot \alpha^2}{1-\alpha+\alpha\cdot\gamma}} \right) \cdot AI_t. \tag{A3}$$

6

Unions in an AK Model

The main drawback of the models in the last sections is that although they deal with the long run impact of unions, they were not suitable for the analysis of the growth effects of union wage bargaining, because the rate of growth had been assumed exogenous or, even worse, there had been no growth at all.

In this section we will fix these shortcomings by incorporating union wage bargaining into a simple endogenous growth model, namely an AK type model. We assume the production function to be linear in K, the stock of capital in the economy, at the macroeconomic level. This assumption will guarantee (in contrast to the Solow or the Diamond type model of the last section) that the economy will grow infinitely in per capita terms only by the means of capital accumulation.

The economic intuition for the linearity of the production function at the aggregate level is the notion of learning-by-doing (see, e.g., Arrow (1962) or Romer (1986)). It is assumed that at the firm-level the production function exhibits declining marginal returns to both factors, capital and labour, but that by production and investment the disembodied knowledge in the economy increases. So the technology parameter increases with K and the economy grows only by the means of the accumulation of capital.

One argument why there will be learning-by-doing and, thus, productivity will increase with a larger stock of capital, is the learning curve effect described, e.g., by Arrow (1962). This effect, which is consistent with empirical observations implies that problems will be solved more easily and efficiently the more often these or related problems are solved, because agents learn solution patterns.

We will analyse the effect of union wage bargaining in a model which is characterised by learning-by-doing. It will be shown that the union has negative effects on the rate of growth, because the rate of capital accumulation (and hence, the rate at which productivity increases) decreases. The model we use to show this point is a simplified variant of the model presented in Daveri and Tabellini (2000).

6.1 The Basic Model

The economy at time t is inhabited by two types of households, old and young. Old households do not work anymore. Their only source of income is the interest their savings (done in $t-1$) pay. So consumption of old households at t, C_t^{old} is fixed. Young households supply (inelastically) labour and get labour income. Moreover, young households have to decide how much to save from their income. The utility function of the young is given by:

$$U_t = (C_t^{young})^{\rho} \cdot (C_{t+1}^{old})^{1-\rho}. \tag{6.1}$$

The young choose consumption today, C_t^{young}, and consumption tomorrow, C_{t+1}^{old}, that maximises their utility. The budget constraint they face is given by:

$$Y_t^{young} = C_t^{young} + \frac{1}{1+r} \cdot C_{t+1}^{old}. \tag{6.2}$$

Equation (6.2) depicts that the present value of consumption cannot exceed the primary income of the young. By maximising the utility function subject to the budget constraint, we get the savings of the young as:

$$S_t^{young} = (1-\rho) \cdot Y_t^{young}. \tag{6.3}$$

So the young will save a constant fraction of their income. This property of the savings function is obviously due to the Cobb-Douglas utility function in which the income and the substitution effect of a change in the rate of interest exactly cancel out.

Firms produce the consumption good using labour, $L(i)_t$ and capital, $K(i)_t$. The production function is assumed to be Cobb-Douglas and reads:

$$Y_i = (K(i)_t)^{\alpha} \cdot (A_t \cdot L(i)_t)^{1-\alpha}, \tag{6.4}$$

where Y_i is the output produced by firm i and A_t is the overall stock of knowledge in the economy. By profit maximisation we get the capital and the labour demand function of firm i:

$$w_t = (1-\alpha) \cdot (K(i)_t)^{\alpha} \cdot (A_t)^{1-\alpha} \cdot (L(i)_t)^{-\alpha}, \tag{6.5}$$

$$r = \alpha \cdot (K(i)_t)^{\alpha-1} \cdot (A_t \cdot L(i)_t)^{1-\alpha}. \tag{6.6}$$

Because all firms are symmetric and we assume the number of firms to be of mass one, the aggregate labour and capital demand functions are given by:

$$w_t = (1-\alpha) \cdot (K_t)^{\alpha} \cdot (A_t)^{1-\alpha} \cdot (L_t)^{-\alpha}, \tag{6.7}$$

$$r = \alpha \cdot (K_t)^{\alpha-1} \cdot (A_t \cdot L_t)^{1-\alpha}. \tag{6.8}$$

The population of young at time t is N. In the basic model there is full employment, so $L_t = N$.

From the production function, the labour market equilibrium and the assumption that population is fixed, the rate of growth in the economy is given by:

$$g_Y = \alpha \cdot g_K + (1-\alpha) \cdot g_A. \tag{6.9}$$

Thus the growth rate is the weighted sum of the rate of growth of the stock of capital and the rate of productivity growth. Investment at the firm-level results via learning-by-doing to an increase in the stock of disembodied knowledge. We assume that at the aggregate level $A_t = K_t$. As such, firms do not take the aggregate positive effects of their investment into account.

The rate of output growth in the economy is equal to the growth rate of the stock of capital. Because a closed economy is considered, savings must be equal to investment. Hence, when the rate of depreciation is zero, the following must hold:

$$K_{t+1} = S_t. \tag{6.10}$$

Plugging equation (6.3) into equation (6.10), we get the rate of growth of the stock of capital. The rate of growth of the economy follows as:

$$\frac{K_{t+1}}{K_t} = (1-\rho) \cdot (1-\alpha) \cdot N^{1-\alpha}. \tag{6.11}$$

The rate of growth in the AK model will be high, when the rate of time preference is low, when population is large and when the labour demand curve is flat. The economic intuition for the two latter points is that savings will be high, when there are many workers in the economy[1] and when the wage decrease due to more workers is very small. So the labour market plays a crucial role in the determination of the rate of growth of the economy. In the next section we will analyse the consequences of union wage bargaining for the rate of growth.

6.2 Union Wage Bargaining

We assume that the young population is represented by unions and that these unions bargain the wage at the firm-level, taking all macroeconomic effects as given. Furthermore, we assume that unions only cover one generation of young workers. Hence, after one period when the young grow old, the union splits up and the then young form new unions.[2] The consequence of this simplifying assumption is that as in the preceding section, the bargaining problem of the union is inherently static.

Union's utility function is given by:

---

[1] This is the well known scale effect in these types of models (see Barro and Sala-i-Martin (1995)).

[2] The assumptions on the bargaining process are basically the same as in the OLG model of the preceding section.

$$U(i)_t = w(i)_t \cdot L(i)_t + (M_i - L(i)_t) \cdot B_t, \tag{6.12}$$

where M_i is membership of the union in firm i, which is exogenously given and B_t is the unemployment benefit a union member receives when not being employed in firm i. Hence, we implicitly assume that union members who do not get a job in firm i are not able to find a job somewhere else in the economy.[3] The bargained wage is given by the maximisation of the Nash product subject to the labour demand curve, equation (6.5). The Nash product is given by:

$$\Omega = (U(i)_t - \bar{U}(i)_t)^{\gamma} \cdot (\Pi(i)_t - \bar{\Pi}(i)_t)^{1-\gamma}, \tag{6.13}$$

where $\Pi(i)_t$ is the profit of firm i and γ is the union's bargaining power. $\bar{U}(i)_t$ and $\bar{\Pi}(i)_t$ is union's utility and the firm's profit, respectively when there is no agreement. We assume that in the case of no agreement, all union members receive the unemployment benefit. The firm's profit when there is no agreement is given by $\bar{\Pi}(i)_t = -r \cdot K(i)_t$.[4] So we assume that the firm hires capital *before* the wage bargain. The bargained firm-level wage is given by (since the simple OLG mode and the AK are quite similar, the solution of the wage bargain of the preceding section could also be applied in this section):

$$w(i)_t = \phi \cdot B_t, \tag{6.14}$$

where $\phi \equiv \left(\frac{1}{1 - \frac{\gamma \cdot \alpha^2}{1 - \alpha + \alpha \cdot \gamma}} \right) > 1$. Equation (6.14) depicts that the bargained wage will be higher, the higher is the bargaining power of unions and the lower is α. In a symmetric equilibrium all unions will bargain the same wage, $w_i = w$.

Equation (6.14) reveals that when the unemployment benefit is assumed constant over time, the bargained wage will be constant, too. This is a problematic point, because by inspecting equation (6.5) we see that labour demand will increase as time goes by, because of the accumulation of capital. So with a constant bargained wage and an outward shifting labour demand curve, employment would increase until full employment is restored. So the unionised economy would converge to the competitive one in the long run. To avoid this feature of the model, we assume the unemployment benefit to be growing over time at the rate of the growth of aggregate production.[5]

As in the competitive economy, we assume learning-by-doing spill-overs so that the productivity parameter A_t is equal to K_t. With this, aggregate

[3] Note, that we could have also assumed that the unemployed members have the chance to find another job as, e.g., done in Layard and Nickell (1990) or Lingens (2002). This would not change the main result, but would have made the algebra more complicated.

[4] Again firms do not have the chance to sell capital goods ex-post.

[5] Another solution would be to assume that the ratio of the unemployment benefit over the wage $\frac{B_t}{w_t}$, the replacement rate, is constant over time. This would yield an equal outcome.

production is linear in the stock of capital and employment at the aggregate level is given by:

$$L_t^{Union} = \left(\frac{1}{\phi} \cdot \frac{K_t}{B_t} \cdot (1-\alpha)\right)^{\frac{1}{\alpha}}. \tag{6.15}$$

Our assumption about the evolution of B_t implies that employment in the unionised case is constant. With aggregate employment at hand, we can eventually determine the rate of growth of the unionised economy.

The change in the capital stock over time is financed by the savings of the young. In contrast to the competitive economy savings are done by the young who are employed and those who are unemployed. Assuming the same utility function as in the preceding section, savings are given by:

$$S_t^{young} = L_t^{Union} \cdot \rho \cdot \phi \cdot B_t + (N - L_t^{Union}) \cdot \rho \cdot B_t. \tag{6.16}$$

With the savings function and equation (6.15), the rate of growth of the stock of capital and as such, the rate of growth of the economy is given by:

$$\frac{K_{t+1}}{K_t} = \frac{B_t}{K_t} \cdot (1-\rho) \cdot \rho \cdot \left(N + \underbrace{\left(\frac{1}{\phi} \cdot \frac{K_t}{B_t} \cdot (1-\alpha)\right)^{\frac{1}{\alpha}}}_{L_t^{Union}} \cdot (\phi - 1) \right). \tag{6.17}$$

Interpreting unionisation of the labour market as a change in the bargaining power of unions (hence, a change in ϕ), equation (6.17) reveals that unionisation has two countervailing effects. On the one hand higher bargaining power will increase the rate of capital accumulation. This is obviously due to the fact that the union raises the income of the employed young. As only the young save, this effect raises savings and hence, the rate of growth. On the other hand unionisation will cause unemployment which dampens the income of the young. So with this savings will decline. By expanding the term in brackets in equation (6.17) it is easy to see that a higher ϕ results in a lower rate of capital accumulation. So unionisation will unambiguously dampen economic growth. The wage increase (caused by a reallocation of resources from the old to the young) will not fully offset the negative income effect caused by unemployment.

A noteworthy point is the effect of a change in α. In the competitive case a lower α resulted in a higher rate of growth. With a lower α, the productivity of labour is higher and thus, the wage will be high. Therefore the income of the young and their savings will increase. In the unionised case, things are not that clear. A lower α will result c.p. in higher employment and hence, higher income of the young. On the other hand the bargained wage will decrease since the labour demand curve becomes flatter as α decreases. The overall effect on the income of the young and hence, on the rate of growth is ambiguous.

Another interesting point is the impact of a change in the unemployment benefit. A decrease in B_t will increase employment, but will decrease the wage of the employed *and* the income of the unemployed. So the effect on aggregate savings of the young and thus, on the rate of growth is ambiguous.[6] But even if the rate of growth would increase in case of an increases in the unemployment benefit, one should be very careful in interpreting this result, because we did not take financing needs, e.g., via taxation for the increase in the unemployment benefit ratio into account.

Summarising we can state that unionisation of the labour market will lead to a decrease in the rate of growth in the presented learning-by-doing growth model. This is due to the fact that the rate of growth of the economy is determined by the rate of capital accumulation which in turn is financed by the savings of the young. If the union bargains the wage, it will be higher than in the competitive case, but there will also be unemployed who only receive the unemployment benefit. The overall effect is that the aggregate income of the young declines and so will savings. This results in a lower rate of growth.

The result of the delineated model crucially hinges (as in all of these type of models, see, e.g., Bean and Pissarides (1993)) on the assumed savings structure. On the one hand the assumption that the young save and the old consume does not seem to be too unrealistic, but if we would allow for a bequest motive, we also would have to integrate a savings function of the old. But even in this case, savings in the economy will decline due to union wage bargaining. In addition to the decrease of the savings of the young, income and hence savings of the old would decline, too. This is because the marginal productivity of capital and hence, the rate of interest will decline when part of the labour force is unemployed. So the model's results would also hold for more general assumptions about the savings structure in the economy.

[6] This can be easily seen by differentiating (6.17) with respect to B_t and remembering that ρ and α are smaller than one and ϕ exceeds one.

7

Summary

In this first part we have analysed the impact of union wage bargaining on the accumulation of capital. As was already shown, capital accumulation is an important determinant of economic growth and as such, it is also important to analyse the impact of collective bargaining in models with capital accumulation.

As a first step, we have analysed the interrelation between unions and the investment behaviour of firms, because investment determines the change of the stock of capital. Applying a simple two-period textbook model it was shown that the wage strategy is time inconsistent. The union would like to set a low wage in period one so that the firm would invest a lot, only to set a high wage in period two to get some of the quasi-rents generated by the investment. Since the firm knows that the union is tempted to set a high wage, it will invest less and hence, investment will be too low. Furthermore it was shown that this result also holds in a more generalised set-up with an infinite planing horizon, but that the time inconsistency problem is alleviated, because the union could built up reputation.

In a next step we have analysed neoclassical growth models with unionised labour markets. It was shown that in a standard Solow model only a steady state with full employment exists. Hence, the union retains to use its monopoly power. This is because in such a model the union faces an intertemporal trade-off. A higher wage today implies lower stocks of capital tomorrow and hence, lower wages tomorrow. But this result only holds if the union is not too impatient. If the rate of time preference of the union exceeds a certain threshold, the union will set a wage that is too high to ensure a steady state. The stock of capital will be ultimately exhausted. In this case the union only cares about higher wages in the near future.

Applying a slightly modified version of the Solow model, i.e., using a convex-concave production technology, it was shown that the result is not robust and that also steady states with unemployment may exist. In this case the steady state stock of capital is lower than with competitive labour markets.

Collective bargaining in an OLG model will also result in a lower stock of capital, because unemployment will lower the income of the young and thus, savings and the marginal product of capital (which is the rate of interest) will decline, too. This latter effect also dampens savings. The interesting feature of the OLG model compared to the Solow model is that even with standard assumption this result holds and there will be a steady state with unemployment. This difference is due to the fact that the union in the OLG model faces no intertemporal trade-off. It only covers one generation of young and thus, the bargaining problem of the union is inherently static.

The main drawback of these models is that growth was exogenous or (at least when concentrating on steady states) the economy was static. To tackle this point we analysed in the last section a simple endogenous growth model, namely an AK model. Because of learning-by-doing spill-overs the production function at the macroeconomic level is linear in capital, which implies that the economy can grow unboundedly only via the accumulation of capital. The effect of collective bargaining is again (as in the OLG) model that savings (done by the young) and therewith also the accumulation of capital declines. Therefore, the rate of growth of the economy declines when labour markets are unionised.

Part IV

Unions and Creative Destruction

Unions and Creative Destruction

In the preceding part, we have analysed the impact of union wage bargaining on the accumulation of capital in various models. The stable result of these models has been that unionisation will decrease the steady state stock of capital in an economy or will decrease the rate at which capital is accumulated.

Without doubt, the accumulation of capital is an important variable in the explanation of the rate of growth of a country. At least since the pioneering work of Young (1995) it is general consent that even miraculous growth experiences (like those of the asian tigers in the 1990s) are mainly caused by the accumulation of capital. So in this respect it was important to analyse in which way unionisation influences this crucial determinant of the rate of growth.

Nevertheless, the rate of capital accumulation is not the only important determinant of the rate of growth. The second one is the rate at which factor productivity grows. Figure 7.1 reveals that in the western countries (on an average basis from 1947-1973) up to 63,5% of the rate of growth were caused by factor productivity growth. Therefore, when we want to draw a complete picture of how unionisation might affect the rate of growth in an economy, we must also analyse in which way unionisation affects productivity growth.

Usually, it is assumed that total productivity of a production process can be raised by the means of research and development. Patents or new products are developed which allow the economy to produce more goods with an unchanged primary resource base. So to analyse the impact of unions on the rate of productivity growth we will have to analyse its impact on R&D.

This will be done in the following and the next part in which two different R&D modelling strategies are analysed. In what follows we have applied a schumpeterian model (which is an extension of the Aghion and Howitt (1992) model) which is characterised by creative destruction.[1] There is a patent race and the winner of this race has the opportunity to produce a new state-of-

[1] Schumpeter (1911) was one of the first to analyse this process of creative destruction.

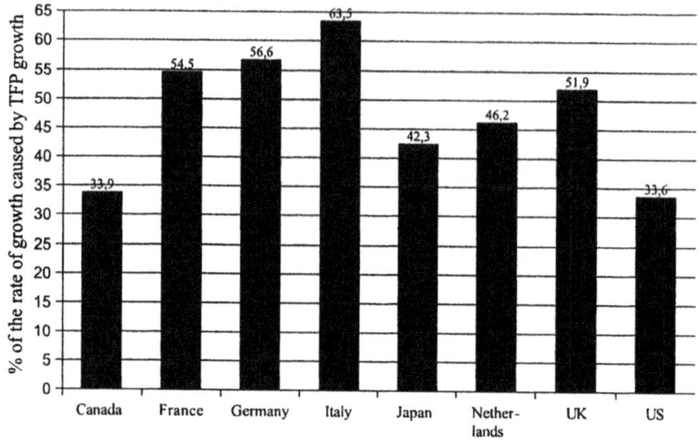

Fig. 7.1. Fraction of the Growth Rate caused by Productivity Growth. Source: Barro and Sala-i-Martin (1995).

the art intermediate good that allows the economy to produce consumption goods using a superior technology. The inventor is able to produce until a new innovator introduces a better technology and replaces the incumbent one. We will analyse in which way unionisation affects this process of creative destruction.

8

The Growth Model

8.1 The Economy

The economy consists of three sectors. A competitive R&D sector where new ideas are produced, a monopolistic intermediate good sector, where the incumbent monopolist supplies the latest generation of the intermediate good to the final goods sector and finally the final goods sector, in which the consumption goods are produced using the "state-of-the-art" intermediate good. The basic inputs of production in the economy are low-skilled labour, L_t, high-skilled labour, H_t, and the intermediate good, X_t. Utility is derived from consuming final goods. The production function of the final goods sector takes the following form:

$$Y_t = A_t \cdot X_t^{\alpha}. \tag{8.1}$$

Y_t is the amount of final goods produced with the intermediate good of generation t. A_t is the efficiency parameter of generation t. The parameter α is restricted to be between 0 and 1. The dynamics of the final goods sector arise from the evolution of the efficiency parameter A_t. Every new generation of the intermediate good causes A to grow by a factor Γ: $A_{t+1} = \Gamma \cdot A_t$. This growth factor Γ is fixed and exogenous to the model. An important point to notice is that only the growth rate of A between two generations of intermediate goods is constant, whereas the time between the innovations is random, i.e., the growth rate per unit of time of A is not constant. With profit maximisation, the demand function of the consumption good sector for the intermediate good is given by (note that we have set $P_Y = 1$):

$$P_{X_t} = \alpha \cdot X_t^{\alpha-1} \cdot A_t. \tag{8.2}$$

In the intermediate sector the leading edge intermediate good generation is produced using low-skilled labour and high-skilled labour. The production function is assumed to be CES and takes the following form:

$$X_t = \left(\delta \cdot L_t^{-\beta} + (1-\delta) \cdot H_t^{-\beta}\right)^{-\frac{1}{\beta}}. \tag{8.3}$$

The parameter δ is usually referred to as the distributional parameter of the production function and β is a measure of the substitutability between the two inputs. Using equation (8.2) and profit maximisation, the factor demands of the monopolist are give by:

$$w^L = \alpha^2 \cdot A_t \cdot \left(\delta \cdot L_t^{-\beta} + (1-\delta) \cdot H_t^{-\beta}\right)^{-\frac{\alpha+\beta}{\beta}} \cdot \delta \cdot L_t^{-\beta-1}, \tag{8.4}$$

for low-skilled labour and

$$w^H = \alpha^2 \cdot A_t \cdot \left(\delta \cdot L_t^{-\beta} + (1-\delta) \cdot H_t^{-\beta}\right)^{-\frac{\alpha+\beta}{\beta}} \cdot (1-\delta) \cdot H_t^{-\beta-1}, \tag{8.5}$$

for high-skilled labour. Using these two demand curves we can determine the elasticity of substitution between low-skilled and high-skilled labour in the intermediate sector. The elasticity of substitution is defined as the change in the high-skilled/low-skilled ratio caused by a change in the factor price proportion (see, e.g., Hamermesh (1993)). With this the elasticity is defined as $\sigma = \frac{d\ln(H_t/L_t)}{d\ln(w^L/w^H)}$. Dividing equation (8.4) by (8.5) we get the following:

$$\frac{w^L}{w^H} = \frac{\delta}{1-\delta} \cdot \left(\frac{H_t}{L_t}\right)^{1+\beta} \Leftrightarrow \frac{H_t}{L_t} = \left(\frac{1-\delta}{\delta} \cdot \frac{w^L}{w^H}\right)^{\frac{1}{1+\beta}}. \tag{8.6}$$

With the definition of the elasticity of substitution we get:

$$\sigma = \frac{1}{1+\beta}. \tag{8.7}$$

Hence, β is a direct measure of the elasticity of substitution and (because σ is always positive due to its definition) it is defined over the interval $[-1, \infty]$.

Equilibrium in both labour markets can be determined employing some additional assumptions. Firstly, it is assumed that low-skilled labour, L, is supplied inelastically and the stock of L is exogenously given and time invariant; thus, the basic model is not characterised by unemployment. Denoting the stock of low-skilled labour by $\bar{L}$, the equilibrium in the low-skilled labour market is given by:

$$w^L = \alpha^2 \cdot A_t \cdot \left(\delta \cdot \bar{L}^{-\beta} + (1-\delta) \cdot H_t^{-\beta}\right)^{-\frac{\alpha+\beta}{\beta}} \cdot \delta \cdot \bar{L}^{-\beta-1}. \tag{8.8}$$

The allocation of the exogenously given and inelastically supplied stock of high-skilled labour $\bar{H}$ is tied down by the assumption of perfect mobility between the intermediate and the R&D sector. This assumption allows to determine the equilibrium by a no-arbitrage condition, which ensures that the high-skilled wage cannot differ between the intermediate and the research sector of the economy.

Researchers use high-skilled labour to develop new generations of the intermediate good. If a researcher is successful in inventing a new product generation, he will be the new intermediate monopolist and replaces the incumbent one. The invention of innovations is governed by a Poisson process. Innovations arrive randomly at the rate $H_t^{R\&D} \cdot \lambda$, where $H_t^{R\&D}$ is the amount of high-skilled labour employed in the research sector and λ is a fixed parameter of the Poisson process. The value of being the new monopolist (at some point in time τ, when generation t is state-of-the-art) is V_{t+1}. This value is given by the following asset equation[1]:

$$V_{t+1} \cdot r = \Pi_{t+1} - \lambda \cdot H_{t+1}^{R\&D} \cdot V_{t+1}, \tag{8.9}$$

where Π_{t+1} is the flow profit of the monopolist and $\lambda \cdot H_{t+1}^{R\&D}$ is the probability of being replaced by a new innovator. In this case the incumbent monopolist gets nothing. Using the intermediate good demand of the final product sector and the labour demand functions, we can derive the monopoly profit as:

$$\Pi_{t+1} = (1-\alpha) \cdot \alpha \cdot X_{t+1}^{\alpha} \cdot A_{t+1}. \tag{8.10}$$

Using (8.10), we can derive the demand for high-skilled labour in the R&D sector:

$$w^{R\&D} = \lambda \cdot \frac{1}{r + \lambda \cdot H_{t+1}^{R\&D}} \cdot (1-\alpha) \cdot \alpha \cdot A_{t+1} \cdot X_{t+1}^{\alpha}. \tag{8.11}$$

Since by the no-arbitrage condition the high-skilled wage must be the identical in both sectors, equations (8.5) and (8.11) determine the allocation of high-skilled labour. By using the full employment condition $\bar{H}_t = H_t + H_t^{R\&D}$ and $A_{t+1} = \Gamma \cdot A_t$, we get a forward looking difference equation in $H^{R\&D}$:

$$\lambda \cdot \frac{1}{r + \lambda \cdot H_{t+1}^{R\&D}} \cdot (1-\alpha) \cdot \alpha \cdot \Gamma \cdot A_t \cdot X_{t+1}^{\alpha} = \alpha^2 \cdot A_t \cdot X_t^{\beta+\alpha} \cdot (1-\delta) \cdot (\bar{H} - H_t^{R\&D})^{-\beta-1}. \tag{8.12}$$

Equation (8.12) determines a steady state equilibrium if we impose $H_t^{R\&D} = H_{t+1}^{R\&D} = H^{R\&D}$. We get a steady state level of high-skilled labour working in the research sector $H_{R\&D}^*$ and this level determines the growth rate of the economy. From Equation (8.3), using $A_{t+1} = \Gamma \cdot A_t$, the (average) growth rate of the economy is given by:

$$g_Y = ln(\Gamma) \cdot \lambda \cdot H_{R\&D}^*. \tag{8.13}$$

Equation (8.12) cannot be solved explicitly for steady state values, but it can be shown that an equilibrium exists. This can be done by showing that the slope of the difference equation (8.12) is strictly negative and that the value of $H_{t+1}^{R\&D}$ is strictly positive when $H_t^{R\&D}$ is zero. The economic intuition for these properties is the following. If innovators expect the employment in the R&D sector to be high when the $t+1$ generation of the intermediate good is state-of-the-art, they know that they will be replaced very soon in case they win the patent race. But this lowers the incentive to perform R&D and hence, $H_t^{R\&D}$ will decline. This explains the negatively sloped difference equation. For the same reasons $H_{t+1}^{R\&D}$ will be positive when $H_t^{R\&D}$ is zero.

[1] For a detailed derivation of this asset equation see the appendix to this chapter

8.2 The Steady State Rate of Growth

Imposing steady state conditions on equation (8.12) and log-linearising this equation yields (where a '$\sim$' denotes the relative change of a variable, hence $\frac{dX}{X} \equiv \tilde{X}$):

$$\tilde{H}^*_{R\&D} = \Psi \cdot \left((1-b) \cdot \tilde{\lambda} + \tilde{\Gamma} - \beta \cdot s^L \cdot \tilde{\bar{L}} + \frac{(1 + \beta \cdot s^L)}{a} \cdot \tilde{\bar{H}} + \left(- \frac{1}{1-\alpha} \right) \cdot \tilde{\alpha} \right), \tag{8.14}$$

with s^L and s^H denoting the steady state production elasticity of low-skilled and high-skilled labour in the intermediate sector; $0 < b \equiv \left(\frac{\lambda \cdot H^*_{R\&D}}{r + \lambda \cdot H^*_{R\&D}} \right) \leq 1$; $(1-a) \equiv \frac{H^*_{R\&D}}{H}$ (hence, $(1-a)$ is the part of the high-skilled labour force employed in the research sector) and $\Psi \equiv b + (\beta \cdot s^L + 1) \cdot \left(\frac{(1-a)}{a} \right)^{-1} \geq 0$.[2]

A rise in the parameter of the Poisson distribution, λ, will increase the steady state level of high-skilled labour employed in the research sector, since $(1-b) \geq 0$. The economic intuition is the following: on the one hand higher λ raises the rate of creative destruction which discourages potential inventors to hire high-skilled labour, but on the other hand the research success will turn up faster; this encourages researchers. The latter effect dominates because of the positive time preference of agents. They care more about getting the profits today than loosing them tomorrow. The higher the growth rate of the efficiency parameter, Γ, the higher is the level of high-skilled labour employed in the research sector, because higher Γ results in higher profit opportunities when becoming a monopolist. The impact of low-skilled labour on the rate of growth is ambiguous and depends (via β) on the elasticity of substitution σ. If σ is bigger (smaller) than one, the impact is positive (negative). Since the economic intuition is also crucial to understand the union effect, we defer the discussion to the next section. A rise in the stock of high-skilled labour causes the steady state level of high-skilled labour in the research sector to rise, because more high-skilled labour is spread uniformly over the intermediate and the research sector. A rise in α results in a higher price elasticity of the demand for the intermediate good and this causes monopoly profits to decline. This lowers marginal productivity of high-skilled labour in the research sector and therefore the amount of high-skilled labour employed in the research sector.

[2] Note that we assume the production function as being constant ($\tilde{\beta} = \tilde{\delta} = 0$).

9

Union Wage Bargaining

9.1 The right-to-manage Case

We assume that the new monopolist has to bargain the low-skilled wage with a labour union. After a wage agreement is settled, the intermediate good monopolist can choose the amount of labour he wants to hire, given the bargained wage. So the sequence of events in the model is depicted in the following figure 9.1: When the incumbent monopolist is driven out of the market, the process

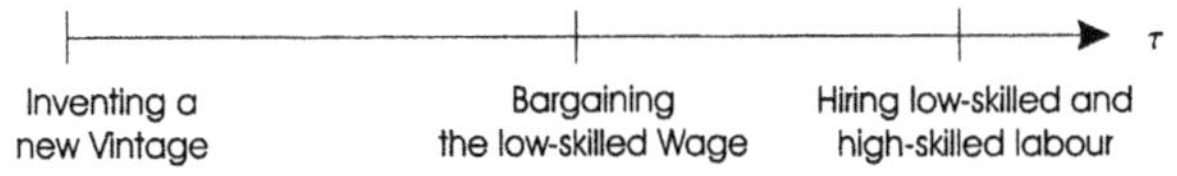

Fig. 9.1. The Sequence of the Bargain in the Creative Destruction Model.

starts anew and the new monopolist has to bargain again with the union. Note that we do not consider insider power which means that after a wage agreement ends (so after the monopolist is driven out of the market), every union member has again the same probability of becoming employed. This is the same as to assume that after the wage agreement, the new monopolist chooses randomly, i.e., history independent from the low-skilled labour force.[1]

After these more general assumptions and institutional settings we have to take a closer look at the utility function the union wants to maximise. To keep the model as simple as possible, we apply the so called "rent maximisation" utility function (this function can be derived from the expected utility function when assuming some sort of income transfer within the union, see Pencavel (1994)). The utility function of the union takes the following form:

$$U = L \cdot \left(w^L - \bar{w}^L\right) . \tag{9.1}$$

[1] This can be legitimated on the grounds that we do not consider specific skills which would be lost during the period of being unemployed.

Hence, the union seeks to maximise the difference between the bargained wage w^L and the competitive wage $\bar{w}^L$ times the number of employed members. The competitive wage is a reference scenario for a union member, which is exogenous to the union. Following the standard approach in the literature on wage bargaining, we assume the Nash bargaining solution to determine the wage for low-skilled labour. The solution to the wage bargain will maximize the following Nash product:

$$\Omega = \left(U - \bar{U}\right)^{\gamma} \cdot \left(\Pi - \bar{\Pi}\right), \tag{9.2}$$

where γ is the (relative) bargaining power of the union, U is union's utility after an agreement is reached, $\bar{U}$ is the disagreement point of the union, Π are the profits of the monopolist after an agreement and $\bar{\Pi}$ is the monopolist's disagreement point.

When applying the Nash solution to a bargaining problem much respect has to be payed how to model the disagreement points (see Binmore, Shaked and Sutton (1989) and Binmore, Rubinstein and Wolinsky (1986)). The disagreement points reflect the utility flow during the bargain. We assume no employment of low-skilled labour during the bargain. Furthermore high-skilled and low-skilled labour are imperfect substitutes, i.e., σ is finite. With these assumptions the impasse utility of both parties is zero, hence $\bar{U} = \bar{\Pi} = 0$. The outside option for the union if the bargain is quit unilaterally will be the competitive outcome. For the monopolist the outside option is zero, because in the case he quits the bargain he is not able to produce anything. As shown in Binmore, Shaked and Sutton (1989) these outside options serve as constrains in the determination of the Nash solution.[2]

Maximisation of the Nash product subject to the labour demand curve (8.4) yields the bargained wage:

$$w^L = \frac{1}{1 + \left(\frac{1}{\frac{1}{\gamma} \cdot \frac{w^L}{\Pi} \cdot \frac{\partial \Pi}{\partial w^L} + \frac{w^L}{L} \cdot \frac{\partial L}{\partial w^L}}\right)} \cdot \bar{w}^L. \tag{9.3}$$

By the envelope theorem, $\frac{\partial \Pi}{\partial w^L} = -L$. Moreover, $-\frac{w^L}{L} \cdot \frac{\partial L}{\partial w^L}$ denotes the wage elasticity of low-skilled labour demand. Due to the assumed bargaining structure, the union has to bear in mind that a wage hike has two consequences for low-skilled employment. Firstly, there is a static effect that the higher the wage the less low-skilled labour will be hired (this is a movement along the low-skilled labour demand curve) and secondly that less low-skilled labour results in a change in the amount of high-skilled labour employed in the intermediate sector in the steady state. This has repercussions on the demand for low-skilled labour, since high-skilled labour employed in the intermediate

[2] See for these points also the remarks in part one, where it was discussed how to identify the disagreement points if we want to interpret the Nash solution as the limiting solution of an alternating offers game.

sector is a shift parameter of the low-skilled labour demand curve. So the constraint the union faces in the bargaining process is the "total labour demand curve". Letting ε denote the (absolute) value of the elasticity of total labour demand, we obtain for the bargained low-skilled real wage:

$$w^L = \frac{1}{1 - \left(\frac{1}{\frac{1}{\gamma} \cdot \frac{w^L \cdot L}{\Pi} + \varepsilon}\right)} \cdot \bar{w}^L, \tag{9.4}$$

which is a mark-up over the wage in the competitive case $\bar{w}^L$. This mark-up depends on union's bargaining power γ, on the total labour demand elasticity ε and on the relation of low-skilled labour income to profits. From equations (8.4) and (8.10) this relation is:

$$\frac{w^L \cdot L}{\Pi} = \frac{\alpha}{1-\alpha} \cdot s^L. \tag{9.5}$$

Equation (8.4) also yields an expression for the wage elasticity of low-skilled labour demand:

$$\varepsilon = -\frac{1}{(\alpha+\beta) \cdot s^L - \beta - 1 + s^H (\alpha+\beta) \cdot \frac{\partial H}{\partial L} \cdot \frac{L}{H}}, \tag{9.6}$$

where $\frac{\partial H}{\partial L} \cdot \frac{L}{H}$ can be derived using equation (8.14). From this equation we know that:

$$\frac{dH^{R\&D}}{H^{R\&D}} = \Psi \cdot (-\beta) \cdot s^L \cdot \frac{dL}{L}. \tag{9.7}$$

Moreover, $\frac{dH}{H}\left(\frac{a}{a-1}\right) = \frac{dH^{R\&D}}{H^{R\&D}}$. Therefore:

$$\frac{\partial H}{\partial L} \cdot \frac{L}{H} = \frac{1-a}{a} \cdot \Psi \cdot \beta \cdot s^L. \tag{9.8}$$

Hence, we obtain the wage elasticity of total labour demand as:

$$\varepsilon = \frac{1}{(1+\beta) - (\alpha+\beta) \cdot s^L - (\alpha+\beta) \cdot \frac{1-a}{a} \cdot \Psi \cdot \beta \cdot s^L}. \tag{9.9}$$

ε reflects the two aforementioned effects. On the one hand a wage hike will result in lower labour demand. On the other hand there will be a reallocation effect of high-skilled labour due to the change in employment of low-skilled labour. If the elasticity of substitution is less than one (implying that lower low-skilled employment results in a decline of high-skilled employment in the intermediate sector), the reallocation effect lowers marginal productivity of low-skilled labour. Thus the low-skilled employment loss due to a wage hike is quite high (the (absolute) value of the elasticity of total labour demand will be high). The opposite is true if σ exceeds one. The mark-up turns out to be:

$$\phi(\gamma, \alpha, s^L) = \frac{1}{1 - \left(\frac{1}{\frac{1}{\gamma} \cdot \left(\frac{\alpha}{1-\alpha} \cdot s^L \right) + \varepsilon} \right)}. \tag{9.10}$$

Log-linearising the mark-up in γ, α and s^L yields [3]:

$$\tilde{\phi} = \phi \cdot \delta_1 \cdot \tilde{\gamma} - \phi \cdot \delta_2 \cdot \tilde{\alpha} - \phi \cdot \delta_3 \cdot \tilde{s}^L, \tag{9.11}$$

with $\delta_1 \equiv \frac{\frac{s^L}{\gamma} \frac{\alpha}{1-\alpha}}{\left(\frac{s^L}{\gamma} \frac{\alpha}{1-\alpha} + \varepsilon \right)^2}$, $\delta_2 \equiv \frac{\frac{s^L}{\gamma} \frac{\alpha}{1-\alpha} \cdot \left(\frac{1}{1-\alpha} \right) + \frac{\partial \varepsilon}{\partial \alpha} \cdot \alpha}{\left(\frac{s^L}{\gamma} \frac{\alpha}{1-\alpha} + \varepsilon \right)^2}$ and $\delta_3 \equiv \frac{\frac{s^L}{\gamma} \frac{\alpha}{1-\alpha} + \frac{\partial \varepsilon}{\partial s^L} \cdot s^L}{\left(\frac{s^L}{\gamma} \frac{\alpha}{1-\alpha} + \varepsilon \right)^2}$.

The coefficient of a change in union power $\tilde{\gamma}$, δ_1, is unambiguously positive. Hence, a rise in union power will raise the mark-up. The same is true for δ_2 since it can be show that $\frac{\partial \varepsilon}{\partial \alpha}$ is positive. This implies that a higher α lowers the mark-up, because a higher price elasticity of the demand for the intermediate good implies lower monopoly profits that the union is able to capture. The coefficient δ_3 is unambiguously positive, because it can be shown that $\frac{\partial \varepsilon}{\partial s^L}$ is positive for all $(\alpha + \beta) \neq 0$. The economic intuition is that due to the assumption of a CRS production function, s^H falls as s^L rises. But a decline in s^H lowers the quasi-rents generated by high-skilled labour. This in turn lowers the bargained wage. Furthermore the demand curve for low-skilled labour becomes flatter with a higher s^L, so that the bargained wage falls.

9.1.1 The Employment Effects of the Labour Union

This subsection examines how parameter changes influence steady state unemployment of low-skilled labour. The preceding analysis of union behaviour has established that the wage in the low-skilled labour market is a mark-up over the competitive wage:

$$w^L = \phi \cdot \bar{w}^L. \tag{9.12}$$

Because of the "right-to-manage" assumption, both wages are given by the labour demand equation (8.4). We restrict our analysis to steady states and assume that steady state employment of high-skilled labour in the intermediate sector is $H^*(\bar{L})$ in the competitive case and $H^*(L^U)$ in the presence of union wage bargaining. Hence, employment in the unionised economy will be time invariant and so will be the unemployment rate.[4] By substituting the wages in equation (9.12) by the labour demand equations, we get:

[3] Throughout the paper we treat s^L and s^H as exogenous variables, although this is only true for the Cobb Douglas case. We justify this simplifying assumption on the basis that firstly we only analyse small changes around some steady state and that secondly these second round effects are small in size. So the underlying error is of "quantitative nature" and very small.

[4] Note that steady state unemployment will only occur if the reference wage (which is in our case $\bar{w}^L$) grows at the same rate as the increased technology shifts out the low-skilled labour demand (see equation (8.4)). If this is not the case the unionised economy will converge with the competitive economy.

$$A_t \cdot \left(\delta \cdot \left(L^U\right)^{-\beta} + (1-\delta)\left(H^*\left(L^U\right)\right)^{-\beta}\right)^{-\frac{\alpha+\beta}{\beta}} \cdot \delta \cdot \left(L^U\right)^{-\beta-1} = \phi \cdot A_t \cdot \left(\delta \cdot \left(\bar{L}\right)^{-\beta} + (1-\delta)\left(H^*\left(\bar{L}\right)\right)^{-\beta}\right)^{-\frac{\alpha+\beta}{\beta}} \cdot \delta \cdot \left(\bar{L}\right)^{-\beta-1}. \tag{9.13}$$

Log-linearisation of equation (9.13) around a steady state (which determines steady state unemployment) yields:

$$\tilde{L}^U = -\varepsilon \cdot \tilde{\phi} + \tilde{\bar{L}}. \tag{9.14}$$

The change in steady state employment of low-skilled labour depends only on the mark-up and on the amount of low-skilled labour in the economy. An increase in the stock of low-skilled labour will raise employment in the unionised economy, but the *rate* of unemployment will remain constant.[5] A rise in the stock of low-skilled labour lowers the reference wage $\bar{w}^L$ and hence, with a constant mark-up, lowers the bargained wage and raises employment. The change in employment will be equal to the change in the stock of low-skilled labour, because the wage elasticity of labour demand is assumed to be constant. In the more general case the wage elasticity determines whether the unemployment rate will rise, remain constant or decline. The intuition for this is that the change in $\bar{L}$ changes the competitive wage which in turn causes a one to one change in the bargained wage. But this will change employment in the unionised case and the strength of this change is determined by the wage elasticity of the labour demand curve. So only in the case of this elasticity being constant, the change in the stock of labour will change employment proportionally. However, the qualitative result, that an increase in the low-skilled labour pool raises low-skilled employment remains unaffected. Finally a higher mark-up, e.g., due to higher union power, γ, raises the bargained wage and lowers employment of low-skilled labour.

9.1.2 The Growth Effects of the Labour Union

It has been shown that the growth rate of the economy depends positively on R&D sector employment (and as such, on the allocation of the stock of high-skilled labour). The equilibrium allocation in the case of a unionised low-skilled labour market is given by equation (8.14) with the only difference that in the unionised case low-skilled labour employment is L^U. So using equation (9.14), the equation determining high-skilled employment labour in the R&D sector modifies to:

$$\tilde{H}^*_{R\&D} = \Psi \cdot \left((1-b)\cdot\tilde{\lambda} + \tilde{\Gamma} + \beta \cdot s^L \cdot \varepsilon \cdot \tilde{\phi} - \beta \cdot s^L \cdot \tilde{\bar{L}}\right) + \Psi \cdot \left((\beta \cdot s^L + 1)\cdot \tilde{\bar{H}} + (-\frac{1}{1-\alpha})\cdot\tilde{\alpha}\right). \tag{9.15}$$

[5] The change in the unemployment rate is by definition $\tilde{U} = \frac{L}{L-\bar{L}}(\tilde{\bar{L}} - \tilde{L}^U)$. If the change in the low-skilled labour pool causes union employment to change proportionally, i.e., $\tilde{\bar{L}} = \tilde{L}^U$, the unemployment rate will not change, see (9.14).

With this equation at hand the growth effects of union wage bargaining can be analysed. Consider first an economy which consists of competitive labour markets for high-skilled as well as for low-skilled labour. This case of the competitive labour market is nested in the unionised model when ϕ equals one. So we can analyse the impact of the union as a change in the mark-up ϕ (the mark-up is obviously an endogenous variable, but let us for the moment assume that we concentrate on a steady state, where we take the mark-up determining parameters as given. Later we will also analyse the effect of changes in these parameters). Equation (9.15) reveals that changes in the mark-up change $\tilde{H}^*_{R\&D}$ and that the effect indirectly depends (via β) on the elasticity of substitution between low-skilled and high-skilled labour in the intermediate goods sector, σ. We can distinguish three cases. In the Cobb Douglas case in which the elasticity of substitution is one and β is zero, a change in the mark-up has no effect on the amount of high-skilled labour employed in the research sector, i.e., a union does not affect steady state growth. If low-skilled and high-skilled labour are very good substitutes (σ exceeds unity and β is negative) unionisation of low-skilled labour will lead to lower steady state high-skilled employment in the research sector and therefore lower growth. The opposite is the case if substitutability between low-skilled and high-skilled labour is low, i.e., σ smaller than one and β exceeds zero. Then steady state growth is faster and the existence of the union may actually foster growth compared to a situation in which the low-skilled labour market is competitive. In this case the economy faces a trade-off between growth and employment. Unemployment will lower the amount of consumable goods but on the other hand it will raise the rate of growth.

What is the economic intuition behind these results? The union rations low-skilled labour, which affects the marginal productivity of high-skilled labour in both the R&D and the intermediate good sector. If the impact of a change in L affects the marginal productivity of high-skilled labour in both sectors asymmetrically this will cause migration of high-skilled labour and the direction of this migration will determine the growth effect of the union. Marginal productivity is given by:

$$\tilde{w}^H = \tilde{A} + (-\beta - 1) \cdot \tilde{H} + (\alpha + \beta) \cdot \underbrace{\left(s^L \cdot \tilde{L} + s^h \cdot \tilde{H}\right)}_{\tilde{X}} + \left(2 - \frac{\alpha \cdot ln(X^{-\beta})}{\beta}\right) \cdot \tilde{\alpha}, \tag{9.16}$$

$$\tilde{w}^{R\&D} = \tilde{A} + (1 - b) \cdot \tilde{\lambda} + \tilde{\gamma} + \alpha \cdot \underbrace{\left(s^L \cdot \tilde{L} + s^h \cdot \tilde{H}\right)}_{\tilde{X}} - b \cdot \tilde{H}_{R\&D} + \left(-\frac{\alpha}{1 - \alpha} + 1 - \frac{\alpha \cdot ln\left(X^{-\beta}\right)}{\beta}\right) \cdot \tilde{\alpha}. \tag{9.17}$$

Using these equations, we can see that the change in low-skilled labour employment has an asymmetric effect on the productivity of high-skilled labour in the two sectors if and only if $\beta \neq 0$. If β is negative ($\sigma > 1$), a decline in L lowers the wage in the intermediate sector by a smaller amount than in the research sector. So we have a wage differential favouring the intermediate sector, causing high-skilled labour to move into the intermediate good sector and thereby lowering growth. The opposite is true if β is positive ($\sigma < 1$). In this case the decline of the wage in the intermediate sector will be higher than the decline in the research sector causing growth enhancing migration of high-skilled labour into the research sector.

The economic intuition is straightforward. The effect of less low-skilled employment is more severe when σ is smaller than one, because a factor substitution which could dampen the negative effect of lower low-skilled employment is hardly possible. So the decline of high-skilled productivity in the intermediate sector is high compared to that in the research sector. The opposite is true when both factors are substitutes.

Since the mark-up is an endogenous variable we can, using equation (9.11) and (9.15), analyse the impact of various parameters that determine the mark-up. Increased union power, γ, results in a higher mark-up and hence, we can apply the previous arguments. The effect of a change in α, the price elasticity of the intermediate good market, is ambiguous. On the one hand, higher α is bad for growth, because more competition in the intermediate good market implies lower monopoly profits. This discourages researchers and the growth rate will decline. On the other hand a rise in α will lower the mark-up. If σ is less than one, a smaller mark-up will lower the growth rate of the economy. Hence, the direct effect is amplified by the existence of a union. However, if σ exceeds unity, a smaller mark-up will raise the growth rate. That is, there are two opposite effects on the rate of growth and it is ambiguous which effect dominates. The coefficient determining the overall effect is given by (using equation (9.11) and (9.15)):

$$\tilde{H}^*_{R\&D} = \Psi \left(\left(-\beta \cdot s^L \cdot \varepsilon \cdot \phi \cdot \frac{\frac{s^L}{\gamma}\frac{\alpha}{1-\alpha} \cdot \left(\frac{1}{1-\alpha}\right) + \frac{\partial \varepsilon}{\partial \alpha} \cdot \alpha}{\left(\frac{s^L}{\gamma}\frac{\alpha}{1-\alpha} + \varepsilon\right)^2} - \frac{1}{1-\alpha} \right) \cdot \tilde{\alpha} \right). \tag{9.18}$$

Equation (9.18) demonstrates the aforementioned effects. If σ is less than one the coefficient of the impact of a change in α on $H^*_{R\&D}$ will be negative. In the case of σ exceeding unity the impact is ambiguous.[6]

[6] An important condition for this to hold is that the absolute labour demand elasticity is positive, i.e., that the low-skilled labour demand curve is negatively sloped. We assume this condition (as in the complete chapter) to hold.

9.2 Efficient Bargaining

In the preceding section we have only analysed the so called right-to-manage model which implied that we have restricted the focus to points on the labour demand curve. What happens when the bargaining between the union and the monopolist is efficient, i.e., they bargain over wages *and* employment? To analyse this question, we apply the same framework (assumptions and bargaining procedure) as in the right-to-manage model. The only difference is that this time we find the bargained wage *and* employment in the economy by maximising the Nash product (for details of the derivation of the equilibrium in efficient bargaining models see, e.g., Booth (1996)). Maximising the Nash product with respect to the wage and to employment gives the following two first order conditions:

$$\frac{\partial \log(\Omega)}{\partial w^L} = \left(\frac{1}{w^L - \bar{w}^L}\right) \cdot \gamma - \frac{L}{\Pi} = 0, \tag{9.19}$$

$$\frac{\partial \log(\Omega)}{\partial L} = \frac{\gamma}{L} + \frac{R'(L) - w^L}{\Pi} = 0, \tag{9.20}$$

where $R'(L)$ is the marginal revenue of low-skilled labour in the intermediate sector. Combining equations (9.19) and (9.20), we get the contract curve which is given by:

$$\bar{w}^L = R'(L), \tag{9.21}$$

This contract curve maps pareto efficient wage and employment combinations. The equilibrium of the economy with efficient bargaining will be on this contract curve. Since we have assumed risk neutral union members, the contract curve will be a vertical line over $\bar{L}$ in wage-employment space.[7] Hence, there will be no unemployment of low-skilled labour.

The wage in the economy is given by equation (9.19), noting that low-skilled labour will be fully employed and so $L = \bar{L}$. The wage in the economy which is characterised by efficient bargaining is given by:

$$w^L_{efficient} = \bar{w}^L + \gamma \cdot \frac{\Pi}{\bar{L}}. \tag{9.22}$$

Although there will be no unemployment in the economy, the bargained wage will be higher than in the competitive case. This wage push drives the growth effect in the efficient bargaining case. Since the wage will be higher than in the competitive case, monopoly profits will be lower, which discourages innovators.

Using equation (9.22) it is easy to show that the profit an intermediate monopolist can earn modifies to:

$$\Pi_{t+1} = \frac{(1-\alpha)\cdot\alpha}{1+\gamma} \cdot X^{\alpha}_{t+1} \cdot A_{t+1}. \tag{9.23}$$

[7] Only in this case equation (9.21) is fulfilled.

With the help of equation (9.23)[8] we can determine the equilibrium allocation of the high-skilled pool in the case with efficient union bargaining. Equilibrium high-skilled employment in the research sector is given by:

$$\tilde{H}^*_{R\&D} = \Psi \cdot \left((1-b) \cdot \tilde{\lambda} + \tilde{\Gamma} - \beta \cdot s^L \cdot \tilde{\bar{L}}\right) + \Psi \cdot \left(\frac{(1+\beta \cdot s^L)}{a} \cdot \tilde{\bar{H}} + \left(-\frac{1}{1-\alpha}\right) \cdot \tilde{\alpha} - \left(\frac{\gamma}{1+\gamma}\right) \cdot \tilde{\gamma}\right). \tag{9.24}$$

Equation (9.24) depicts that research sector employment and therewith the rate of growth will decline in case of efficient bargaining.

The economic intuition for this property is the following: the marginal value product of high-skilled labour in the research sector will decline, because profits in the intermediate sector decline. Hence, the high-skilled labour demand curve in the research sector is shifted downwards. The demand for high-skilled labour in the intermediate sector remains unchanged. By the no-arbitrage condition, this implies a reallocation of high-skilled labour from the research sector towards the intermediate sector. So the rate of growth will unambiguously decline in the presence of union wage bargaining.

[8] Note the similarities to equation (8.10) in the non-union case.

10

Appendix

In this appendix we will derive the asset equation a potential innovator faces. The presentation follows Weiß (2001) and Dixit and Pindyck (1994): the reward for being the new monopolist is the (expected) stream of monopoly profits. So in discrete time, the value of being the new monopolist is given by:

$$V(A_{t+1})_\tau = \Pi(A_{t+1})_\tau + \frac{1}{1+r} \cdot E_\tau \left(V(A_{t+1})_{\tau+1} \right), \tag{A1}$$

where E is the expectation operator. Equation (A1) reveals that the value of being a new innovator at time τ is the profit stream during period τ plus the expected value as of tomorrow. Because we analyse a continuous time model, we have to transform the discrete time form (A1) into continuous time. This is done by assuming the length of periods of time not to be one, but infinitesimally small:

$$V(A_{t+1})_\tau = \Pi(A_{t+1})_\tau \cdot dt + \frac{1}{1+r \cdot dt} \cdot E_\tau \left(V(A_{t+1})_{\tau+dt} \right). \tag{A2}$$

We can rearrange equation (A2) and get:

$$\frac{V(A_{t+1})_\tau}{dt} \cdot (1 + r \cdot dt) = (1 + r \cdot dt) \cdot \Pi(A_{t+1})_\tau + E_\tau \left(\frac{V(A_{t+1})_{\tau+dt}}{dt} \right). \tag{A3}$$

Further algebraic manipulations of equation (A3) yield:

$$V(A_{t+1})_\tau \cdot r = (1+r \cdot dt) \cdot \Pi(A_{t+1})_\tau + E_\tau \left(\frac{V(A_{t+1})_{\tau+dt} - V(A_{t+1})_\tau}{dt} \right). \tag{A4}$$

We know that the invention of new innovations follows a Poisson process. Hence, we can rewrite the expectation term of the difference between the value of being an innovator in τ and in $\tau + dt$. The probability that the innovator is replaced between τ and $\tau + dt$ is given by $\lambda \cdot H_{t+1}^{R\&D}$. In the replacement case, the innovator is pushed out of the market and gets nothing. When he is not pushed out of the market, he gets the value of being a monopolist at $\tau + dt$. So the following holds:

$$E_\tau \left(\frac{V(A_{t+1})_{\tau+dt} - V(A_{t+1})_\tau}{dt} \right) = \\ (1 - \lambda \cdot H_{t+1}^{R\&D}) \cdot V(A_{t+1})_{\tau+dt} + \lambda \cdot H_{t+1}^{R\&D} \cdot 0 - V(A_{t+1})_\tau . \tag{A5}$$

Plugging equation (A5) into (A4), taking limits on (A4), because we are interested in the continuous time value equation ($\lim_{dt \to 0}$) and doing some algebraic manipulations, we get the value equation given in the text.

Part V

Unions and Expanding Product Variety

Unions and Expanding Product Variety

In the last part, we have analysed the effects of union wage bargaining in a model in which growth was driven by creative destruction. This creative destruction model only represents one strand of the literature on models in which the rate of growth is determined by R&D. Another important strand of this literature are the so called expanding product variety models, firstly analysed by Romer (1990). In these models new blueprints are produced in the research sector that allow the production of more diversified intermediate goods. With this increase in intermediate good varieties, the division of labour will be deeper, enabling the economy to produce more consumption goods with an unchanged primary resource base. Thus, the economy can grow unboundedly. The main advantages of the latter modelling strategy over the creative destruction models are that they are more easy to handle, because no stochastic component is needed and that they take a more general equilibrium point of view, allowing to interpret the results as being macroeconomic.

In the following we will integrate union wage bargaining into various versions of the standard growth model with expanding product varieties. In the first chapter, we will analyse a model whose structure is very similar to that of the creative destruction type. It will be shown that this model mimics the results of the preceding part. Furthermore this model will be extended to allow for taxation. This extended model will be used to evaluate revenue neutral tax reforms and their impact on growth and employment. The purpose of this extension is that in the standard model, we assume that unemployed union members will get unemployment benefit, but do not discuss in which way this benefit is financed. This is a clear shortcoming of the basic model which is healed by the explicit incorporation of the government's budget constraint and taxation.

We can show that taxation dampens low-skilled employment, but that the effects on the allocation of the high-skilled pool and thus on the rate of growth are ambiguous. The analysis of revenue neutral tax reforms reveals that the effects of these reforms on low-skilled employment and growth are not clear cut.

In the last section we will analyse a model in which we allow for two sector wage bargaining, i.e., the wage in the intermediate as well as in the research sector will be bargained. We will show that the results differ substantially from that of the growth model with one sector wage bargaining. This is due to the fact that although in this model we also observe a reallocation of resources between sectors, the union will ration the resource employed in the research sector. This rationing effect in the research sector was not present in the one-sector bargaining models, but it dominates all other effect if taken into account. Hence, the results on the impact of union wage bargaining on the rate of growth react very sensitive to the assumption which factors of production are covered by collective bargaining and where these are employed.

11

One Sector Bargaining

In this section we will analyse the impact of union wage bargaining when the union covers low-skilled labour and low-skilled labour is only employed in the manufacturing sector. So from the set up, this model is rather close to Palokangas (1996) and (2000)[1] and to the in the preceding section presented schumpeterian growth model. Interestingly enough the results of this section reproduce more or less the results shown in the schumpeterian growth model. This is due to the well known fact that the structure of the two R&D growth models is very much the same and so the results which hold for the schumpeterian model in general also hold for the expanding product variety type (see, Grossman and Helpman (1991)).

In the following model the consumption good sector employs intermediate good varieties as input factors. The number of these varieties rise and so, due to specialisation (see, Ethier (1982)) it is possible to produce a larger amount of the consumption although the primary production factors are fixed.

11.1 The Basic Model

Consider a standard expanding product variety growth model as, e.g., in Grossman and Helpman (1991), Romer (1990) or Barro and Sala-i-Martin (1995), where the consumption good Y_t is produced using varieties of an intermediate good x. The production function takes the following CES form:

$$Y_t = \left(\int_0^{n_t} x(i)^{\alpha} di \right)^{\frac{1}{\alpha}}. \qquad (11.1)$$

The consumption good Y_t is the only utility generating good in the economy and it is sold on competitive markets at a price P_Y. Because we assume this good as numéraire of the economy, the price P_Y will be one. The demand

[1] Although in these models the union covers the whole manufacturing sector.

of the consumption good sector for an intermediate good of variety i can be derived from profit maximisation and is given by:[2]

$$P_x(i) = x(i)^{\alpha-1} \cdot \left(\int_0^{n_t} x(i)^{\alpha} di \right)^{\frac{1}{\alpha}-1} . \tag{11.2}$$

When looking at two arbitrary intermediate good varieties from the continuum of existing ones (let us call them 1 and 2) and, using the demand equations, we get an equation that allows us to derive the elasticity of substitution between two arbitrary varieties:

$$\frac{P(1)}{P(2)} = \left(\frac{x(1)}{x(2)} \right)^{\alpha-1} . \tag{11.3}$$

From the definition of the elasticity of substitution[3] we get for this elasticity $\frac{1}{\alpha-1}$, which is equal to the price elasticity of the intermediate goods demand curve.

Intermediate goods are produced using low-skilled and high-skilled labour. We assume the production function to be of the CES type, which is important when analysing the effect of union wage bargaining. Hence, the production function takes the following explicit form:

$$x(i) = \left(\delta \cdot l(i)^{-\beta} + (1-\delta) \cdot h(i)^{-\beta} \right)^{-\frac{1}{\beta}} , \tag{11.4}$$

where $l(i)$ is the amount of low-skilled labour employed in an intermediate sector firm i, $h(i)$ is the amount of high-skilled labour employed, δ is a parameter of the production function usually referred to as the distribution parameter. As was shown in the last chapter, β is a parameter reflecting the elasticity of substitution between high-skilled and low-skilled labour.

The intermediate good firm is a monopolist and sells the intermediate good variety to the final goods sector. Every intermediate good producer has to buy a blueprint from the research sector. To finance this, he can get money on the capital market (savings from households), but has to repay the debt indefinitely at a rate of interest r. So at every point in time a monopolist has to repay $P_n \cdot r$. With this, the profit function reads $\Pi(i) = x(i) \cdot p_x(i) - w^L \cdot l(i) - w^H \cdot h(i) - r \cdot P_n$. Using this and the demand curve given by equation (11.2), we can derive the demand for the two types of labour as:

$$w^L = \alpha \cdot P_x(i) \cdot \delta \cdot \left(\frac{x(i)}{l(i)} \right)^{1+\beta} , \tag{11.5}$$

for low-skilled labour (with w^L as the low-skilled wage) and

---

[2] Consumption good sector firms maximise $\Pi^C = Y_t - \left(\int_0^{n_t} x(i) \cdot P_x(i) di \right)$. Maximising this with respect to $x(i)$ results in equation (11.2).

[3] This is given by: $\frac{d(x(1)/x(2))}{d(P(1)/P(2))} \cdot \frac{(P(1)/P(2))}{(x(1)/x(2))}$.

$$w^H = \alpha \cdot P_x(i) \cdot (1+\delta) \cdot \left(\frac{x(i)}{h(i)^x}\right)^{1+\beta}, \tag{11.6}$$

for high-skilled labour (with w^H as the high-skilled wage).

The third sector of the economy is the R&D sector where blueprints of new intermediate good varieties are produced using high-skilled labour. The production function takes the following form:

$$\Delta n_t = n_t \cdot H^n, \tag{11.7}$$

where Δn_t are the new blueprints produced during an interval of time of length one, H^n is aggregate employment of high-skilled labour in the research sector and n_t are the already existing blueprints. This catches the notion of research spill-overs. The more blueprints already exist, the easier it is to develop new blueprints (or the less high-skilled labour is needed to develop a fixed amount of new blueprints). Research firms sell the blueprints competitively at a price P_n to new intermediate good producers. So the high-skilled labour demand of the research sector follows from profit maximisation as:[4]

$$w^H = n_t \cdot P_n. \tag{11.8}$$

The price of blueprints P_n can be determined using a zero profit condition for the intermediate sector. In an equilibrium with free-entry into the intermediate goods sector, the following must hold:

$$P_n \cdot r = P_x(i) \cdot x(i) - w^L \cdot l(i) - w^H \cdot h(i). \tag{11.9}$$

Plugging the labour demand equations (11.5) and (11.6) into the zero profit condition (11.9), we get the price of a blueprint as:

$$P_n = \frac{(1-\alpha) \cdot P_x(i) \cdot x(i)}{r}. \tag{11.10}$$

Now that we have determined the high-skilled labour demand of the research sector, we can turn to the equilibrium allocation of high-skilled labour between the intermediate and the research sector. We assume the amount of high-skilled labour in the economy to be exogenously given at $\bar{H}$ and to be supplied inelastically. Furthermore we assume that high-skilled labour is freely mobile between sectors of the economy and that the whole stock of high-skilled labour is allocated between the two sectors $\bar{H} = H^n + H^x$. Because of this perfect mobility, the intersectoral high-skilled wage differential must be zero. As such, the following no-arbitrage condition governs the allocation:

$$\alpha \cdot P_x(i) \cdot (1+\delta) \cdot \left(\frac{X}{H^x}\right)^{1+\beta} = \frac{(1-\alpha) \cdot P_x(i) \cdot X}{r}, \tag{11.11}$$

[4] The profits in the research sector are given by $\Pi^{R\&D} = P_n \cdot \Delta n_t - w^H \cdot H^n$.

where $X = n \cdot x$ is aggregate intermediate goods production and H^x is aggregate high-skilled employment in the intermediate sector. The lhs of equation (11.11) is the aggregate high-skilled labour demand in the intermediate sector and the rhs is the research sector's high-skilled demand. Equilibrium employment of high-skilled labour in the intermediate sector follows from equation (11.11) as a function of β, α, r, δ and $L = n \cdot l$, the total employment of low-skilled labour in the intermediate sector.

Equation (11.11) cannot be solved explicitly for H^x due to the assumed CES production function, but we can log-linearise the equation. When linearising we assume the form of the production function as being constant, hence $\tilde{\beta} = \tilde{\delta} = 0$. Remembering that the linearised version of the intermediate sector production function reads $\tilde{X} = s^L \cdot \tilde{L} + s^H \cdot \tilde{H}^x$ (with s^L and s^H being the production elasticity of low-skilled and high-skilled labour), the log-linearised version of (11.11) is:

$$\tilde{H}^x = \varphi \cdot \left(\frac{1}{1-\alpha} \cdot \tilde{\alpha} + \beta \cdot s^L \cdot \tilde{L} + \tilde{r} \right), \tag{11.12}$$

with $\varphi \equiv \frac{1}{1+\beta \cdot s^L} > 0$. Equation (11.12) reveals that equilibrium high-skilled employment in the intermediate sector will be the higher, the higher is the price elasticity of the intermediate goods demand and the higher is the rate of interest. The effect of a change in low-skilled employment is ambiguous and depends on the elasticity of substitution. Using the resource constraint of high-skilled labour $\bar{H} = H^n + H^x$, equation (11.12) modifies to:

$$\tilde{H}^n = \frac{c}{1-c} \cdot \varphi \cdot \left(-\frac{1}{1-\alpha} \cdot \tilde{\alpha} - \beta \cdot s^L \cdot \tilde{L} - \tilde{r} \right) + \frac{1}{1-c} \cdot \tilde{\bar{H}}, \tag{11.13}$$

where $c = \frac{H^x}{\bar{H}}$ denotes equilibrium high-skilled labour in the intermediate sector as part of the stock of high-skilled labour. Since in this case the low-skilled labour market is perfectly competitive, the whole stock of low-skilled labour will be employed. Hence, $\tilde{L} = \tilde{\bar{L}}$. With this, the relative change in H^n is only a function of exogenous variables.

With the help of equation (11.13) we can determine the steady state rate of growth of the economy. Consider a symmetric equilibrium; moreover assume that along a balanced growth path the allocation of high-skilled labour between the sectors of the economy does not change. With this the consumption good production is:

$$Y_t = n_t^{\frac{1}{\alpha}-1} X_t, \tag{11.14}$$

where X_t is aggregate intermediate good production at time t. Because we assume that along the balanced growth path employment (low-skilled as well as high-skilled) is constant in every sector, the aggregate intermediate goods production will not change over time. Using equation (11.14) we can determine the balanced growth rate of output as[5]:

[5] Note that we have used the approximation $\log(1 + x) = x$ for small x.

$$g_Y = \frac{1-\alpha}{\alpha} \cdot g_n, \tag{11.15}$$

where g_Y and g_n denote the growth rate of consumption good output and of intermediate good varieties, respectively. Log-linearising equation (11.15) and using equations (11.7) and (11.13), we get the equilibrium rate of growth in relative changes:

$$\tilde{g}_Y = -\frac{1}{\alpha} \cdot \tilde{\alpha} + \left(\frac{c}{1-c} \cdot \varphi \cdot \left(-\frac{1}{1-\alpha} \cdot \tilde{\alpha} - \beta \cdot s^L \cdot \tilde{\bar{L}} - \tilde{r}\right) + \frac{1}{1-c} \cdot \tilde{\bar{H}}\right). \tag{11.16}$$

In the following section we will deviate from the assumption of perfectly competitive labour markets and will introduce union wage bargaining. We will only analyse the effects of unionisation on the allocation of the stock of high-skilled labour. But as we have seen, there is a one-to-one relation between high-skilled employment in the research sector and the rate of growth of the economy.

11.2 The Unionised Economy

In this section we assume the union bargaining the wage at the firm-level. As such, there are n unions at every point in time and the whole low-skilled work force $\bar{L}$ is organised. Furthermore, we assume that membership is exogenous to the union. At some point in time t the union bargains the wage with an intermediate good firm as to maximise the utility of its members. Union's utility function takes the following form:

$$U = l(i) \cdot w^L(i) + (m(i) - l(i)) \cdot AI, \tag{11.17}$$

where $m(i)$ is the membership of the union and AI is the income the union members get, when not finding a job in firm i (i.e. the alternative Income). After a wage agreement between a firm and a union has been settled, the firm chooses low-skilled employment and high-skilled employment. We assume that the wage agreement lasts for a period of length one. After this period of time, the wage bargain starts over again. Again everyone of the workforce has the same probability of being (re)employed.

To determine the bargained wage we apply the Nash bargaining solution which implies the following Nash product:

$$\Omega = (U - \bar{U})^{\gamma} \cdot (\Pi - \bar{\Pi})^{1-\gamma}, \tag{11.18}$$

where γ is the bargaining power of the union. $\bar{U}$ and $\bar{\Pi}$ are union's utility and the profit of the firm respectively in the case of permanent dispute. We assume that in this case the union members can get the alternative income AI. So $\bar{U} = m(i) \cdot AI$. This stands in contrast to the assumption in the part on creative destruction where we assumed that the impasse utility for the union was zero. To make the model a bit more realistic and to discuss taxation later on, we assume that the disagreement point is not zero. In the case of permanent dispute the firm is not able to produce anything. Worse than that, the firm has to repay the debt every period. Hence, $\bar{\Pi} = -r \cdot P_n$.[6] Keeping this in mind we get the bargained wage by maximising the Nash product subject to the low-skilled labour demand curve (11.5). This yields (see the appendix):

$$w^L(i) = \phi \cdot AI, \tag{11.19}$$

where $\phi \equiv \frac{1}{1 - \frac{1}{\frac{1-\gamma}{\gamma} \cdot \frac{\alpha}{1-\alpha} \cdot s^L + \eta}}$. So the wage the union and the firm will agree upon is a mark-up over the alternative income. This mark-up depends positively on union's bargaining power γ, negatively on the demand elasticity α, on the production elasticity s^L and on the (absolute) labour demand elasticity η. The intuition for these properties is by and large the same as in the preceding part.

Up to this point we have only determined the firm-level wage. To analyse the macroeconomic effects of unionisation we have to aggregate and analyse the general equilibrium. Assuming a symmetric equilibrium and aggregating over the n firms, we get for the economy wide low-skilled labour demand curve, using equation (11.5):

$$w^L = \alpha \cdot P_x \cdot \delta \cdot \left(\frac{X}{L}\right)^{1+\beta}, \tag{11.20}$$

which is usually referred to as the price setting relation of the intermediate sector (see, e.g., Jerger and Michaelis (1999)).

When aggregating equation (11.19) we have to endogenise the alternative income AI which is exogenous to the union during the bargain, but is endogenous at the macroeconomic level. We assume the alternative income to be the weighted average of the low-skilled wage and the unemployment benefit. The weights are $(1-u)$ and u respectively where u denotes the unemployment rate in the economy. The rationale behind this assumption is that when a union member becomes unemployed, he can find a job somewhere else in the economy with probability $(1-u)$, earning w^L or with probability u he does not find a job, in which case he gets the unemployment benefit B. Plugging the alternative income into (11.19) and assuming symmetry, we get:

$$w^L = \frac{\phi \cdot u}{1 - \phi \cdot (1-u)} \cdot B. \tag{11.21}$$

This equation, which is called the wage setting curve, shows the aggregate low-skilled wage that will be bargained in the economy for alternative unemployment rates. The higher the unemployment rate the lower will be the

[6] As in Part II on capital and collective bargaining, we assume that the firm is not able to sell the patent in case of a dispute, because, e.g., there exists no secondary market for patents.

wage. This is because with a high unemployment rate it is harder to find a job elsewhere in the economy and thus, being unemployed is more costly. This lowers wage demands of the union.

The unemployment rate is given by $u = \frac{\bar{L}-L}{\bar{L}}$ hence, equations (11.20) and (11.21) determine equilibrium low-skilled employment in the economy (and thereby equilibrium unemployment).

An important point is that the price-setting curve is not constant over time in the wage-employment space, but will be shifted outwards. This is because the symmetric price of an intermediate good variety, $P_x = n_t^{\frac{1-\alpha}{\alpha}}$ will rise every period. This price increase is due to the increased specialisation. With more intermediate good varieties, the marginal efficiency of every variety will rise and so will the price which the consumption good sector is willing to pay.

If the wage setting curve was fixed over time, this growth process would result in ever increasing low-skilled employment until the whole low-skilled stock $\bar{L}$ would be employed in the intermediate sector. To avoid this unpleasant feature, we assume that the unemployment benefit B_t is growing over time at the same rate as the growth rate of the economy. So the bargained wage will rise every period but employment will remain constant.

The assumption of a growing unemployment benefit can be legitimated on the grounds that the unemployed should participate in the growing well being of the economy. Another way to avoid this feature is to assume a constant replacement rate (as, e.g., done in Layard et al. (1990)), i.e., that the unemployment benefit is a constant part of the wage. The main drawback of this assumption is that in this case the wage setting curve is vertical in the wage-employment space.[7] Thus, low-skilled employment would be solely determined by the wage-setting curve. So this assumption seems to be too restrictive. Furthermore empirical evidence (see, e.g., Blanchard and Wolfers (2000)) suggest that at least in continental europe, the benefit replacement ratio is not constant over time.

Log-linearising both curves yields the following:[8]

$$\tilde{w}^L = \tilde{\alpha} + \tilde{P}_x + (1+\beta)\cdot(s^L \cdot \tilde{L} + s^H \cdot \tilde{H}^x) - (1+\beta)\cdot \tilde{L}, \tag{11.22}$$

$$\tilde{w}^L = \varrho_\phi \cdot \tilde{\phi} - \varrho_u \cdot \left(\frac{\bar{L}}{U} - 1\right) \cdot \tilde{\bar{L}} - \varrho_u \cdot \frac{L}{U} \cdot \tilde{L} + \tilde{B}_t, \tag{11.23}$$

with $\varrho_\phi \equiv \frac{1}{1-(1-u)\cdot\phi} > 0$ and $\varrho_u \equiv \frac{\phi-1}{1-(1-u)\cdot\phi} > 0$, U denoting unemployment and B_t is the (growing) unemployment benefit at some point in time t. These two equations can be solved for the (change) of equilibrium low-skilled employment, which yields:

---

7 Because in this case unemployment is only a function of the union mark-up.

8 Remember that we assumed that the unemployment benefit will grow at the same rate as the economy. Hence, $B_t = g_Y \cdot B$. Furthermore remember that in a symmetric equilibrium $P_x = n_t^{\frac{1-\alpha}{\alpha}} = g_Y$. With these assumptions B_t/P_x will be equal to B.

$$\left((1+\beta) \cdot s^H + \varrho_u \cdot \frac{L}{U} \right) \cdot \tilde{L} = \\ \tilde{\alpha} + (1+\beta) \cdot s^H \cdot \tilde{H}^x - \varrho_\phi \cdot \tilde{\phi} - \varrho_u \cdot \left(\frac{\bar{L}}{U} - 1 \right) \cdot \tilde{\bar{L}} - \tilde{B}. \tag{11.24}$$

So low-skilled employment will increase as the amount of high-skilled labour which is employed in the intermediate sector rises. This is because with higher high-skilled employment, marginal productivity of low-skilled labour will be higher which results in an outward shift of the price setting curve. This effect is the stronger, the lower is the elasticity of substitution between high-skilled and low-skilled labour. The economic intuition is that when both types of labour are complements in the intermediate goods sector's production function, the change in marginal productivity of one factor caused by a change in employment of the other factor will be very high, because it will be hardly possible to compensate this change. A very interesting point is that in the case where both factors are perfect substitutes ($\beta = -1$) high-skilled employment will have no effect on the equilibrium employment of low-skilled labour.

A higher mark-up, e.g., due to higher union power will cause low-skilled employment to decline. The same is true if the employment benefit in terms of the intermediate good rises, because in this case the utility loss due to unemployment will be small and the union will bargain a high wage.

The equation for equilibrium low-skilled employment in the union case (11.24) and the equation for the equilibrium allocation of the stock of high-skilled labour (11.12) determine the general equilibrium in the economy.

To solve for the equilibrium level of high-skilled employment in the intermediate goods sector (which, by the resource constraint also determines equilibrium employment in the research sector which in turn determines the equilibrium rate of growth of the economy) we can plug equation (11.24) into (11.12) and get the following equation:

$$\tilde{H}^x \cdot \left(\frac{(1+\beta) \cdot s^H}{s^H \cdot (1+\beta) + \varrho_u \cdot \frac{L}{U}} - \frac{1}{\varphi \cdot \beta \cdot s^L} \right) = \\ \left(\tilde{B} + \varrho_\phi \cdot \tilde{\phi} - \varrho_u \cdot \left(\frac{\bar{L}}{U} - 1 \right) \cdot \tilde{\bar{L}} \right) \cdot \frac{1}{s^H \cdot (1+\beta) + \varrho_u \cdot \frac{L}{U}} \\ - \left(\frac{(1-\alpha) \cdot \beta \cdot s^L + 1}{(1-\alpha)} \cdot \tilde{\alpha} + \tilde{r} \right) \cdot \frac{1}{\beta \cdot s^L}. \tag{11.25}$$

If we are able to determine the sign of the coefficient of $\tilde{H}^x$ we can analyse parameters influencing the equilibrium high-skilled employment in the intermediate sector and hence, influencing (with reversed signs) the growth rate of the economy. With this at hands we can also analyse the impact of union wage bargaining on the rate of growth of the economy.

First of all consider the case in which β is zero, i.e. the production function in the intermediate sector is Cobb-Douglas. Using this, equation (11.25) can be simplified, yielding:

$$\tilde{H}^x = \left(\frac{(1-\alpha) \cdot s^L + 1}{(1-\alpha) \cdot s^L} \right) \cdot \tilde{\alpha} + \tilde{r} \cdot \frac{1}{s^L}. \tag{11.26}$$

Equation (11.26) shows that in the Cobb-Douglas case only the rate of interest and α (assuming that the production function and its parameters are constant) determine equilibrium employment of high-skilled labour in the intermediate sector. A rise in the interest rate will result in higher high-skilled employment in the intermediate sector. The economic intuition of this property is the following. When the rate of interest rises the demand of the intermediate sector for new blueprints will decline. But this in turn dampens high-skilled labour demand of the research sector; so the wage which research sector firms are able to pay will decline. High-skilled labour is perfectly mobile between sectors, so high-skilled labour will migrate into the intermediate sector and with this the wage will decline and employment will rise.

A similar analysis can be applied in the case of a change in α. Consider a decline in this parameter which is a measure of the elasticity of substitution between two intermediate goods in the consumption good production function. In this case the profits of the intermediate good firms will increase which implies that the price for blueprints will rise and hence, the high-skilled labour demand in the research sector will be higher. On the other hand (see equation (11.6)) the high-skilled labour demand in the intermediate sector will decline because the mark-up α declined. The first effect results in a wage differential favouring the research sector and this effect is amplified by the second effect.[9] So high-skilled labour will move into the research sector and thereby lowering equilibrium high-skilled labour employment in the intermediate goods sector and fostering the rate of growth.

In the cases in which the production function is not Cobb-Douglas, labour market parameters and as such, unionisation have an impact on equilibrium high-skilled employment in the intermediate sector and thus on the growth rate of the economy.

To analyse these effects we can distinguish two cases. Firstly, the case in which high-skilled and low-skilled labour in intermediate sector are good substitutes ($\sigma > 1$, $\beta < 0$) and secondly the case in which they are bad substitutes ($\sigma < 1$, $\beta > 1$). Inspecting equation (11.25), it is easy to see that we have to determine the sign of the coefficient $\left(\frac{(1+\beta) \cdot s^H}{s^H \cdot (1+\beta) + \varrho_u \cdot \frac{L}{U}} - \frac{1}{\varphi \cdot \beta \cdot s^L} \right)$ to analyse the impact of collective bargaining (e.g., a change in ϕ) on high-skilled employment in the intermediate sector and hence, on the rate of growth. Using the following equation, we can analyse the sign of the coefficient:

$$\left(\frac{(1+\beta) \cdot s^H}{s^H \cdot (1+\beta) + \varrho_u \cdot \frac{L}{U}} - \frac{1}{\varphi \cdot \beta \cdot s^L} \right) \gtrless 0. \tag{11.27}$$

[9] Note that the coefficient exceeds one so that the change in α is disproportionately to the resulting change in high-skilled labour employment.

Remembering that $\varphi = (1 + \beta \cdot s^L)$ and doing some algebraic manipulations on equation (11.27) yields the following equation:

$$-\frac{(1+\beta)s^H + \varphi_u \cdot \frac{L}{U} \cdot (1 + \beta \cdot s^L)}{\varphi \cdot \beta \cdot s^L \cdot \left(s^H \cdot (1+\beta) + \varrho_u \cdot \frac{L}{U}\right)} \gtrless 0. \tag{11.28}$$

Equation (11.28) depicts that as long as β is negative (positive), the coefficient is positive (negative). With this at hand, we can analyse the impact of collective bargaining and labour market parameters on the rate of growth.[10]

Consider, e.g., a change in the union mark-up which might have been caused by a change in the union's bargaining power or by a change in the labour demand elasticity. In this case employment of high-skilled labour in the intermediate sector will change, too. But the direction of the change depends on the elasticity of substitution. If β is negative, a rise (decline) of the mark-up will lead to higher (lower) high-skilled labour employment in the intermediate sector and hence, to a lower (higher) growth rate of the economy. The opposite will be true if β is positive. A higher mark-up in this case will cause high-skilled employment in the intermediate sector to decline, so the growth rate will rise due to unionisation (or stronger unions). The economic intuition for this point is that due to union wage bargaining the high-skilled labour demand curve in both sectors of the economy will shift downwards. The asymmetry of these shifts causes a reallocation of the stock of high-skilled labour between sectors, which will in turn also change the rate of growth. We will analyse this point in more detail below.

The same arguments can be applied when analysing the impact of a change in the unemployment benefit. A higher unemployment benefit will result in a higher bargained wage, because being unemployed is less costly. Hence, a higher B has the same effects as a higher mark-up. It will cause low-skilled employment to decline and change the allocation of high-skilled labour accordingly.

Very similar arguments hold true for a change in the low-skilled resource pool $\bar{L}$. With a higher $\bar{L}$, the probability of being employed will decline. Hence, the union will be reluctant to bargain a high wage, because the unemployed union members will find it hard to find a new job in the economy. So low-skilled-employment will be high, which in turn will lead to lower high-skilled employment in the intermediate sector if β is negative and to higher employment if β is positive.

Summarising, we can state that in the case of $\sigma < 1$ ($\sigma > 1$) the growth rate of the economy will be higher (lower), the higher is low-skilled unemployment. Thus, higher unionisation might result in a higher rate of economic growth, at least in the case of low-skilled and high-skilled labour in the intermediate

[10] The impact of α and the rate of interest are in the case of $\beta \neq 0$ the same as they were in the Cobb-Douglas case, because a change in the sign of the coefficient of $\tilde{H}^x$ and the sign of $\frac{1}{\beta \cdot s^L}$ (which determines the sign of the coefficients of a change in α and r) will change accordingly.

sector being bad substitutes. Figure 11.1 shows the impact of union wage bar-

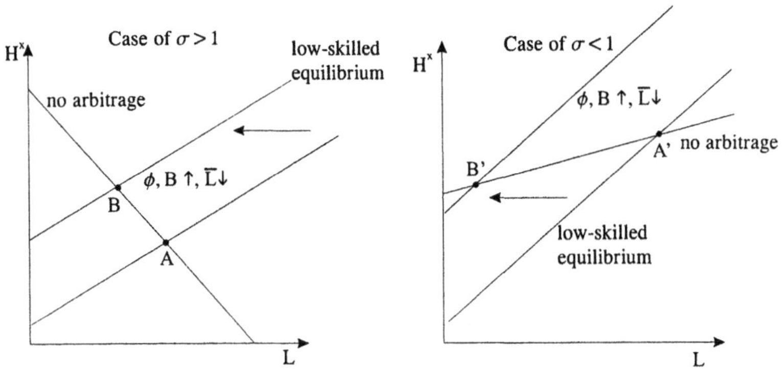

Fig. 11.1. Growth and Employment Effects of Unions in a Model with Expanding Product Variety

gaining on equilibrium low-skilled and high-skilled employment in the intermediate goods sector. Due to unionisation the curve showing the equilibrium in this market (the upward sloping curve labelled "low-skilled equilibrium") will be shifted upwards because at any given level of high-skilled employment, employment of low-skilled labour will decline.

The high-skilled labour equilibrium (downward respectively upward sloping curve labelled "no-arbitrage") is not affected by unionisation. The figure shows the above mentioned effects. If σ exceeds one, the equilibrium high-skilled employment in the intermediate sector will rise (the move from point A to point B). Hence, given the stock of high-skilled labour, the rate of growth will decline. The opposite will be true if σ is smaller than one.[11]

What is the economic intuition behind these effects? To analyse this we concentrate on the high-skilled labour market equilibrium. In the following we will analyse the impact of low-skilled labour employment on the high-skilled labour demand curve in the intermediate and in the research sector.

The effect of lower low-skilled employment on the high-skilled labour demand can be depicted when differentiating equation (11.6) with respect to L (and for the ease of exposition multiply by $\frac{L}{w^H}$). With this we get:

[11] For this case the figure reveals the interesting point that the slope of the "no-arbitrage" curve (which is actually, due to the log-linearisation, the elasticity) must not exceed the slope of the low-skilled equilibrium curve to guarantee an equilibrium to exist. By inspecting equations (11.12) and (11.24) this is always true, because the slope of the no-arbitrage curve will be smaller than one, whereas the slope of the low-skilled equilibrium curve exceeds unity.

$$\frac{dw^H}{dL} \cdot \frac{L}{w^H} = (1+\beta) \cdot s^L > 0. \tag{11.29}$$

This elasticity shows in which way the relative marginal productivity of high-skilled labour in the intermediate sector changes due to a relative change in low-skilled employment. So equation (11.29) depicts the shift of the high-skilled labour demand curve. We can see that a decline in low-skilled labour employment will unambiguously shift the high-skilled labour demand curve downwards, i.e., at a given high-skilled wage w^H the intermediate goods sector will demand less high-skilled labour.

There are two variables driving this inward shift. On the one hand this is the elasticity of substitution between the two factors of production and on the other hand this is the productivity of low-skilled labour.

With a high elasticity of substitution[12] the shift of the high-skilled labour demand curve will be small. This is because the effect of a change in low-skilled labour on marginal productivity will be small since the decrease in low-skilled employment can be substituted very easily (see also Hamermesh (1993)). The opposite will be true if the elasticity of substitution is small. In this case a decline in one factor obviously has a strong impact on marginal productivity of the other factor.

The second parameter influencing the impact of changes in low-skilled employment on the productivity of high-skilled employment is the production elasticity of low-skilled-labour. An increase in this parameter will cause a large shift of the high-skilled demand curve. This is because with a high production elasticity of low-skilled labour, a decline in low-skilled employment will have a strong impact on production which will lead to a strong decline in marginal productivity.

Hence, we can interpret the first effect as the substitution effect and the second one as the rationing effect of a change in low-skilled employment on the high-skilled labour demand in the intermediate sector.

The important point is that the strength of the impact of a decline of low-skilled employment on high-skilled labour demand in the intermediate goods sector is positively related to the elasticity of substitution of the production function in this sector.

We can do the same analysis for the effect of lower low-skilled employment on the high-skilled labour demand in the research sector. To do this we take the rhs of equation (11.11) and apply the same elasticity approach as was done before:

$$\frac{dw^H}{dL} \cdot \frac{L}{w^H} = s^L. \tag{11.30}$$

The equation depicts that in this case high-skilled labour demand also shifts downwards due to a decline in low-skilled employment. But interestingly enough the strength of the effect in this case is only determined by the production elasticity of low-skilled labour. The economic intuition for this is clear.

[12] Remember that $\beta = \frac{1-\sigma}{\sigma}$ and thus $(1+\beta) = \sigma^{-1}$.

High-skilled labour demand in the research sector is only affected by unionisation via a decline of profits in the intermediate goods sector. But this decline of profits is due to a decline in production which can be measured using the low-skilled labour production elasticity.

The rationing of low-skilled labour by the union will shift the high-skilled labour demand in the intermediate as well as in the research sector downwards. The important point is that the shift of these two curves is asymmetric and that this asymmetry depends on the elasticity of substitution of the intermediate goods production function.

Now consider the change from a competitive equilibrium to one in which low-skilled labour is unionised for the case of β being negative. So the inward shift of the high-skilled labour demand curve in the intermediate goods sector is smaller (because $(1 + \beta) < 1$) than the shift of the high-skilled demand curve in the research sector. With the old allocation of the high-skilled labour pool, the high-skilled wage in the intermediate sector will be higher than that in the research sector. So the unionisation of the low-skilled labour market will result in a high-skilled wage differential between the research and the intermediate sector, favouring the latter one. Obviously this cannot be an equilibrium because high-skilled labour is mobile between sectors and any wage differential will result in arbitrage.

The wage differential will trigger off a migration of high-skilled labour towards the intermediate goods sector and thereby lowering the wage in the intermediate sector and raising it in the research sector (due to the negatively sloped labour demand curves). This migration process will cease when the high-skilled wage is again the same in both sectors. At the end of this process the equilibrium high-skilled employment will be higher in the intermediate sector and lower in the research sector, which will lead to a decline of the equilibrium rate of growth of the economy.

The opposite will be true if β is positive. The shift of the high-skilled labour demand curve in this case will be larger than the shift of the high-skilled demand curve in the research sector. Hence, there will be a wage differential in favour of the research sector. This wage differential will result again in a reallocation of the high-skilled labour force. But this time high-skilled labour will move from the intermediate into the research sector. Hence, high-skilled employment will rise in the research sector and the equilibrium rate of growth will rise, too.

If the production function in the intermediate sector is Cobb-Douglas (β is zero), unionisation of the low-skilled labour market will have no effect on the rate of growth. This was already analysed above, but now we can give the economic intuition. In the Cobb-Douglas case both high-skilled labour demand curves will be shifted by the same extend when low-skilled employment decreases. So unionisation does not result in a wage differential and hence, there is no reallocation of the stock of high-skilled labour, leaving the growth rate unchanged.

Up to this point we have only analysed the growth effects of unionisation. Besides these effects the union will cause unemployment in the economy. To determine the equilibrium rate of unemployment we can use the resource constraint of the low-skilled labour pool which states that all low-skilled labour is either employed in the intermediate sector or unemployed, hence $\bar{L} = L + U$. Log-linearising this equation yields the change in unemployment as: $\tilde{U} = -\left(1 - \frac{\bar{L}}{U}\right) \cdot \tilde{L} + \frac{\bar{L}}{U} \cdot \tilde{\bar{L}}$. The change in low-skilled employment can be determined using equations (11.24) and (11.12). With this we get for the equilibrium rate of unemployment:

$$\begin{aligned} \tilde{U} = \nu_L \cdot \left(-\varphi \cdot \left(\frac{(1-\alpha) \cdot \beta \cdot s^L + 1}{1-\alpha} \cdot \tilde{\alpha} + \tilde{r} \right) + \varrho_\phi \cdot \tilde{\phi} \right) + \\ \nu_L \left(\varrho_u \cdot \left(\frac{\bar{L}}{U} - 1 \right) \cdot \tilde{\bar{L}} + \tilde{B} \right) + \left(\frac{\bar{L}}{U} - \nu_L \cdot \varrho_u \cdot \left(\frac{\bar{L}}{U} - 1 \right) \right) \cdot \tilde{\bar{L}}, \end{aligned} \tag{11.31}$$

where $\nu_L \equiv \left(\frac{\bar{L}}{U} - 1 \right) \cdot \left(\frac{1}{\frac{(1+\beta) \cdot s^H + \varrho_u \cdot \frac{\bar{L}}{U}}{(1+\beta) \cdot s^H} - \beta \cdot s^L \cdot \varphi} \right) > 0$ (see the appendix).

Unemployment in the economy is first of all affected by the usual labour market variables in a way that is very standard in nearly all (static) models with unionised labour markets (see, e.g., Layard et al. (1990) or Booth (1996)). Higher unemployment benefits lead to higher unemployment, because unions will bargain a higher wage and with unchanged labour demand this will result in lower low-skilled employment. The same is obviously true for a higher mark-up. A higher mark-up will drive up bargained wages and this will also lead to lower employment. More subtle effects are caused by changes of the low-skilled pool, the rate of interest and the competitiveness parameter α. A high low-skilled pool has two effects on unemployment. On the one hand (and this follows from the definition of unemployment) a larger resource pool will raise c.p. unemployment, but on the other hand it will dampen the wage demands of unions, because with this it is less costly to be unemployed. The latter effect raises employment. The overall effect of a larger stock of low-skilled labour on unemployment is ambiguous.

Another parameter having ambiguous effects on unemployment is α. On the one hand, the mark-up will be lower with higher α. So the union will bargain a lower wage which clearly raises low-skilled employment. But this increase in low-skilled employment changes the allocation of the stock of high-skilled labour between the two sectors of the economy. This again has repercussions on low-skilled demand. The arguments for this are the same as in the preceding part. If σ is smaller than one high-skilled labour in the intermediate sector will increase as low-skilled employment increases. Thus, the impact will be amplified. The opposite is true if σ exceeds one. In this case the overall effect will be ambiguous.

The last parameter influencing unemployment is the rate of interest. A higher rate of interest will lead to a decline in the demand for blueprints.

Hence, high-skilled labour demand in the research sector will decline and (because of the full employment assumption) high-skilled labour employment in the intermediate sector will rise. But this in turn will shift the low-skilled labour demand curve outwards with the effect that for a given bargained wage[13] low-skilled employment will rise and this obviously lowers unemployment.

The analysis of the impact of union wage bargaining in a model of expanding product variety has shown that the growth rate is influenced by wage bargaining. We have seen that lower low-skilled employment and the higher wage caused by the union will result in a downward shift of high-skilled labour demand in the intermediate as well as in the research sector, implying a possible reallocation of the stock of high-skilled labour. If the elasticity of substitution in the research sector will be lower than one there will be a reallocation towards the research sector. In this case the growth rate will rise. The opposite will be true if this elasticity exceeds one. In the Cobb-Douglas case there will be no reallocation, as such, the union has no effect on the rate of growth. Moreover we have analysed unemployment and have shown the unemployment influencing parameters.

11.3 Appendix

The bargained wage

In this part of the appendix we will derive the bargained wage from the maximisation of the Nash product.

$$\frac{d\Omega}{dw^L(i)} = (l(i)(w^L(i) - AI))^\gamma \cdot (1-\gamma) \cdot (\Pi - r \cdot P_n)^{-\gamma} \cdot \left(\frac{d\Pi}{dw^L(i)}\right) +$$

$$\gamma \cdot (l(i)(w^L(i) - AI))^{\gamma-1} \left(\frac{dl(i)}{dw^L(i)} \cdot (w^L(i) - AI) + l(i)\right) \cdot (\Pi - r \cdot P_n)^{1-\gamma} = 0. \tag{A1}$$

With $\frac{d\Pi}{dw^L(i)} = -l(i)$ and some algebraic manipulations equation (A1) modifies to:

$$\frac{d\Omega}{dw^L(i)} = \gamma \cdot \frac{1}{(l(i)(w^L(i) - AI))} \left(\frac{dl(i)}{dw^L(i)} \cdot (w^L(i) - AI) + l(i)\right) \\ +(1-\gamma) \cdot (\Pi - r \cdot P_n)^{-1} \cdot -l(i) = 0. \tag{A2}$$

Multiplying both sides by $w^L(i)$ and using the fact that $\Pi - r\ P_n = (1-\alpha) \cdot P_x(i)x(i)$, (A2) modifies to:

[13] As long as the *slope* of the labour demand curve is unchanged, the bargained wage of the union will be unchanged. We assume that with the outward shift of the low-skilled labour demand curve, the slope will not change.

$$\frac{d\Omega}{dw^L(i)} = \gamma \cdot \frac{dl(i)}{dw^L(i)} \cdot \frac{w^L(i)}{l(i)} + \frac{w^L(i)}{w^L(i) - AI} - (1-\gamma) \cdot \frac{l(i) \cdot w^L(i)}{(1-\alpha) \cdot P_x(i) \cdot x(i)} = 0. \tag{A3}$$

Finally using the equation for low-skilled labour demand (11.5) and the fact that $\frac{\delta \cdot l(i)^{-\beta}}{x(i)^{-\beta}}$ is the production elasticity of low-skilled labour. The bargained wage follows after some straightforward algebraic manipulations as:

$$w^L(i) = \frac{1}{1 - \frac{1}{\frac{1-\gamma}{\gamma} \cdot \frac{\alpha}{1-\alpha} \cdot s^L + \eta}} \cdot AI. \tag{A4}$$

The sign of the coefficient ν_L

In this part we will show that ν_L is positive as stated in the text. The first part of the coefficient $\left(1 - \frac{L}{U}\right)$ is unambiguously positive, because unemployment cannot exceed the whole stock of low-skilled labour. To determine the sign of the second part, take the denominator and assume for the moment that it would be positive. This yields:

$$\frac{(1+\beta) \cdot s^H + \varrho_u \cdot \frac{L}{U}}{(1+\beta) \cdot s^H} - \beta \cdot s^L \cdot \varphi > 0. \tag{B1}$$

Remembering that $\psi = \frac{1}{1+\beta \cdot s^L}$ and after some algebraic manipulations, equation (B1) modifies to:

$$\left((1+\beta) \cdot s^H + \varrho_u \cdot \frac{L}{U}\right) \cdot (1 + \beta \cdot s^L) > \beta \cdot s^L \cdot (1+\beta) \cdot s^H. \tag{B2}$$

Because ϱ_u is positive and it is always true that $(1+\beta) \cdot s^L > \beta \cdot s^L$ the statement that ν_L is positive is also always true.

12

Tax Policy

We have argued in the preceding part that union members who do not find a job will get unemployment benefit. But this begs the question how this unemployment benefit is financed. To focus the arguments in the last section, we have not implemented this financing need into the analysis. What we want to do now is to implement taxation into the analysis to enrich the model. We assume that a government exists that pays the unemployment benefit and has the power to levy taxes to finance its expenditures.

In this sense the government is only an institution to redistribute resources from the employed to the unemployed. We do not consider the government as a device of providing public goods (e.g., infrastructure and the like) as done in Barro (1990) or Barro and Sala-i-Martin (1995) because we want to keep the model as simple as possible.

The enrichment of the last section's model via the implementation of the government offers two main advantages:

1. It closes the model and allows us to take a more general equilibrium view; e.g., when we stated that higher wage bargaining power of unions might be growth enhancing (in the case of the elasticity of substitution smaller than one) this was obviously a c.p. conclusion. But this conclusion might not hold in the case when we explicitly integrate the need to finance higher unemployment via higher taxes into the model. In this case the effect might be dampened or even reversed.
2. Furthermore, a model with explicit taxation can be used to judge economic policy. In times in which most western european governments face high budget deficits, the question whether the economic performance of an economy could be increased using revenue neutral tax reforms is high on the agenda. The model with taxation allows us to study simultaneously the growth and employment effects of these reforms.

The discussion of the dynamic effects of taxation and of tax reforms is quite old and was first analysed in standard neoclassical growth models (see, e.g., Atkinson and Stiglitz (1980)). The main problem of these studies is that in the neoclassical framework there is no room for influencing the rate of growth of the economy since this is exogenously given by the rate of population growth or some exogenous technological change. As such effects of taxation are limited to changes of the steady state capital stock (and so to the level of output) or the rate of growth during the transition from the old steady state to the new one.[1]

With the emergence of the endogenous growth theory the interest in the impact of taxes and tax reforms awoke again. Compared to the neoclassical growth models, the new models at hands offered potential impact of taxes or of tax reforms on the rate of growth in these models.

One of the early contributions in the discussion of the effects of tax policy on the rate of growth is a paper by Sergio Rebelo (1991) in which a model is presented where growth is driven by the accumulation of capital. By introducing a spill-over effect, the economy can grow unboundedly only by the accumulation of capital (similar to the AK growth model presented in the second part "Unions and Capital"). To analyse fiscal policy he introduces a tax on consumption and a tax on investment (the tax revenue is used to provide a public good which does not affect the structure of the economy). The impact of these taxes is that the investment tax lowers the rate of growth and that the tax on consumption only changes the level of consumption but is neutral with respect to the rate of growth.

More sophisticated models in which growth is driven by the accumulation of physical and human capital (some with endogenous labour supply) and in which more different taxes are distinguished show less clearer results. There are papers where tax policies have at best marginal effects (like in Lucas (1990)). But there are also papers in which tax policy is a very important factor in determining the rate of growth (see, e.g., Kim (1998) in which a model is calibrated with data of the US economy and where it is shown that the rate of growth will rise by 0.85 percentage points when all taxes are eliminated or Jones et al. (1993) who suggest that in such a case the growth rate could rise by 8 percentage points).[2]

Beside the analysis of the "total" impact of taxation, there are also papers in which reforms of the tax structure (taking explicitly the governmental budget constraint into account or implicitly by assuming revenue neutral tax reforms) are analysed. The paper by Kim (1998) does not only analyse the ef-

[1] Nevertheless also in these models in which taxation does not affect the rate of growth, some very interesting results concerning the effects of taxation can be analysed, e.g., that an income transfer to workers, financed by a tax on capital will not necessarily lead to an increase in the share of income wage earners will get (see Atkinson and Stiglitz (1980)).

[2] A nice comparison of some different growth models implementing tax reforms and some explanations why the results between quite similar models differ so much, can be found in Stockey and Rebelo (1995). They support the Lucas (1990) view and argue that the strong impact of taxes found in Jones et al. (1993) is due to a labour supply elasticity that is unrealistically high.

fect of the elimination of all taxes in the economy, but also depicts the impact of revenue neutral tax reforms, where he considers the optimal "allocation" of taxation to labour and capital. He finds that the rate of growth might increase by 0.28 percentage points and hence, also revenue neutral tax reforms might have substantial impact on the rate of growth.

As the theoretical (and calibrated) models on the effects of taxation on the rate of growth suggest also the empirical evidence is mixed. In a paper by Mendoza et al. (1997) the Harberger conjecture is analysed, which states that changes of the tax structure have only minor effects on the growth rate of an economy. Their analysis shows that tax rates are generally not significant in explaining economic growth, although they state that the hypothesis that the coefficients of the taxes (consumption tax, tax on labour and capital income) are jointly zero is rejected by the data. The method used by Mendoza et al. (among others) is criticised in a recent paper by Kneller et al. (1999) who suggest that some of the results are driven by the incomplete specification of the governmental budget constraint, i.e., some of the studies neglect that a change in a tax will be accompanied by a change in another tax to compensate for the original change in order to keep the budget balanced (see, e.g., also the paper by Easterly and Rebelo (1993) who assume that tax changes will be accompanied by changes of lump-sum taxes or subsidies.)[3] Taking these implicit budget financing effects into account, Kneller et al. (1999) find that higher (distortionary) taxation will significantly reduce the rate of economic growth in an economy.

A serious drawback of all of the aforementioned (theoretical) models analysing the impact of taxation on economic growth is that they assume perfectly competitive labour markets. But especially in continental europe we observe substantial equilibrium unemployment, so the question begs in which way the standard results are modified when implementing labour market distortions (a notable exception is Birk and Michaelis (2002) who analyse green tax reforms in a dynamic economy with unemployment caused by costly search).

To analyse this point we employ the model of expanding product variety that was analysed in the preceding section. We integrate four taxes into the model, namely a payroll tax on low-skilled and high-skilled labour, an income tax on low-skilled labour income and a tax on the usage of the intermediate good. These taxes are levied in order to finance the unemployment benefit. We analyse which effects these taxes (if any) have on the equilibrium rate of growth of the economy. Furthermore, we analyse the effects of revenue neutral tax reforms and distinguish *ex-ante* neutrality (taking the endogenous

[3] The problem of this assumption is that it will change the estimated coefficient (for a nice exposition of this point, see the paper by Kneller et al. (1999) p 174). Not the coefficient of a change in one tax on the growth rate is estimated, but the effect of a change in the tax minus the effect of the tax that compensates for the change.

variables as unchanged) and *ex-post* neutrality (accounting for all adjustments of the endogenous variables caused by the reform).

12.1 The Basic Model

When analysing the growth and employment effects of the various taxes within the framework of the last section's model, we have to focus on how the price setting and the wage setting curve and the no-arbitrage relation are affected by these taxes.

The tax on the usage of the intermediate goods, t_x, will obviously change the demand function of the final goods sector. In the case that the final sector has to pay a tax on the usage of intermediate goods, the optimisation problem modifies to:

$$\Pi^C = Y_t - \left(\int_0^{n_t} x(i) \cdot (1 + t_x) \cdot P_x(i) di \right), \tag{12.1}$$

where t_x is the tax on the usage of the intermediate good. With this, we get a modified demand function of the final goods sector for an intermediate good variety:

$$P_x(i) = \frac{1}{1 + t_x} \cdot x(i)^{\alpha - 1} \cdot \left(\int_0^{n_t} x(i)^\alpha di \right)^{\frac{1}{\alpha} - 1}. \tag{12.2}$$

The prices the final good sector has to pay for the intermediate goods implicitly increase due to taxation and hence, demand will fall. The tax will shift the intermediate goods demand curve downwards. But this shift will also affect the labour demand curves of the intermediate goods producers (equations (11.5) and (11.6)). Due to the intermediate goods tax these two labour demand curves will shift downward, too. This is quite intuitive. Since the price which the final good firms are willing to pay for a given quantity of an intermediate good declines, the marginal value product of labour employed in an intermediate firm will decline, too.

The payroll taxes on low-skilled and high-skilled labour, t_L and t_H, respectively, will obviously influence the labour demand curves in the intermediate goods as well as in the research sector. With payroll taxation, profits in the intermediate sector will be:

$$\Pi_x = P_x(i) \cdot x(i) - w^L \cdot (1 + t_L) \cdot l(i) - w^H \cdot (1 + t_H) \cdot h(i)^x - P_n \cdot r, \tag{12.3}$$

with this, the labour demand curves in the intermediate sector will modify to:

$$w^L(i) = \frac{1}{1 + t_L} \cdot \alpha \cdot P_x(i) \cdot \delta \cdot \left(\frac{x(i)}{l(i)} \right)^{1+\beta}, \tag{12.4}$$

$$w^H(i) = \frac{1}{1 + t_H} \cdot \alpha \cdot P_x(i) \cdot (1 + \delta) \cdot \left(\frac{x(i)}{h(i)^x} \right)^{1+\beta}. \tag{12.5}$$

An interesting and important feature can be derived when the demand equations (12.4) and (12.5) are plugged into the profit function (12.3). This reveals that profits in the optimum are given by $\Pi_x = (1-\alpha) \cdot P_x(i) \cdot x(i) - r \cdot P_n$.[4]

High-skilled labour demand in the research sector is also modified in the presence of payroll taxation and is given by:

$$w^H = \frac{1}{1+t_H} \cdot P_n \cdot n_t. \tag{12.6}$$

We assume that the payroll tax on high-skilled labour is the same in both sectors of the economy, because it seems hard to justify why the same factor should be taxed differently depending on whether it is employed in one or the other sector of the economy.[5] With the zero profit assumption and the high-skilled demand curves of the two sectors of the economy, the no arbitrage relation can be derived. This is the same as given in the no-tax case by equation (11.11). This result should be intuitively clear; because the high-skilled payroll tax is the same in both sectors, the downward shift of the high-skilled labour demand curves (which governs the allocation of the stock of high-skilled labour) is the same. Moreover the impact of intermediate goods taxation is the same in both sectors (the price $P_x(i)$ declines, but also the price of blueprints[6]). Hence, the allocation of high-skilled labour (at a given level of low-skilled employment) will not change due to the taxation of the high-skilled payroll or the taxation of the intermediate goods.

The other determinant of the equilibrium allocation of the stock of high-skilled labour is equilibrium low-skilled employment in the economy. This is given by the interception of the price and the wage setting curve.

The impact of the low-skilled payroll tax and of the intermediate goods tax on the price setting curve is given by equation (12.4) (remember that the intermediate goods tax affects the low-skilled demand indirectly via a change in the price $P_x(i)$), the price setting curve will shift downward. So the wage which the intermediate firms are willing to pay (given low-skilled employment) will decline. This is because the payroll tax has the same effects as an increase in low-skilled labour costs and the intermediate goods tax will lead to a decline in the price.

---

[4] But note that the price $P_x(i)$ will be lower in this case given $x(i)$, because the intermediate goods demand will be lower due to the tax t_x. Hence overall profits in the economy will be lower than in the no-tax case.

[5] The assumption of different taxation of the same factor might lead to interesting results as, e.g., shown in Kolm (1998). Although we generally suppress these effects we refer now and then to the case when the payroll taxes might differ.

[6] This can be shown very easily, when remembering that the price of blueprints is driven by the zero profit condition in the intermediate sector. So in an equilibrium the following must hold: $P_n \cdot r = P_x(i) \cdot x(i)(1-\alpha)$. Hence, a change in the price of an intermediate good variety will change the price of a blueprint by the same extend.

The impact of the tax on low-skilled labour income,[7] t_I^L, is a bit more subtle. It leaves the price setting curve unchanged, but affects the wage setting relation. Union's utility function changes with a tax on low-skilled labour income, because the union is only interested in the net wage the union members will get. So the utility function modifies to:

$$U = l(i) \cdot (1 - t_I^L) \cdot w^L(i) + (m(i) - l(i)) \cdot AI, \tag{12.7}$$

with this union utility function, the bargained wage (at the firm-level) turns out to be:

$$w^L(i) = \phi \cdot \frac{1}{1 - t_I^L} \cdot AI, \tag{12.8}$$

where ϕ is the in the preceding section defined mark-up, $\phi \equiv \frac{1}{1 - \frac{1}{\frac{1-\gamma}{\gamma} \cdot \frac{\alpha}{1-\alpha} \cdot s^L + \eta}}$ and AI is the alternative income of a union member who is not employed in the intermediate goods firm i. The alternative income will be the average income when not employed, i.e., the wage paid in another firm and the unemployment benefit, B_t. Hence, $AI = (1 - t_I^L) \cdot w^L \cdot (1 - u) + u \cdot B_t$. Assuming symmetry and aggregating over all intermediate firms in the economy yields the wage setting curve:

$$w^L = \frac{1}{1 - t_I^L} \cdot \frac{\phi \cdot u}{1 - (1 - u) \cdot \phi} \cdot B_t. \tag{12.9}$$

We assume that the unemployment benefit is tax free.[8] Equation (12.9) reveals that the bargained wage increases with the income tax rate. The economic intuition for this effect is the following. The higher the tax on low-skilled wage income, the less it pays to become employed or the lower is the loss of utility due to unemployment. Therefore, the union is eager to bargain a higher wage. The wage setting curve will shift upwards in presence of a low-skilled income tax. In figure 12.1 these two effects of taxation are depicted. The figure shows that employment in the presence of a low-skilled payroll, an intermediate goods and an income tax will unambiguously decline. The low-skilled wage will increase with a higher income tax, because in this case the union will bargain a higher wage. An increase in the payroll tax will lead c.p. to a decrease in the low-skilled wage.

With this in mind we can conclude that the positively sloped curve in the $L - H^x$–space (shown in figure 11.1) that depicts combinations of low-skilled and high-skilled employment in the intermediate sector for which the low-skilled labour market is in equilibrium will shift upwards. This implies that at any given level of high-skilled employment in the intermediate sector, low-skilled employment will be lower than in the case without taxation.

---

[7] We do not incorporate a tax on high-skilled labour income, because this would only have lump-sum effects as we assume the supply of high-skilled labour to be totally inelastic.

[8] If this is not the case it is easy to show that the wage setting curve would be unaffected by the introduction of a tax on labour income.

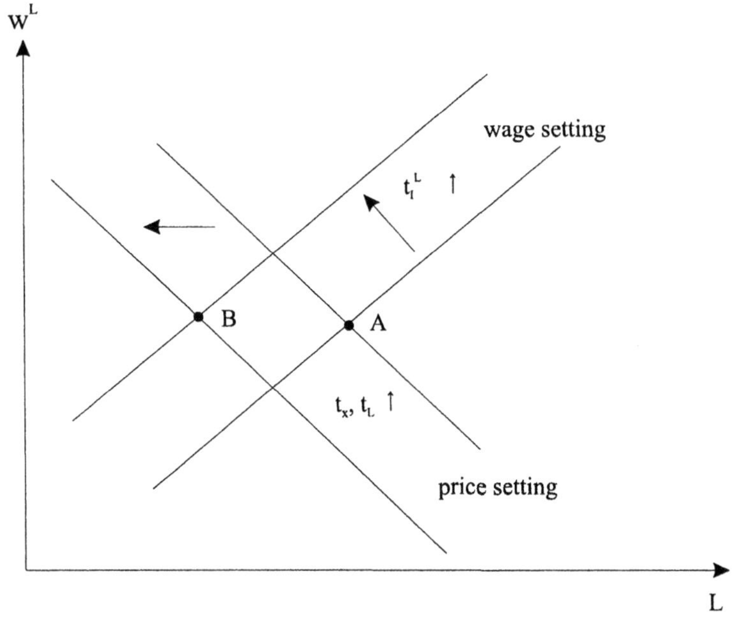

Fig. 12.1. The Impact of Taxation on Wage and Price Setting

We can derive this relation algebraically by merging equation (12.4) which gives the price setting curve with the wage setting curve given in equation (12.9). With this the following (which is the counterpart of equation (11.24) in the no-tax case) holds:

$$\frac{1}{1-t_I^L}\cdot\frac{\phi\cdot u}{1-(1-u)\cdot\phi}\cdot B_t=\frac{1}{1+t_L}\cdot\alpha\cdot P_x^{pt}\cdot\frac{1}{1+t_x}\cdot\delta\cdot\left(\frac{X}{L}\right)^{1+\beta}, \quad (12.10)$$

where P_x^{pt} is the pre-tax price of the intermediate good, which is in the aggregate basically $n_t^{\frac{1-\alpha}{\alpha}}$. Log-linearising this equation gives:[9]

$$\frac{t_I^L}{1-t_I^L}\cdot\tilde{t}_I^L+\varphi_\phi\cdot\tilde{\phi}+\varphi_u\cdot\tilde{u}+\tilde{B}=-\frac{t_x}{1+t_x}\cdot\tilde{t}_x+\tilde{\alpha}+(1+\beta)\cdot\left(\tilde{X}-\tilde{L}\right). \quad (12.11)$$

Using this equation, the definition of the rate of unemployment, the fact that $\tilde{X}=s^L\cdot\tilde{L}+s^H\cdot\tilde{H}^x$ and the linearised version of the no-arbitrage relation

[9] Remember that as in the preceding section we assume that the unemployment benefit grows at the same rate as the economy. Hence, $B_t=B\cdot n_t^{\frac{1-\alpha}{\alpha}}$. Since $P_x^{pt}=n_t^{\frac{1-\alpha}{\alpha}}$ the following condition $\frac{B_t}{P_x^{pt}}=B$ will hold.

(11.11), we can determine the equilibrium of the economy[10] and get the following two equations for the equilibrium values of low-skilled and high-skilled employment in the intermediate sector:

$$\tilde{H}^x \cdot h_1 = \left(\frac{t_L}{1+t_L} \cdot \tilde{t}_L + \frac{t_I^L}{1-t_I^L} \cdot \tilde{t}_I^L + \tilde{B} + \frac{t_x}{1+t_x} \cdot \tilde{t}_x + \varrho_\phi \cdot \tilde{\phi}\right) h_2 - \left(\varrho_u \cdot \left(\frac{\bar{L}}{U} - 1\right) \cdot \tilde{\bar{L}}\right) \cdot h_2 - \left(\frac{(1-\alpha) \cdot \beta \cdot s^L + 1}{(1-\alpha)} \cdot \tilde{\alpha} + \tilde{r}\right) \cdot \frac{1}{\beta \cdot s^L}, \tag{12.12}$$

$$\tilde{L} \cdot l_1 = -\frac{t_I^L}{1-t_I^L} \cdot \tilde{t}_I^L - \frac{t_L}{1+t_L} \cdot \tilde{t}_L - \frac{t_x}{1+t_x} \cdot \tilde{t}_x - \varrho_\phi \cdot \tilde{\phi} + \left(\frac{\bar{L}}{U} - 1\right) \cdot \varrho_u \cdot \tilde{\bar{L}} + \tilde{B} + \left(\varphi \cdot \frac{1}{1-\alpha} - 1\right) \cdot \tilde{\alpha} + \varphi \cdot \tilde{r}, \tag{12.13}$$

where $\varphi = (1 + \beta\ s^L)$ and the coefficients h_1, h_2 and l_1 are given in the appendix. An interesting point is that the coefficient h_1 is positive for small elasticities of substitution ($\sigma < 1$) and vice versa. The coefficients h_2 and l_1 are both positive.

The two equations (12.12) and (12.13) reveal the impact of taxation on the equilibrium of the economy. As was already shown diagrammatically, equilibrium low-skilled employment will decline if the low-skilled payroll tax, the intermediate goods tax or the income tax increases. The effect of taxation on the equilibrium allocation of the high-skilled labour pool is less clear and depends on the elasticity of substitution. In the case of σ exceeding (smaller than) one, higher taxation will result in higher (lower) high-skilled employment in the intermediate sector and via the resource constraint lower (higher) employment in the research sector and therewith to lower (higher) growth. The economic intuition for this property is straightforward. Taxation affects the allocation of high-skilled labour only indirectly via a change in low-skilled employment. Hence, the effect of higher taxation on high-skilled employment is the same as the impact of lower low-skilled employment. But this impact was already analysed in the preceding section.

Summarising, we can say that the direct effect of various taxes on the growth rate of the economy is limited. High-skilled labour payroll taxes have no effect on the rate of growth, because their impact is symmetric. Only taxes which affect low-skilled labour employment can affect (via this indirect effect) the growth rate of the economy. An interesting point is that although the

[10] As before this equilibrium can only be determined explicitly in changes and not in levels. Due to the solution method of log-linearisation, we can only discuss the effect of infinitesimally small changes of already existing taxes. We cannot discuss the effects of the introduction of a tax.

impact of taxation on the rate of growth is ambiguous, unemployment will always increase with an increase in taxation.[11]

12.2 Tax Reforms

Up to this point we have only analysed the effects of taxation on the rate of growth and on unemployment. In this analysis we did not take the governmental budget constraint into account.

The explicit consideration of the interrelation between taxation and spending on the unemployment benefit (i.e., the governmental budget constraint) will be analysed in the following section. An interesting point arising in this context is which effect tax reforms, i.e., changes of the structure of taxation have on unemployment and the rate of growth of the economy. Especially revenue neutral tax reforms, i.e., tax reforms that leave the governmental budget unchanged have become fashionable among economists. This is firstly because only revenue neutral reforms seem to be feasible in the political process and secondly the notion that just by changing the structure of taxation employment or growth might rise is very appealing.[12] There is a lot of literature dealing with the effects of changes of the tax structure on unemployment and it seems to be consensus that revenue neutral tax reforms have an impact on unemployment. Pflüger (1997), e.g., argues that a reduction of the payroll tax, financed by a heavier taxation of consumption will lead to lower unemployment. This is because the reduction of the payroll tax will be cost dampening for the firms (hence, the demand for labour will increase) whereas the consumption tax is neutral with respect to the labour demand curve. Very similar arguments are put forward by Sørensen (1997) when he argues that a shift of taxation away from low income earners (i.e., low-skilled labour) might increase employment. The main shortcoming of the standard literature is that this issue of revenue neutral tax reforms is only analysed in static models (the exception to this rule is again the paper by Birk and Michaelis (2002), but in their model growth is either exogenous and so tax reforms only have transitory effects or they apply a simple AK structure).

In the following we will analyse revenue neutral tax reforms in the delineated model in which unemployment and growth are endogenously determined. The tax reforms analysed in the following are:

---

[11] Equation (12.13) depicts this property, because low-skilled employment will always decline when tax rates are raised. So unemployment, which is by definition the difference between the (exogenously) given stock of low-skilled labour and low-skilled employed will increase.

[12] Because employment and/or growth might increase due to the revenue neutral reform one is tempted to conclude that these tax reforms imply a free lunch. But this is obviously not true as the tax reform will nevertheless distort other parts of the economy (see, e.g., Sørensen (1997) for this point for the case of a more progressive tax structure).

1. a decline in the low-skilled payroll tax financed by a higher low-skilled income tax,
2. an equal decline in the low-skilled payroll and the low-skilled income tax financed by a heavier taxation of the use of the intermediate goods,
3. and finally a swap from the low-skilled and high-skilled payroll tax to the intermediate goods tax.

The first tax reform analyses the tax incidence of the income tax and the payroll tax. We will analyse whether it makes any difference if an economy taxes labour demand or labour "supply".[13] Hence, we will analyse if tax shifts are neutral with respect to low-skilled employment, or not.

The second and third reform are devoted to the question which effect a shift of taxation away from labour has in this economy. An important point of these reforms is that there exists a dual interpretation for the growth models of the expanding product variety type (see, Grossman and Helpman (1991)). The first one is the interpretation applied in the text. The second one is that it is assumed that the intermediate goods are not inputs into the production process, but are varieties of a consumption good which are consumed by agents who have CES preferences. Qualitatively the same properties hold, but in the latter case the intermediate goods tax can be interpreted as a tax on consumption. Hence, the second and third tax reform could be interpreted as a shift of taxes away from labour to consumption.

We will distinguish two forms of revenue neutrality: an ex-ante neutral reform, i.e., a reform where only the impact effect of a lower tax must be financed by a higher rate of another tax, assuming the tax base as being constant (ex-post this reform needs not to be revenue neutral) and an ex-post neutral reform, where all general equilibrium effects (all adjustments of the tax bases due to the change in the tax structure) are taken into account. These two points are often mixed up in the literature (see, e.g., Goerke (2002) who distinguishes these two forms but performs two different tax reforms within the two neutrality frameworks; hence, he is not able to compare the different effects these two neutrality assumptions have). Moreover, we will analyse whether these two concepts differ only in quantity or also in quality.

12.2.1 Ex-Ante Revenue Neutrality

We assume that the government only finances the unemployment benefit and that the budget must be balanced. Hence, the budget constraint of the government reads:

$$B_t \cdot U = w^L \cdot L \cdot (t_L + t_I^L) + w^H \cdot \bar{H} \cdot t_H + P_x \cdot X \cdot t_x. \tag{12.14}$$

The budget can be kept in balance over time although the unemployment benefit increases in a steady state, because the tax base grows at an identi-

[13] Note, that we could interpret the wage setting curve as the (union induced) labour supply in the economy.

cal rate as the unemployment benefit.[14] Log-linearisation of equation (12.14) gives:

$$\tilde{B}_t + \tilde{U} = \frac{w^L \cdot L \cdot (t_L + t_I^L)}{B_t \cdot U}\left(\tilde{w}^L + \tilde{L}\right) + \frac{w^L \cdot L \cdot t_L}{B_t \cdot U} \cdot \tilde{t}_L +$$
$$\frac{w^L \cdot L \cdot t_I^L}{B_t \cdot U} \cdot \tilde{t}_I^L + \frac{w^H \cdot \bar{H} \cdot t_H}{B_t \cdot U}\left(\tilde{\bar{H}} + \tilde{w}^H + \tilde{t}_H\right) + \frac{P_x \cdot X \cdot t_x}{B_t \cdot U} \cdot \left(\tilde{P}_x + \tilde{X} + \tilde{t}_x\right). \quad (12.15)$$

Using this equation we are able to analyse the ex-ante neutral reforms.

When the government lowers the low-skilled payroll tax and wants to finance this tax cut by an increase in the low-skilled income tax, the following relation (given by the budget constraint (12.15)) must hold in order to keep the budget ex-ante balanced:

$$\tilde{t}_L = -\frac{t_I^L}{t_L} \cdot \tilde{t}_I^L. \quad (12.16)$$

This equation shows that the absolute changes of the two taxes must be identical in order to keep the budget balanced. The intuition for this is that both tax rates have the same tax base, namely low-skilled labour income.

Plugging this relation into the equilibrium equations (12.13) and (12.12) and assuming the relative change of all other variables as being zero, we get the following equations:

$$\tilde{H}^x \cdot h_1 = \frac{t_L}{1+t_L} \cdot \left(-\frac{t_I^L}{t_L}\right) \cdot \tilde{t}_I^L + \frac{t_I^L}{1-t_I^L} \cdot \tilde{t}_I^L, \quad (12.17)$$

$$\tilde{L} \cdot l_1 = -\left(\frac{t_I^L}{1-t_I^L} - \frac{t_I^L}{1+t_L}\right) \cdot \tilde{t}_I^L. \quad (12.18)$$

The employment effects of this tax policy are determined by the sign of the coefficient $\frac{t_I^L}{1-t_I^L} - \frac{t_I^L}{1+t_L}$. Straightforward algebra implies that this coefficient is unambiguously positive. As such, low-skilled employment will unambiguously decline if the low-skilled income tax increases. The economic intuition for this effect is the following. With a higher low-skilled income tax, the union will bargain a higher wage (given low-skilled employment). So the wage setting curve is shifted upwards. On the other hand the price setting curve will shift outwards due to the decrease in the low-skilled payroll tax. So the good employment effect caused by the decline of the payroll tax will be outweighed by the bad employment effect caused by a higher income tax. Hence, this switch of taxation is not neutral with respect to low-skilled employment. This result is due to the fact that we can only analyse relative changes. It was already said

[14] Remember that in a steady state the low-skilled wage, the high-skilled wage and the price of an intermediate good variety grow at the same rate. Hence, tax revenues increase over time.

that the absolute change in both taxes must be equal. The relative impact is given by the absolute change relative to $(1 - t_I^L)$ and $(1 + t^L)$, respectively. Since the first one is smaller than one and the second one exceeds one, the relative impact of a change in the income tax exceeds that of the change in the payroll tax.

This lower low-skilled employment implies that high-skilled employment in the intermediate sector will increase (decrease) if the elasticity of substitution is smaller than (exceeds) one. So this kind of tax policy is bad for low-skilled employment, but the effect on economic growth (as is standard in this model) is ambiguous.

The next policy experiment is the switch from low-skilled labour taxation (payroll and income) to the taxation of intermediate goods.[15] From the budget constraint we can derive the following relation between the payroll taxes and the tax on intermediate goods that will keep the budget ex-ante in balance (note that we assume that the relative decrease in both taxes is the same, hence $\tilde{t}_I^L = \tilde{t}_L$):

$$\begin{aligned} \left(\frac{w^L \cdot L \cdot t_L}{B_t \cdot U} + \frac{w^L \cdot L \cdot t_I^L}{B_t \cdot U}\right) \tilde{t}_L &= -\frac{P_x \cdot X \cdot t_x}{B_t \cdot U} \cdot \tilde{t}_x \\ \Rightarrow \tilde{t}_L &= -\frac{P_x \cdot X}{w^L \cdot L} \cdot \frac{t_x}{t_L + t_I^L} \cdot \tilde{t}_x. \end{aligned} \tag{12.19}$$

The above given tax swap implies a change in employment given by the following equations:

$$\tilde{H}^x \cdot h_1 = \left(\left(\frac{t_L}{1+t_L} + \frac{t_I^L}{1-t_I^L}\right) \cdot -\frac{P_x \cdot X}{w^L \cdot L} \cdot \frac{t_x}{t_L + t_I^L} + \frac{t_x}{1+t_x}\right) \cdot \tilde{t}_x, \tag{12.20}$$

$$\tilde{L} \cdot l_1 = \left(\left(\frac{t_I^L}{1-t_I^L} + \frac{t_L}{1+t_L}\right) \cdot \frac{P_x \cdot X}{w^L \cdot L} \cdot \frac{t_x}{t_L + t_I^L} \cdot -\frac{t_x}{1+t_x}\right) \cdot \tilde{t}_x. \tag{12.21}$$

Again there are two countervailing effects of the tax policy on low-skilled employment. On the one hand employment will rise, because low-skilled labour costs decline (this will shift the price setting curve downwards) and the bargained wage will be lower (this shifts the wage setting curve downwards). On the other hand, due to the higher intermediate goods tax, revenues of intermediate firms will decline and hence, the price setting curve will shift inwards. The dominating effect of this tax policy is determined by the following coefficient:

$$\left(\frac{t_I^L}{1-t_I^L} + \frac{t_L}{1+t_L}\right) \cdot \frac{P_x \cdot X}{w^L \cdot L} \cdot \frac{t_x}{t_L + t_I^L} - \frac{t_x}{1+t_x}. \tag{12.22}$$

If this coefficient is positive the tax policy of lowering taxes on low-skilled labour financed by a higher intermediate goods tax will lead to higher low-

[15] As aforementioned this could also be interpreted as a switch from low-skilled labour taxation to the taxation of consumption.

skilled employment. Using the fact that $P_x = \frac{P_x^{pt}}{1+t_x}$ we get the following condition, which ensures that the above given coefficient will be positive:

$$\frac{P_x^{pt} \cdot X}{w^L \cdot L} \cdot \frac{1}{(1 - t_I^L) \cdot (1 + t_L)} > 1. \tag{12.23}$$

Let us only concentrate on equilibria in which the revenue of an intermediate good firm will exceed total low-skilled labour costs (direct costs plus taxation).[16] It is easy to see that in this case (remember that $1 - t_I^L < 1$) the above given relation is always satisfied. Hence, a shift from labour taxation to indirect taxation will lead to higher low-skilled employment. The intuition for this property is that changes in the intermediate tax rate do not change the allocation of the pool of high-skilled labour to the sectors of the economy. Hence, the only distortionary effect is that the price for intermediate goods will decline. But this distortion is small compared to the one that will be reduced due to lower low-skilled income *and* payroll taxation. When interpreting the intermediate goods tax as a consumption tax, these results are in line with the ones existing in the literature. Thus, it seems that the finding that a switch to more indirect taxation could alleviate the employment problem is quite robust.

The growth effects of this tax policy depend on the elasticity of substitution. The rate of growth will increase as long as low-skilled and high-skilled labour are good substitutes ($\sigma > 1$) and vice versa. The economic intuition for this is the same as for an increase in low-skilled employment.

The last policy experiment considers a decline in payroll taxes on low-skill and high-skill labour financed by an increase in the intermediate goods tax. With the change in the low-skilled payroll tax equal to the change in the high-skilled tax, $\tilde{t}_L = \tilde{t}_H$, the ex-ante budget neutral relation is:

$$\tilde{t}_L = -\frac{X \cdot P_x \cdot t_x}{w^L \cdot L \cdot t_L + w^H \cdot \bar{H} \cdot t_H} \cdot \tilde{t}_x. \tag{12.24}$$

Using this to substitute $\tilde{t}_L$ and $\tilde{t}_H$ in equation (12.12) and (12.13), we get the following equations, showing the impact of this tax swap:

$$\tilde{H}^x \cdot h_1 = \left(-\frac{t_L}{1+t_L} \cdot \left(\frac{X \cdot P_x \cdot t_x}{w^L \cdot L \cdot t_L + w^H \cdot \bar{H} \cdot t_H} \right) + \frac{t_x}{1+t_x} \right) \cdot \tilde{t}_x, \tag{12.25}$$

$$\tilde{L} \cdot l_1 = \left(\frac{t_L}{1+t_L} \cdot \left(\frac{X \cdot P_x \cdot t_x}{w^L \cdot L \cdot t_L + w^H \cdot \bar{H} \cdot t_H} \right) - \frac{t_x}{1+t_x} \right) \cdot \tilde{t}_x. \tag{12.26}$$

For this coefficient determining the effect of a swap from payroll taxation to intermediate good taxation the following relation must hold:

[16] The legitimation for this assumption is that only these equilibria seem to be the realistic ones, since in all other cases the profit would be negative. Remember that the intermediate firm employs in addition to low-skilled labour, high-skilled labour and has to repay the debt.

$$\frac{t_L}{1+t_L} \cdot \left(\frac{X \cdot P_x^{pt}}{w^L \cdot L \cdot t_L + w^H \cdot \bar{H} \cdot t_H} \right) > 1. \tag{12.27}$$

The first factor on the lhs is unambiguously smaller than one, whereas the second expression is indeterminate, although it seems reasonable to assume that the tax revenue from low-skilled and high-skilled payroll taxation is smaller than the (net) revenue of intermediate goods producers. As such, we assume the second expression to exceed one. So the sign of the coefficient showing the impact of this tax swap is ambiguous.

Nevertheless, we can show that equation (12.27) is more likely satisfied when the original low-skilled payroll tax is high, the original tax revenues from payroll taxation are low and the (net) revenues of intermediate firms are high. The economic intuition for these arguments is the following. A high low-skilled payroll tax implies that the absolute decline of the tax rate (given some relative change) is very high. Hence, in this case the outward shift of the price setting curve will be very high too, making it more likely that this shift will (over)compensate the inward shift of this curve due to the higher intermediate goods tax.

Low payroll tax revenues make it more likely that the coefficient is positive, because in this case the relative decline of tax revenues due to lower payroll taxation is low and hence, the increase in the intermediate goods tax can be lower, too. So c.p. the inward shift of the price setting curve due to a higher t_x will be small. Similar arguments can be applied for the (net) revenue of intermediate firms. When these are high, the tax base of the intermediate goods tax is very high. Thus, the increase in the intermediate goods tax, given the decrease in the payroll taxes, could be low without hurting the budget constraint.

So the success of the policy of reducing payroll taxation and financing this reduction by increased intermediate goods taxation in terms of higher employment crucially depends on the economic situation at the beginning of the tax reform.

12.2.2 Ex-Post Revenue Neutrality

The major drawback of the preceding analysis was that we have assumed the tax base as being constant. So the repercussions that the change of the structure of taxation has on the tax bases (e.g., that employment rises or falls) were not taken into account. As a consequence, the financing needs due to the cut of a tax derived from the budget constraint might be misleading. Actually, after all repercussions, the budget in the ex-ante case does not need to be in balance. To have a tax reform which is revenue neutral from a general equilibrium point of view, one has to take these second round effects into account.

What we want to do in this section is to analyse the above given tax policies, but assuming that the reforms must be ex-post revenue neutral. Moreover we will compare these effects with the effects of the tax reforms in the ex-ante neutral case and analyse whether there are only quantitative or also qualitative differences.

To analyse ex-post revenue neutral tax reforms, we first of all have to derive the governmental budget constraint that takes all repercussions on the tax bases due to tax changes into account. Taking the log-linearised budget constraint (equation (12.15)) and substitute the relative change in the low-skilled and the high-skilled wage, using the log-linearised versions of the (aggregate) low-skilled and high-skilled demand equations of the intermediate sector (equations (12.4) and (12.5)) and substituting the relative change in unemployment by the log-linearised version of the definition of unemployment ($U = \bar{L} - L$), we get a modified budget constraint, which reads:

$$\begin{aligned} \tilde{B}_t + \frac{\bar{L}}{U}\cdot\tilde{\bar{L}} - \frac{L}{U}\cdot\tilde{L} = b_1\cdot\left(-\frac{t_L}{1+t_L}\cdot\tilde{t}_L + \tilde{\alpha} + \tilde{P}_x + (1+\beta)\cdot(\tilde{X}-\tilde{L}) + \tilde{L}\right) + \\ b_2\cdot\tilde{t}_L + b_3\cdot\tilde{t}_I^L + \\ b_4\cdot\left(\tilde{\bar{H}} - \frac{t_H}{1+t_H}\cdot\tilde{t}_H + \tilde{\alpha} + \tilde{P}_x + (1+\beta)\cdot(\tilde{X}-\tilde{H}^x) + \tilde{t}_H\right) + \\ b_5\cdot\left(\tilde{P}_x + \tilde{X} + \tilde{t}_x\right), \end{aligned} \tag{12.28}$$

with the $b_i > 0$ coefficients given in the appendix.

Equation (12.28) depicts the balanced budget of the government as a function of the two endogenous variables low-skilled and high-skilled employment in the intermediate sector (remember that $\tilde{X} = s^L\cdot\tilde{L} + s^H\cdot\tilde{H}^x$). This equation determines an additional curve in the low-skilled-high-skilled employment space along which the government's budget is in balance. The slope of this curve can be determined by assuming that the change in all other variables except low-skilled and high-skilled labour is zero. Hence, we assume that these (exogenous) parameters are constant. This yields (using (12.28))[17]:

$$\begin{aligned} -\frac{L}{U}\cdot\tilde{L} = b_1\cdot\left((1+\beta)\cdot(\tilde{X}-\tilde{L}) + \tilde{L}\right) + \\ b_4\cdot\left((1+\beta)\cdot(\tilde{X}-\tilde{H}^x)+\right) + b_5\cdot\left(\tilde{X}\right). \end{aligned} \tag{12.29}$$

Using the fact that $\tilde{X} = s^L\cdot\tilde{L}+s^H\cdot\tilde{H}^x$ and collecting terms, equation (12.29) modifies to:

$$\tilde{L} = \frac{s_1}{s_2}\cdot\tilde{H}^x, \tag{12.30}$$

where the coefficients s_1 and s_2 are given in the appendix.

[17] Due to the solution method of log-linearisation we are only able to determine the elasticity given by this curve. So we cannot derive the slope explicitly, but we can derive the sign of the slope.

Equation (12.30) reveals that the slope given by $\frac{s_1}{s_2}$ can be positive as well as negative. Nevertheless, we assume $\frac{s_1}{s_2}$ to be negative. The arguments for this assumption are firstly, that this is the only one that makes sense from an economic point of view. If, e.g., high-skilled employment rises (and hence, the tax revenues) low-skilled employment can decline without hurting the balanced budget constraint. Secondly there are only two factors which give rise to this ambiguity: $(1-\beta)\cdot b_4$ and $\beta\cdot(-s^L)$. The economic intuition for this ambiguity is (for the first factor) that as high-skilled employment in the intermediate sector rises the high-skilled wage will decline. This affects the tax base of the high-skilled payroll tax with the consequence that low-skilled employment cannot decline by that much when H^x rises without hurting the budget constraint, hence the curve reflecting a balanced budget in the low-skilled high-skilled employment space will become flatter. The intuition for the second factor is that when σ is smaller than one (β is positive) lower low-skilled employment will result in lower high-skilled employment in the intermediate sector. So c.p. the curve will be flatter, implying that the rise of high-skilled employment due to a decline of low-skilled employment must be larger to keep the budget in balance.[18]

The equilibrium of the model with taxation and with a balanced budget constraint is given by the three equations (12.28), (12.13) and (12.12).[19] The first equation restricts the equilibria given by the other two equations to equilibria that fulfil the balanced budget constraint.[20]

With these three equations at hand, we can derive a balanced budget constraint that incorporates all repercussions due to changes in taxation. By assuming the changes of all other variables except the tax variables as being zero, we get the following (budget constraint) relation:

$$-t_1 \cdot \tilde{t}_L = t_2 \cdot \tilde{t}_I^L + t_3 \cdot \tilde{t}_H + t_4 \cdot \tilde{t}_x, \tag{12.31}$$

where the coefficients t_i are given in the appendix. By assuming Laffer efficiency, all tax coefficients are positive. Hence, a decline in one tax lowers tax revenues. This implies that the economy is on the positively sloped part of the Laffer-curve, i.e., the economy is not overtaxed.

As in the section on ex-ante revenue neutrality, we will perform the same tax experiments and we will focus on how these change low-skilled and high-skilled employment in the intermediate sector. Take, e.g., the first tax reform which considers a shift from low-skilled payroll taxation to income taxation. This policy will not affect high-skilled employment in the intermediate sector

[18] In the extreme case this latter effect could theoretically overcompensate all other effects (β can be infinite) with the result that the balanced budget curve would be positively sloped, but we defer from analysing this case.

[19] Remember that for intermediate good production the following holds: $\tilde{X} = s^L \cdot \tilde{L} + s^H \cdot \tilde{H}^x$ and that as before $\tilde{B} = \tilde{B}_t - \tilde{P}_x$, since $b_1 + b_4 + b_5 = 1$.

[20] Hence, the equilibrium derived in the preceding section only using equations (12.13) and (12.12) was not restricted by this balanced budget constraint.

directly, but will change low-skilled employment (which in turn obviously changes the allocation of the high-skilled labour force according to the above given scheme). Using equation (12.13) (and assuming that the change in all other variables is zero), we get the following:

$$\tilde{L} \cdot l_1 = \left(-\frac{t_I^L}{1 - t_I^L} + \frac{t_2}{t_1} \cdot \frac{t_L}{1 + t_L} \right) \cdot \tilde{t}_I^L. \tag{12.32}$$

Using the definition of t_1 and t_2, we can determine the sign of the coefficient. Applying this definition, it can be shown that the impact of the tax shift boils down to the question whether the following holds:

$$b_3 \cdot \frac{1 - t_I^L}{t_I^L} + b_1 - \frac{t_L}{1 + t_L} \cdot b_2 > 0. \tag{12.33}$$

If this relation holds, the coefficient will be positive, i.e., the tax shift (a reduction of the payroll tax financed by a higher low-skilled income tax, $\tilde{t}_I^L > 0$) will result in higher low-skilled employment. To show that the coefficient is positive, remember that $b_1 = b_2 + b_3$. Since $\frac{t_L}{1+t_L}$ is always smaller than one, the relation (12.33) will be true.

In the case of ex-post neutrality, the tax swap will result in higher low-skilled employment. This is interesting as this finding stands in stark contrast to the result found in the ex-ante neutral case. So all repercussion effects of the tax swap into account will qualitatively change the results.

The economic intuition why the ex-post case generates such different results is easy to see. There are two countervailing effects on low-skilled employment as in the ex-ante case. The lower low-skilled payroll tax shifts the price setting curve outwards. On the other hand, the wage setting curve will shift upwards. But in the ex-post case the first effect, which fosters low-skilled employment, results in lower expenditures for unemployment benefits. Hence, the income tax increase will be low, because the financing needs decreased. So the good employment effect will always dominate. As the effect of this tax reform is increasing low-skill employment, the growth effects are that the rate of growth will increase (decrease) as long as $\sigma > 1$ ($\sigma < 1$). The intuition is the same as in the basic model.

For the second tax policy (an equal decline of the low-skilled payroll and income tax financed by an increase in the intermediate goods tax) we get the following balanced budget relation:

$$\tilde{t}_L = \tilde{t}_I^L = -\frac{t_4}{t_1 + t_2}. \tag{12.34}$$

Plugging this into the low-skilled labour determining equation (12.13), we get the following:

$$\tilde{L} \cdot l_1 = \tilde{t}_x \cdot \left(\frac{\left(\frac{t_I^L}{1-t_I^L} + \frac{t_L}{1+t_L} \right) \cdot t_4}{t_1 + t_2} - \frac{t_x}{1 + t_x} \right). \tag{12.35}$$

This equation can be simplified further when plugging in the definition of t_4 from the appendix. With this we get:

$$\tilde{L} \cdot l_1 = \frac{t_x}{1+t_x} \cdot \tilde{t}_x \cdot \left(\frac{\frac{s_1 \cdot h_2}{h_1} + \frac{s_2}{l_1} + b_5 \cdot \frac{1}{t_x} - b_4 - b_1}{t_1 + t_2} - 1 \right). \tag{12.36}$$

Equation (12.36) reveals, after some algebraic manipulations that the coefficient determining the effect of a higher intermediate goods tax is positive as long as the following relation holds:

$$\frac{b_5}{t_x} - b_2 - b_3 - b_4 \cdot \left(\frac{t_I^L}{1-t_I^L} + \frac{t_l}{1+t_l} \right) - b_1 \cdot \frac{t_I^L}{1-t_I^L}. \tag{12.37}$$

Remembering that $b_1 = b_2 + b_3$ and plugging in the b coefficients, we get the following relation:

$$P_x \cdot X - \left(\frac{1}{1-t_I^L} \right) \cdot w^L \cdot L \cdot t_L - \left(\frac{1}{1-t_I^L} \right) \cdot w^L \cdot L \cdot t_I^L - w^H \cdot \bar{H} \cdot t_h \cdot \left(\frac{t_I^L}{1-t_I^L} + \frac{t_l}{1+t_l} \right). \tag{12.38}$$

In contrast to the ex-ante revenue neutrality case, the sign of the coefficient is ambiguous. We can only state that the coefficient is more likely to be positive, the higher the revenue of intermediate good firms (which is the tax base for the intermediate goods tax) and the lower the tax revenue from the low-skilled and the high-skilled payroll tax and from the low-skilled income tax.

The economic intuition is basically the same as in the ex-ante case. When tax revenues from low-skilled payroll and income taxation are low, the tax revenue loss due to the decline of these taxes is small. Hence, the increase in the intermediate goods tax does not need to be that large to finance the loss. So in this case the bad employment effect due to higher intermediate goods taxation will be low and consequently it is more likely that the coefficient will be positive, i.e., that low-skilled employment will increase.

The same arguments can be applied for the intermediate goods revenue. When these are very high, the increase in the intermediate goods tax rate that finances the decline of the low-skilled payroll and income tax can be small.

The economic intuition of the impact of the high-skilled payroll tax revenues on the coefficient is a bit more subtle. The point is that these revenues will decline as the intermediate good tax rises. This is because a higher intermediate goods tax implies a lower intermediate goods price and this in turn will lower the high-skilled wage as marginal revenue of high-skilled labour declines (in both sectors). So with a higher intermediate goods tax, the tax revenues from the high-skilled payroll tax will decline. But this implies that the low-skilled payroll tax and the income tax cannot decline by that much as they could if the high-skilled payroll tax base would be constant. So implementing all repercussions implies in this case an additional negative effect on the increase in the intermediate goods tax. Thus, it is not clear whether the new effects in the ex-post case (due to the repercussions of the tax policy on the tax base of the various taxes) change the ex-ante results only qualitatively or quantitatively.

The last policy experiment to be analysed is the swap from payroll taxation (low-skilled and high-skilled) to the intermediate goods tax. In this case the relation that keeps the budget ex-post in balance is given by:

$$\tilde{t}_L = \tilde{t}_H = -\frac{t_4}{t_1 + t_3}. \tag{12.39}$$

Plugging this into equation (12.13), we get the following equation:

$$\tilde{L} \cdot l_1 = \tilde{t}_x \cdot \left(\frac{t_l}{1 + t_L} \cdot \frac{t_4}{t_1 + t_3} - \frac{t_x}{1 + t_x} \right). \tag{12.40}$$

By substitution and some manipulations, equation (12.40) modifies to:

$$\tilde{L} \cdot l_1 = \tilde{t}_x \cdot \frac{t_x}{1 + t_x} \cdot \left(\frac{\frac{s_1 \cdot h_2}{h_1} + \frac{s_2}{l_1} + b_5 \cdot \frac{1}{t_x} - b_4 - b_1}{\frac{s_2}{l_1} + \frac{s_1 \cdot h_2}{h_1} - b_1 + b_2 \cdot \frac{1+t_L}{t_L} + b_4 \cdot \frac{1}{1+t_H} \cdot \frac{1+t_L}{t_L}} - 1 \right). \tag{12.41}$$

The following relation (which is derived from equation (12.41)) determines the sign of the impact on low-skilled employment of this third tax policy. If the following relation is true the coefficient will be positive implying that the tax swap increases low-skilled employment.

$$b_5 \cdot \frac{1}{t_x} - \left(1 + \frac{1 + t_L}{1 + t_H} \cdot \frac{1}{t_L} \right) \cdot b_4 - b_2 \cdot \frac{1 + t_l}{t_L} > 0. \tag{12.42}$$

By plugging in the b coefficients, equation (12.42) can also be written as:

$$P_x \cdot X - \left(1 + \frac{1 + t_L}{1 + t_H} \cdot \frac{1}{t_L} \right) \cdot w^H \cdot \bar{H} \cdot t_H - w^L \cdot L \cdot (1 + t_L) > 0. \tag{12.43}$$

(12.43) shows that the sign of the coefficient is ambiguous. But the coefficient is more likely to be positive as long as the revenues in the intermediate goods sector are large and the tax revenue from the low-skilled and the high-skilled payroll tax is small. The economic arguments for these properties are again basically the same as in the ex-ante case.

High revenues in the intermediate goods sector imply that the rise of the intermediate goods tax in order to finance the payroll tax cut can be modest since the tax base is broad. So the bad employment effect (caused by the higher intermediate goods tax) is low. Hence, the coefficient is more likely to be positive. The exact opposite is true for the low-skilled and high-skilled labour payroll tax revenues. When these are very big, the decline of the payroll tax rates will result in a large loss of tax revenues. So to finance this loss the intermediate goods tax rate has to increase a lot with the consequence that it is more likely that the bad effect dominates the good one.

Compared to the ex-ante case, there are more effects present in the ex-post case. E.g., the bad effect will be large in comparison to the good effect when the payroll tax revenues are large, because the lower tax rates will result in high revenue losses, but also due to the fact that a higher intermediate goods tax will affect the tax base of the payroll taxes (i.e., a higher intermediate goods tax will cause the low-skilled and the high-skilled wage and thus, the tax base to decline). So the negative effect is even stronger in the case when all repercussions are taken into account. But since we are not able to derive clear cut results, we are also not able to state whether the ex-post results are qualitatively or quantitatively different than the ex-ante results.

An interesting point is that in both latter tax reforms, the effect on high-skilled employment in the intermediate sector (and as such, indirectly on the rate of growth) is ambiguous, too. This is obviously, because the direct effects of taxation on the rate of growth are very limited to non-existing. Hence, the channel for a potential impact is via the change in low-skilled employment. But as long as the sign of this change is not clear, the growth effect is ambiguous, too.

Summarising we can state the following. Taxation affects low-skilled employment in the economy, because with higher payroll taxes the labour demand of firms will decline and the bargained wage will increase with a higher low-skilled income tax. Furthermore taxation also distorts the allocation of the pool of high-skilled labour. Interestingly enough this distortion is only caused indirectly by the effect of lower low-skilled employment on the allocation of high-skilled labour. The high-skilled payroll tax, which could have direct effects on the allocation, is neutral with respect to the rate of growth. The economic intuition for this point is that this tax affects high-skilled labour demand symmetrically in both sectors of the economy.

Moreover, we have analysed the effects of revenue neutral tax reforms. Alas, only one of the three analysed tax swaps had clear cut effects, namely the effect of a swap from low-skilled payroll taxation to low-skilled income taxation. The other two tax reforms have ambiguous effects on low-skilled employment and the rate of growth (at least in the ex-post neutrality case) which is partly due to the complex structure of the model. But it is safe to say that in the ambiguous cases the starting conditions are extremely important determinants for the reforms to be successful in terms of employment or growth gains or not.

12.3 Appendix

h_1	$\left(\frac{(1+\beta)\cdot s^H}{s^H\cdot(1+\beta)+\varrho_u\cdot\frac{L}{U}} - \frac{1}{\varphi\cdot\beta\cdot s^L}\right) \begin{cases} > 0 & \text{for } \beta > 0 \\ < 0 & \text{for} \beta < 0 \end{cases}$
h_2	$\frac{1}{s^H\cdot(1+\beta)+\varrho_u\cdot\frac{L}{U}} > 0$
l_1	$\left(s^H \cdot (1+\beta) + \varrho_u \cdot \left(\frac{L}{U}\right) - (1+\beta)\cdot s^H \cdot \varphi \cdot \beta \cdot s^L\right) > 0$
b_1	$\frac{w^L\cdot L\cdot(t_L+t_I^L)}{B\cdot U}$
b_2	$\frac{w^L\cdot L\cdot t_L}{B\cdot U}$
b_3	$\frac{w^L\cdot L\cdot t_I^L}{B\cdot U}$
b_4	$\frac{w^H\cdot H\cdot t_H}{B\cdot U}$
b_5	$\frac{P_x\cdot X\cdot t_x}{B\cdot U}$
s_1	$b_1 \cdot (1+\beta)\cdot s^H + b_4 \cdot (1+\beta) \cdot s^H - b_4 \cdot (1+\beta) + b_5 \cdot s^H$
s_2	$-\left(\frac{L}{U} + (s^L - s^H \cdot \beta)\cdot b_1 + b_4 \cdot (1+\beta)\cdot s^L - b_5 \cdot s^L\right)$
t_1	$\frac{t_L}{1+t_L}\left(\frac{s_2}{l_1} + \frac{s_1\cdot h_2}{h_1} - b_1 + b_2 \cdot \frac{1+t_L}{t_L}\right)$
t_2	$\frac{t_I^L}{1-t_I^L}\cdot\left(\frac{s_1\cdot h_2}{h_1} + \frac{s_2}{l_1} + b_3 \cdot \frac{(1-t_I^L)}{t_I^L}\right)$
t_3	$b_4 \cdot \frac{t_H}{1+t_H}$
t_4	$\frac{t_x}{1+t_x}\cdot\left(\frac{s_1\cdot h_2}{h_1} + \frac{s_2}{l_1} + b_5 \cdot \frac{1}{t_x} - b_4 - b_1\right)$

13

Simultaneous Wage Bargaining

In the preceding sections we focused on the effects of union wage bargaining on the rate of growth of an economy in which the union bargained the wage for a factor that was only employed in one sector of the economy. With this assumption we found that the rationing effect of the union had ambiguous effects on the allocation of the stock of high-skilled labour to the intermediate and the research sector and hence, on the rate of growth of the economy. This is a quite extreme assumption since the union does not ration labour in the growth driving research sector. Therefore, the result that the union might foster economic growth could be too optimistic.

In the following section we will analyse the other extreme position in which the migration effect of high-skilled labour is missing. Instead of assuming that bargaining only takes place in one sector, we assume that the wage for the whole stock of labour is bargained by unions and that labour is employed in the research as well as in the production sector of the economy. Thus, the union affects the allocation of resources in a more direct way compared to the models in the preceding sections. To focus on these effects we assume in this chapter that high-skilled labour is only employed in the research sector.

The modification of the one sector bargaining model is important for two reasons. Firstly, from a theoretical point of view we want to know the robustness of the results derived from the one sector bargaining models and how these will be modified by considering the new assumption. Secondly, a two sector simultaneous bargaining model seems to better match with real world observations. It seems straightforward to assume that low-skilled labour is not only employed in the production sector of the economy, but also in the research sector.[1] Furthermore we know that unions do not only bargain the wage in one sector of the economy. We observe substantial wage differentials, even when controlling for individual and workplace characteristics (see, e.g., Edin and Zetterberg (1992)). Hence, the same "type" of labour is paid dif-

[1] Remember that low-skilled labour was assumed to be craftsmen and alike.

ferently in the various sectors of an economy. This might be explained by the fact of institutionally different wage bargains in the sectors of the economy.

One of the main problems when analysing wage bargaining in two sector economies is that additional frictions have to be implemented to generate unemployment.[2] Consider that the bargained wage in one sector will exceed the competitive outcome and thus there will be unemployment. With perfect arbitrage all unemployed workers could move into the second sector of the economy and find a new job, eliminating the unemployment problem. So the labour market imperfection would only result in a sectoral wage differential and would not in unemployment. To avoid this feature we assume that there is no possibility of job-to-job change. When agents try to find a new job in the other sector of the economy, they face a risk of being unemployed. The economic legitimation for this assumption could be that once working in a sector, it is harder to switch jobs, because agents face time constraints. Because of the lack of time, employed agents cannot search as intensive as unemployed workers (who do nothing else than searching). Therefore, it seems to be a straightforward assumption that the probability of finding a job for an unemployed worker exceeds that for an employed one. The assumption of no job-to-job change reflects only the polar case of this observation in which we assume that employed workers can spare no time to look for new jobs.

So in an equilibrium in which expected incomes in the two sectors are identical, there will be a wage differential *and* unemployment.

13.1 The Growth Model

As in the one sector case, we consider a standard growth model with expanding product varieties that follows Grossman and Helpman (1991). But in the following model, we implement simultaneous union wage bargaining in the intermediate and the research sector of the economy.

13.1.1 The Consumption Good Sector

The consumption good is the only utility generating good in the economy. The production function takes the following form:

$$Y_t = \left(\int_0^{n_t} x_t(i)^\alpha \quad di \right)^{\frac{1}{\alpha}}, \tag{13.1}$$

where Y_t is the amount of the consumption good produced at t, $x_t(i)$ is the intermediate variety i used at t and n_t is the number of intermediate good

[2] If this is not the case we will have the same problem as MacDonald and Solow (1985) where there is no unemployment, although the union bargains the wage in one sector of the economy.

varieties available at time t. By maximising the profit function $\Pi^Y = P_Y \cdot Y_t - \int_0^{n_t} x_t(i) \cdot P_{x(i)}$ with respect to $x(i)$, the demand for variety i of the intermediate good is given by:

$$P_{x(i)} = \left(\int_0^{n_t} x_t(i)^{\alpha} \quad di \right)^{\frac{1-\alpha}{\alpha}} \cdot x(i)^{\alpha-1} \cdot P_Y, \qquad (13.2)$$

where $P_{x(i)}$ denotes the price of an intermediate good of variety i and P_Y denotes the price of the consumption good. As usual we assume the latter good to be the numéraire, hence $P_Y = 1$.

13.1.2 The Intermediate Good Sector

A variety of the intermediate good is produced using low-skilled labour with a CRS technology. With this the production function is linear and reads:

$$x(i) = l_{x(i)}, \qquad (13.3)$$

where $l_{x(i)}$ denotes the amount of low-skilled labour employed in an intermediate good firm.[3] The intermediate good producer is monopolist of variety i. The profit of an intermediate producer is given by:

$$\Pi^{x(i)} = P_{x(i)} \cdot x(i) - w_x^L \cdot l_{x(i)} - r \cdot P_n. \qquad (13.4)$$

Note that a monopolist can only start producing when a blueprint of a new intermediate good variety has been bought. To get a blueprint he has to borrow money on the capital market to buy the blueprint at price P_n. He has to repay the debt infinitely, so the repayment every period is $r \cdot P_n$. With profit maximisation the labour demand of a monopolist is given by:

$$w_x^L = \alpha \cdot P_{x(i)}. \qquad (13.5)$$

The elasticity of this low-skilled labour demand curve is given by $\frac{1}{\alpha-1}$. This is straightforward, because of the linear production function. The (physical) marginal product will not decline, but the price will decline due to higher production. So the elasticity of the low-skilled labour demand curve and the price elasticity of the intermediate good demand curve will coincide.[4] Because all intermediate good firms are symmetric (they face the same demand function, produce using the same technology and so on), the same amount is produced in every intermediate good firm. Hence, $x(i) = x$ and $P_{x(i)} = P_x$. Low-skilled labour demand of an intermediate good firm in a symmetric equilibrium reads:

$$w_x^L = \alpha \cdot (n_t)^{\frac{1-\alpha}{\alpha}}. \qquad (13.6)$$

[3] This form of the production function reflects the above mentioned approach that we solely want to focus on the direct effects of union wage bargaining. Hence, we defer from considering (as we did in the last sections) from a "spill-over" effect of the labour market imperfection.

[4] All these results are derived under the assumption that so many intermediate good firms exists that no strategic interaction is possible between them.

13.1.3 The Research Sector

The research sector produces blueprints using low-skilled labour and high-skilled labour that is only used in the research sector. We assume that the production function of the research sector is Cobb-Douglas:

$$\Delta n_t = n_t \cdot (L_n^\lambda \cdot H_n^{1-\lambda}), \tag{13.7}$$

where Δn_t denotes the number of new blueprints produced in a time interval of length one and H_n is the amount of high-skilled labour employed in the research sector. Note that we have incorporated the usual research spill-over by assuming that the number of new varieties produced depends on the number of already existing ones. So it is easier (in terms of resources used) to produce a new blueprint when the number of already existing ones is large. With profit maximisation, low-skilled labour demand in the research sector is given by:

$$w_n^L = P_n \cdot n_t \cdot \lambda \cdot L_n^{\lambda-1} \cdot H_n^{1-\lambda}. \tag{13.8}$$

The demand for high-skilled labour is given by:

$$w_n^H = P_n \cdot n_t \cdot (1-\lambda) \cdot L_n^\lambda \cdot H_n^{-\lambda}. \tag{13.9}$$

13.1.4 Households

The two types of households in the economy (households that supply low-skilled and high-skilled labour) consume final goods and have to decide how much to save and how much to consume. The life time utility function (independently of the type of household) is given by:

$$V = \sum_{t=0}^{\infty} (1+\rho)^{-t} \cdot ln(C_t^j), \tag{13.10}$$

where ρ is the rate of time preference and C_t^j is consumption of household of type j at t, where $j \in [H; L]$. Households maximise (13.10) subject to an intertemporal budget constraint which is given by:

$$A_{t+1} = (1+r) \cdot A_t + w_t^j - C_t^j, \tag{13.11}$$

where A_t is the stock of assets of a household at time t. In the aggregate there is only one asset in the economy, namely the debt given to the intermediate firms (in the aggregate consumption loans cancel out). By solving the intertemporal decision problem of households, we get an equation relating the growth rate of consumption to the difference between the rate of interest and the rate of time preference (using the simplification of $log(1+x) = x$ for small x).

$$g_{C_t^j} = r - \rho, \tag{13.12}$$

where $g_{C_t^j}$ is the growth rate of consumption of a household of type j. Equilibrium in the goods market implies that $C_t^L + C_t^H$ equals Y_t at every point in time. So for the growth rates of output and the consumption of the two types of households the following must hold:

$$g_{Y_t} = \frac{C_t^L}{Y_t} \cdot g_{C_t^L} + \frac{C_t^H}{Y_t} \cdot g_{C_t^H}. \tag{13.13}$$

Equation (13.13) reveals that the growth rate of consumption (which is by equation (13.12) the same for both types of households) must be equal to the rate of output growth (so $g_{Y_t} = g_{C_t^L} = g_{C_t^H}$).

13.1.5 Steady State Equilibrium

In a steady state the allocation of labour between the intermediate good and the research sector is constant. Hence, g_{n_t} is constant over time as well as aggregate production in the intermediate sector $X = n_t \cdot x$. The steady state growth rate of final output is given by $g_{Y_t} = \frac{1-\alpha}{\alpha} \cdot g_{n_t}$. To determine the equilibrium allocation of the stock of low-skilled labour (which determines production and the rate of growth) we use a slightly different approach as, e.g., applied in Grossman and Helpman (1991), because our approach makes comparing the competitive with the unionised situation easier.

Let us divide the labour demand in the research sector (13.8) by the labour demand in the intermediate sector (13.5) and denote the relative research sector wage (the research sector wage in terms of the intermediate sector wage) $\frac{w_n^L}{w_x^L}$ by z. This yields:

$$z = \frac{P_n \cdot n_t \cdot \lambda \cdot L_n^{\lambda-1} \cdot H_n^{1-\lambda}}{\alpha \cdot n_t^{\frac{1-\alpha}{\alpha}}}. \tag{13.14}$$

Note that we assume free-entry into the intermediate goods market, so in an equilibrium, profits in this sector will be zero. This zero profit condition determines the price of blueprints as:

$$P_n = \frac{P_x \cdot x - w_x^L \cdot l_x}{r}. \tag{13.15}$$

Euler's theorem implies that $P_x \cdot x - w_x^L \cdot l_x = (1-\alpha) \cdot P_x \cdot x$. Furthermore the rate of interest is given by (13.12) and the price of an intermediate good in a symmetric equilibrium is given by $P_x = n^{\frac{1-\alpha}{\alpha}}$. Plugging all this into (13.14) this equation modifies to:

$$z = X \cdot (1-\alpha) \cdot \frac{\lambda}{\alpha} \cdot \frac{L_n^{\lambda-1} \cdot H_n^{1-\lambda}}{g_{n_t} \cdot \frac{1-\alpha}{\alpha} + \rho}. \tag{13.16}$$

Because we assume (in this competitive framework) that low-skilled labour is perfectly mobile between sectors, the relative wage, z, must be equal to one. Furthermore we assume that high-skilled labour is supplied inelastically with the consequence that it is always fully employed at the exogenously given level $\bar{H}_n$. So equation (13.16) establishes a relation between the amount of low-skilled labour employed in the production process and the amount of low-skilled labour devoted to the research sector (remember that aggregate production in the intermediate sector X is determined by $n \cdot l_{x(i)} = L_x$). To close the model we need an additional equation which is the resource constraint of the economy (the amount of labour employed in both sectors of the economy cannot exceed the resource base):

$$\bar{L} = L_x + L_n, \tag{13.17}$$

so there is only an exogenous amount of labour $\bar{L}$ that can be allocated to both sectors. Combining equations (13.17) and (13.16) and substituting X and g_{n_t} by the production functions (13.3) and (13.7), we get the following equilibrium condition for employment in the research sector (and this also determines (indirectly) the rate of growth of the economy):

$$n \cdot L_n^{\lambda} \cdot \bar{H}_n^{1-\lambda} \cdot \frac{1-\alpha}{\alpha} + \rho = \frac{1-\alpha}{\alpha} \cdot \left(\bar{L} - L_n\right) \cdot \lambda \cdot L_n^{\lambda-1} \cdot \bar{H}_n^{1-\lambda} \tag{13.18}$$

Equation (13.18) depicts equilibrium employment in the research sector. Due to the assumed structure of production, equation (13.18) is not analytically solvable for the levels of employment in the two sectors. But we can log-linearise the equation and argue for relative changes.

Log-linearising equation (13.18) (where a '$\sim$' over a variable denotes a relative change, hence $\tilde{x} = \frac{dx}{x}$) gives:

$$\left(1 - \lambda + \lambda \cdot b_1 + \frac{L_n}{\bar{L} - L_n}\right) \cdot \tilde{L}_n = (1-\lambda) \cdot b_2 \cdot \tilde{\bar{H}}_n + \frac{\bar{L}}{\bar{L} - L_n} \cdot \tilde{\bar{L}} - b_2 \cdot \tilde{\rho} - \frac{b_2}{1-\alpha} \cdot \tilde{\alpha}, \tag{13.19}$$

where the coefficients b_1 and b_2 are given in the appendix (both are positive and add up to one, hence, $b_1 + b_2 = 1$). With equation (13.19) at hand we can analyse the impact of the various parameters on the growth rate of the economy. A larger stock of high-skilled labour will foster the rate of growth, because marginal productivity of low-skilled labour in the research sector will rise. A larger stock of low-skilled labour will also raise employment in the research sector and therewith growth, because additional labour will be allocated evenly between the two sectors of the economy, thus raising production and research output. A more impatient economy (higher ρ) will have less employment in the research sector and hence, will grow slower. This is because in an economy with impatient inhabitants savings are low and this tends to increase the (steady state) rate of interest. Thus, borrowing is expensive and so there will be less entrepreneurs in the intermediate goods sector. Therefore, the price of patents will be low causing the marginal value product of labour in the research sector to decline. This dampens employment in the research sector. Similar arguments hold true for a change in α. An increase in α implies that the market for intermediate goods is more competitive.[5] So the profit of an intermediate good firm declines, implying that fewer entrepreneurs enter the market and the demand for blueprints (and as such, the price for blueprints) will be low. This will dampen employment in the research sector.

13.2 The Unionised Economy

In this section we derive the equilibrium of the economy when we have union wage bargaining in the research as well as in the intermediate goods sector.[6] We assume, starting from an arbitrary steady state equilibrium with perfectly competitive labour markets, that unions form in every firm of the economy. All employed workers in a firm are members of the union and membership is exogenous. Every union bargains at the firm-level a wage for its members which maximises their life time utility given by equation (13.10). Because we consider a perfectly decentralised wage setting, all macroeconomic effects are taken as exogenous during the bargain. Life time utility of a typical union member depends (via the indirect utility function) solely on the state dependent income of that member. The union members might experience different states, namely being employed in the intermediate sector, being employed in the R&D sector or being unemployed.[7] The value attached to those states is given by the following Bellmann's equations:

$$V_t^{x(i)} = \left(w_t^{x(i)} + D_t + a \cdot V_{t+1}^u + (1-a) \cdot V_{t+1}^{x(i)}\right) \cdot \frac{1}{1+\rho}, \tag{13.20}$$

$$V_t^{n(i)} = \left(w_t^{n(i)} + D_t + e \cdot V_{t+1}^u + (1-e) \cdot V_{t+1}^{n(i)}\right) \cdot \frac{1}{1+\rho}, \tag{13.21}$$

$$V_t^u = \left(B_t + D_t + c \cdot V_{t+1}^n + c \cdot V_{t+1}^x + (1-c-c) \cdot V_{t+1}^U\right) \cdot \frac{1}{1+\rho}, \tag{13.22}$$

where $V^{x(i)}$, $V^{n(i)}$ is the value of working in a specific intermediate firm and a specific research firm, respectively. V^x and V^n are the values of working in the intermediate sector and in the research sector, respectively. V^u is the value of being unemployed, B_t is the unemployment benefit, D_t are the dividends

[5] Remember that the elasticity of substitution between two intermediate good varieties is given by $\frac{1}{1-\alpha}$. Hence, with a higher α the intermediate goods become better substitutes.

[6] The modelling of this two sector wage bargain follows rather closely Holmlund (1997) and Kolm (1998).

[7] It is important to note that a direct switch from one sector to another is not possible without frictions, i.e., being unemployed. This is because both sectors are dominated by union wage bargaining. So an agent who quits a job in one sector cannot be sure to find a job in the other immediately because the union rations jobs.

a union member gets (which is independent of the employment status)[8] and a, e, c are the probabilities of loosing a job in the intermediate sector, loosing a job in the research sector and finding a job in the intermediate or the research sector, respectively. Note that we assume the probability of finding a job to be the same in both sectors. One might argue that, once unemployed, it is harder to find a job in the research sector, because more sector specific skills are needed, which are lost during the time being unemployed. To keep the model as simple as possible we do not consider different probabilities of finding a job.

Note that the value of being employed (in any firm) is growing in a steady state, because the wages the firms are willing to pay will grow.[9] The growth rate of the wage is given by $\frac{1-\alpha}{\alpha} \cdot g_n = g_Y$ (see equation (13.5)). In the following we assume that the unemployment benefit is indexed to the wage in the intermediate goods sector and that this ratio is constant $\left(\frac{B_t}{w_t^{x(i)}}\right)$. This assumption implies that the unemployment benefit must also grow at the above given rate. If this would not be the case the value of being unemployed would decrease over time and so would the bargained wage. The unionised economy would converge to the competitive one.

As in the competitive case we concentrate on steady states, which implies that $V_{t+1}^{x(i)} = (1+g_Y) \cdot V_t^{x(i)}$, $V_{t+1}^{n(i)} = (1+g_Y) \cdot V_t^{x(i)}$ and $V_{t+1}^U = (1+g_Y) \cdot V_t^U$.[10]

13.2.1 Wage Bargaining in the Intermediate Sector

The union bargains the wage with a firm in the intermediate sector. Union's utility function is given by:

$$U^{union} = l_{x(i)} \cdot V_t^{x(i)} + (m - l_{x(i)}) \cdot V_t^U, \tag{13.23}$$

so when bargaining the wage, the union maximises life time utility of all its members m taking into account that some might become unemployed. To determine the firm-level wage in the intermediate sector, we apply the (asymmetric) Nash bargaining solution. The Nash product is given by:

$$\Omega_x = (U^{union} - \bar{U}^{union})^{\gamma} \cdot (\Pi_x - \bar{\Pi}_x)^{1-\gamma}, \tag{13.24}$$

[8] These dividends are debt repayment of the intermediate good firms.

[9] This growth of wages is due to the fact that as the number of varieties grows the consumption goods sector is willing to pay a higher price for the intermediate goods. But with this, the wage, which intermediate good firms are willing to pay, increases. Furthermore the demand for blueprints increases. Thus, research firms are also willing to pay higher wages.

[10] Dividends in the economy are the debt repayment of the intermediate good firms. Hence, the sum of dividend payments to all members of the economy $(\bar{H}+\bar{L}) \cdot D_t = n_t \cdot (P_n \cdot r)$. Differentiating this with respect to time it is easy to see that in the steady state dividends grow at the same rate as, e.g., wages.

where γ is the bargaining power of the labour union, Π_x is the profit of the intermediate firm and $\bar{U}^{union}$ is union's utility in the case that no agreement is reached (in this case all union members "get" the value of being unemployed). $\bar{\Pi}_x$ is the profit of the firm if there is no agreement. In such a situation the firm is not able to produce output, so revenue is zero, but because the firm had to buy a patent in advance (to get the chance of bargaining with the union and start production) there will be costs of $r \cdot P_n$. Maximising the Nash product Ω_x with respect to the wage and subject to the labour demand curve (13.5) gives the bargained wage (see the appendix):

$$w^L_{x(i)} = \phi_x \cdot \left((\rho - g_Y) \cdot V^U_t - D_t \right), \tag{13.25}$$

where $\phi_x = \left(\frac{(1-\gamma)\cdot\alpha+\gamma}{\alpha} \right)$. The bargained wage is a mark-up over the present value of being unemployed (net of dividends). The mark-up depends (positively) on the bargaining power of unions and negatively on the price elasticity of the intermediate goods demand (which in turn determines monopoly profits, so the higher these profits are, the higher will be the wage). Furthermore equation (13.25) reveals that the competitive case is nested in the union case. When bargaining power γ is zero, ϕ_x will be one and the wage will be equal to the competitive wage.

13.2.2 Wage Bargaining in the R&D Sector

To determine the wage, w^L_n, in the R&D sector, we follow the same approach, we have already applied to determine the wage in the intermediate sector. We assume that the union in the research sector has the same utility function as the union in the intermediate sector.[11] The following Nash product determines the bargained wage:

$$\Omega_n = (U^{union} - \bar{U}^{union})^{\mu} \cdot (\Pi_n - \bar{\Pi}_n)^{1-\mu}. \tag{13.26}$$

In this case, μ denotes the bargaining power of the union, $\bar{U}^{union}$ is again the utility of the union when there is no agreement and this is, as in the intermediate sector, $m \cdot V^U$. The profit of a research firm in the case of a dispute, $\bar{\Pi}_n$, is $-w^H_n \cdot H_n$. So we assume that in the case of a dispute with the labour union nothing can be produced (which is obviously a result of the assumed production function), but that high-skilled labour must be paid accordingly. This last assumption can be justified on the basis that we consider a bargaining structure where on the first stage the firm hires high-skilled labour and as such, ties its hands for the second stage of the bargain.[12] So

[11] Since low skilled labour is homogeneous this seems to be a straightforward assumption.

[12] Another, may be more plausible argument for this assumption would be that high-skilled labour owns the firms and receives the difference between revenues and labour costs as income. This would result in the same Nash product, assuming that the firm wants to maximise income and cannot produce without labour.

the firm faces a hold-up problem (similar to that described in the part on "Unions and Capital") and anticipates the bargained low-skilled wage at the second stage. This sequence of events is very important for the outcome of the bargain. There are only (quasi-) rents in the research sector as long as there is a fixed factor employed. The union will bargain a wage that exceeds the value of being unemployed if there are rents that could be captured. So only if the firm has tied its hands by employing high-skilled labour at the first stage, the union will bargain a wage that exceeds the competitive one.

In the case that the bargain is at the first stage, the union has to take adjustments in the amount of high-skilled labour into account. Hence, the constraint in this case is the total low-skilled labour demand curve (see, e.g., the chapter on "Unions and Creative Destruction" for similar arguments) and this curve is totally elastic. This implies that the union is not able to push the wage above the competitive one.

The wage that maximises the Nash product (which is the bargained wage) is given by (see the appendix):

$$w^L_{n(i)} = \phi_n \cdot (\rho - g_Y) \cdot (V^U - D), \tag{13.27}$$

where $\phi_n = \left(\frac{(1-\mu)\cdot\lambda+\mu}{\lambda}\right)$. As in the intermediate sector the bargained wage in the research sector will be a mark-up over the value of being unemployed (net of dividends). This mark-up depends positively on the bargaining power of unions in the research sector and it depends negatively on the labour demand elasticity (reflected by the parameter λ). The economic intuition is, as in all of the bargaining models of this kind, that with a flatter labour demand curve (hence, with a more elastic labour demand curve) the bargained wage will be lower, because a given wage hike of the union will be punished by a greater loss of employment. So in this case the union is reluctant to bargain a high wage.

13.2.3 General Equilibrium

Up to this point we have only derived the bargained wage at the firm-level for the research and the intermediate sector. Now we have to aggregate these wage equations to the macroeconomic level. This is done by deriving an explicit equation for the value of being unemployed and assuming symmetry within the research and the intermediate goods sector, i.e., $w^L_{x(i)} = w^L_x$ and $w^L_{n(i)} = w^L_n$. To derive an explicit equation for $(\rho - g_Y) \cdot V^U$ we use the above given value equations (13.20), (13.21), (13.22). From these equations we get:

$$V_t^x - V_t^U = \left(\frac{1}{\rho - g_Y + a \cdot g_Y + c \cdot g_Y}\right) \cdot (w_x^L - B - c \cdot g_Y \cdot (V_t^n - V_t^U)), \tag{13.28}$$

$$V_t^n - V_t^U = \left(\frac{1}{\rho - g_Y + e \cdot g_Y + c \cdot g_Y}\right) \cdot (w_n^L - B - c \cdot g_Y \cdot (V_t^x - V_t^U)). \tag{13.29}$$

These two equations can finally be solved for $V_t^x - V_t^U$ and $V_t^n - V_t^U$. The solutions can be plugged into equation (13.22). This yields an equation for the present value of being unemployed net of dividends as a function of the unemployment benefit, the wages in the two sectors of the economy, the exogenous probabilities of finding jobs and getting unemployed, respectively and as a function of the wage growth and the discount rate of agents. This equation would be very messy and little is lost when assuming that the discount rate approaches the steady state growth rate (so we analyse the model for a special valued discount rate).[13] Doing this we get the following equation for the value of being unemployed net of dividends:

$$\lim_{\rho \to g_Y} (\rho - g_Y) \cdot (V_t^U - D) =$$
$$B_t \cdot (1 - c \cdot \frac{a + e}{\Gamma - (c \cdot g_y)^2}) + \frac{g_Y \cdot c \cdot g_Y \cdot a}{\Gamma - (c \cdot g_y)^2} \cdot w_n^L + \frac{g_Y \cdot c \cdot g_Y \cdot e}{\Gamma - (c \cdot g_y)^2} \cdot w_x^L, \tag{13.30}$$

with $\Gamma \equiv (g_Y \cdot a + g_Y \cdot c) \cdot (g_Y \cdot e + g_Y \cdot c)$. Because we focus on steady states, we also assume a flow equilibrium on the labour market. This implies that $a \cdot L^x = c \cdot U$ and $e \cdot L^n = c \cdot U$. Using this to substitute for the probabilities of changing between states from equation (13.30) and plugging this into equation (13.25) we get the following equation[14]:

$$w_x^L = \left(\frac{(1-\gamma) \cdot \alpha + \gamma}{\alpha}\right) \cdot \left(\frac{U}{\bar{L}} \cdot B + \frac{L_n}{\bar{L}} \cdot w_n^L + \frac{L_x}{\bar{L}} \cdot w_x^L\right). \tag{13.31}$$

Factoring out w_x^L on the rhs of equation (13.31) and collecting terms we get the following (note that we also used the following definition of unemployment $U = \bar{L} - L_n - L_x$):

$$L_x = \bar{L}\left(\frac{\alpha}{(1-\gamma) \cdot \alpha + \gamma} - b\right) \cdot \frac{1}{1-b} - L_n \cdot (z - b) \cdot \frac{1}{1-b}, \tag{13.32}$$

where z is the relative research sector wage $\frac{w_n^L}{w_x^L}$ and $b = \frac{B}{w_x^L}$, so b is the replacement ratio in terms of the intermediate sector wage. By equations (13.27) and (13.25) the relative research sector wage is given by:

[13] This simplification is also applied in Holmlund (1997) or Kolm (1998).

[14] Note that we could have also plugged it into equation (13.27) without any substantial change in the equations. Which approach to take to determine the equilibrium is a matter of taste.

$$z = \frac{\alpha}{(1-\gamma)\cdot\alpha+\gamma}\cdot\frac{(1-\mu)\cdot\lambda+\mu}{\lambda} = \frac{\phi_n}{\phi_x}. \tag{13.33}$$

The relative research sector wage in the unionised economy is solely a function of the mark-ups in the two sectors. This is because all other parameters affect the bargaining situations symmetrically and thus will not change the relative wage. We assume in the following that $z > b$. If this condition was hurt no individual would like to work in the research sector, because the wage in this sector would be lower than the unemployment benefit. Note that in the unionised case z needs not to be equal to one as in the competitive case.

If labour markets were competitive any wage differential would result in worker flows until the wage in both sectors is equalised. But if unions bargain the wage, there will be unemployment in the economy and every worker who quits a job faces the risk of being unemployed for a certain amount of time. So there is no perfect mobility between the two sectors with the result that arbitrage can only equalise expected life time utility between the two states: being employed in the intermediate goods and in the research sector. As shown in equation (13.33) the wage differential will be a function of the parameters $\alpha, \gamma, \lambda, \mu$. The higher the union's bargaining power and the lower the price elasticity in the intermediate goods market, the higher will be the bargained wage in the intermediate sector and the lower will be z. The opposite will be true if bargaining power in the research sector is high and the wage elasticity of the labour demand curve is low. In this case the bargained wage in the research sector will be high and z will c.p. be high.

Equation (13.32) determines a curve which is in the one sector union literature (see, e.g., Carlin and Soskice (1990)) usually referred to as the wage setting curve. The wage setting curve in the one sector models depicts the bargained wage as a function of employment. A similar interpretation can be applied for equation (13.32). Since there is an additional sector, this equation reflects the bargained wage in the intermediate sector (remember equation (13.31)) as a function of employment opportunities in both sectors of the economy, given the bargained wage in the other sector. The wage setting curve is downward sloping in the L_x-L_n-space. The intuition for this is the following. Consider an increase in low-skilled employment in the intermediate sector and thus, an increase in the value of being employed. With this the bargained wage in both sectors will increase, but the wage increase will be asymmetric. The wage in the sector with the higher bargaining power will increase by more than the one in the other sector. Hence, the relative wage z would change. Since wage setting curve depicts combinations of L_x and L_n for which the wage is constant, low-skilled employment in the other sector must decrease, to keep the relative wage constant.

The equilibrium in the economy is determined by the wage setting curve (given by equation (13.31)) and the relative labour demand in the two sectors, given by equation (13.16) (which is the pendant to the price setting curve in one sector models). The price setting curve is upward sloping in L_x-L_n-space.

The intuition for this property is that this curve depicts low-skilled employment combinations for which the relative research sector wage is constant. If low-skilled employment in the intermediate sector increased the wage in this sector would decrease. In such a situation, low-skilled employment in the research sector must increase too, in order to ensure the the relative wage to be constant.

In figure 13.1 the equilibrium of the economy and the resource constraint are shown.

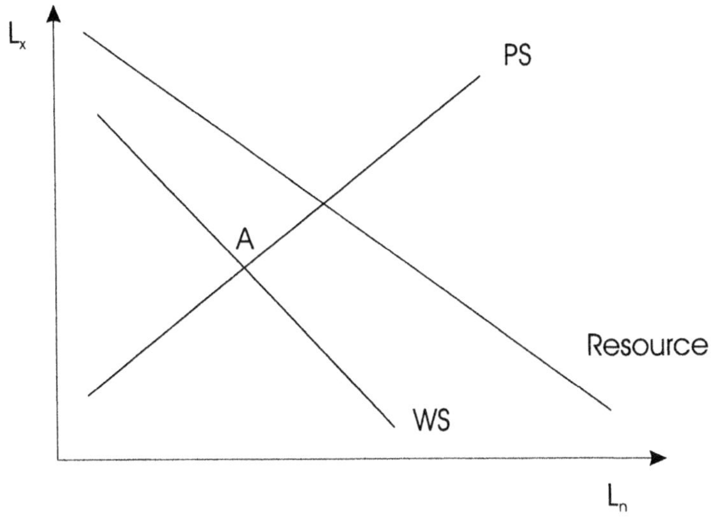

Fig. 13.1. The Equilibrium in the Unionised Economy

In this figure PS denotes the price setting curve, WS the wage setting curve and *Resource* the resource constraint. The interception of the wage and the price setting curve constitutes the equilibrium in the economy (point A in the figure). Obviously only points to the left of the resource constraint are feasible. Moreover the resource constraint can be used as a measure of the distortion caused by union wage bargaining, because the distance between the resource constraint and the wage setting curve shows the level of unemployment.

As equations (13.31) and (13.16) are not explicitly solvable in levels, we again log-linearise the equations and get:

$$\tilde{z} = \tilde{L}_x - \left(\frac{b_2}{1-\alpha}\right) \cdot \tilde{\alpha} - (1 - \lambda \cdot b_2) \cdot \tilde{L}_n + ((1-\lambda) \cdot b_2) \cdot \tilde{\bar{H}}_n - b_2 \cdot \tilde{\rho}, \tag{13.34}$$

$$\tilde{L}_x = c_1 \cdot \tilde{\bar{L}} - c_2 \cdot \tilde{\gamma} + c_3 \cdot \tilde{\alpha} - \frac{U}{L_x} \cdot \tilde{b} - c_4 \cdot \tilde{z} - c_5 \cdot \tilde{L}_n, \tag{13.35}$$

where the coefficients c_1, c_2, and c_3 are given in the appendix. Note that all coefficients are positive. Finally, using (13.35) and (13.34) we can determine equilibrium employment in the intermediate and the research sector:

$$\begin{aligned} \tilde{L}_n \cdot (1 - \lambda \cdot b_2 + c_5) = \left(c_3 - \frac{b_2}{1-\alpha}\right) \cdot \tilde{\alpha} + ((1-\lambda) \cdot b_2) \cdot \tilde{\bar{H}}_n \\ -b_2 \cdot \tilde{\rho} + c_1 \cdot \tilde{\bar{L}} - c_2 \cdot \tilde{\gamma} - \frac{U}{L_x} \cdot \tilde{b} - (c_4 + 1) \cdot \tilde{z}, \end{aligned} \tag{13.36}$$

$$\begin{aligned} \tilde{L}_x \cdot \left(\frac{1}{1-\lambda \cdot b_2} + \frac{1}{c_5}\right) = \frac{c_1}{c_5} \cdot \tilde{\bar{L}} - \frac{c_2}{c_5} \cdot \tilde{\gamma} + \left(\frac{b_2}{1-\alpha} \cdot \frac{1}{1-\lambda \cdot b_2} + \frac{c_3}{c_5}\right) \cdot \tilde{\alpha} \\ -\frac{U}{L_x \cdot c_5} \cdot \tilde{b} - \left(\frac{c_4}{c_5} - \frac{1}{1-\lambda \cdot b_2}\right) \cdot \tilde{z} - \frac{b_2 \cdot (1-\lambda)}{1-\lambda \cdot b_2} \cdot \tilde{\bar{H}}_n + \frac{b_2}{1-\lambda \cdot b_2} \cdot \tilde{\rho}. \end{aligned} \tag{13.37}$$

13.3 Equilibrium Unemployment

In the preceding section we have determined equilibrium employment in both sectors given simultaneous union wage bargaining. In this section we will determine unemployment in the economy and analyse in which way parameter changes affect unemployment.

By definition the relative change in unemployment is given by:

$$\tilde{U} = \frac{\bar{L}}{U} \cdot \tilde{\bar{L}} - \frac{L_x}{U} \cdot \tilde{L}_x - \frac{L_n}{U} \cdot \tilde{L}_n. \tag{13.38}$$

Plugging equations (13.37) and (13.36) into equation (13.38) we get equilibrium unemployment in the economy:

$$\begin{aligned} \tilde{U} = \left(\frac{\bar{L}}{U} - \frac{1}{1 - b_2 \cdot \lambda + c_5} \cdot d_5\right) \cdot \tilde{\bar{L}} + \\ \frac{1}{1 - b_2 \cdot \lambda + c_5} \cdot \left(-d_1 \cdot \tilde{\alpha} + d_2 \cdot \tilde{\gamma} + d_3 \cdot \tilde{z} + d_4 \cdot \tilde{\rho} + d_6 \cdot \tilde{b} + d_7 \cdot \tilde{\bar{H}}_n\right). \end{aligned} \tag{13.39}$$

Note that $\tilde{z}$ is an endogenous variable given by the relative change in the mark-ups in the two sectors. To economise on space and to make the argumentation clearer, we did not plug in for z. When doing this one has to keep in mind that, e.g., changes in union bargaining power have direct effects, but also indirect effects via the change in z. The coefficients d_1 to d_7 are given in the appendix.

Firstly, we analyse the effects of changes of the resource base of the economy on unemployment. A bigger stock of low-skilled labour has ambiguous effects on unemployment. On the one hand a higher $\bar{L}$ will increase employment in both sectors, because a union member that is unemployed will face longer unemployment spells, because there are more people competing for jobs. So there will be wage moderation. On the other hand $\bar{L}$ increases which increases U by definition. If the employment increase overcompensates the increase in $\bar{L}$, unemployment will decrease. This will be the case if the following holds:

$$\frac{\bar{L}}{U} - \frac{1}{1 - b_2 \cdot \lambda + c_5} \cdot d_5 < 0. \tag{13.40}$$

The sign of the coefficient is ambiguous, as is the overall effect on unemployment. Diagrammatically, a larger stock of labour results in an outward shift of the wage setting curve and in an outward shift of the resource constraints.

A larger stock of high-skilled labour implies that the marginal productivity of labour in the research sector increases. Hence, (given the mark-ups) relative labour demand increases; the price setting curve shifts downwards. As figure 13.1 depicts, this downward shift will raise unemployment if the wage setting curve is flat, because in this case the distance between the equilibrium and the resource constraint will increase. Using the definition of c_5 in d_7 gives $\frac{L_n}{U} \cdot \left(\frac{z-b}{1-b} - 1\right)$. Hence, if z exceeds one, unemployment will rise with a bigger stock of human capital and unemployment will decrease if z is smaller than one. What is the economic intuition behind this property? The increased low-skilled labour demand in the research sector implies that the wage which research sector firms are willing to pay increases. So there are workers who find it optimal to move from the intermediate into the research sector. z smaller than one implies that the research sector labour market is more competitive than the intermediate sector one, the workers who moved will find it easy to get a new job, because the rationing effect of the union is not so strong. So with a higher demand in the research sector, resources are shifted into the sector with the less unionised labour market. The employment loss in the intermediate sector caused by this "migration" is overcompensated by the employment gain in the research sector. So overall employment will increase (the opposite is true when z exceeds one).

A change in the rate of the rate of time preference has very similar effects. Higher ρ results in an upward shift of the price setting curve, because labour demand in the research sector has fallen. This is because the marginal value product of labour has fallen as the price of blueprints declined (see, the competitive case). We observe a reallocation of resources from the research into the intermediate sector. Using the definition of c_5 we get $d_4 = \left(\frac{L_n}{U} \cdot \left(1 - \frac{z-b}{1-b}\right)\right)$. If z exceeds one, unemployment will decrease. If it is smaller than one, unemployment will increase. The economic intuition behind this is the same as in the case of a higher pool of high-skilled. Resources are shifted into the more (less) competitive sector of the economy, implying that total employment increases (decreases).

A higher replacement ratio will increase unemployment. This is the standard result also present in one sector models. With a higher replacement ratio, being unemployed is less costly in terms of foregone income. So unions in both sectors will push for higher wages and this will dampen employment. Diagrammatically, a higher b implies an inward shift of the wage setting curve. Figure 13.1 depicts that in this case the distance between the wage setting curve and the resource constraint (and thus, unemployment) increases.

The last parameters influencing unemployment in the economy are the competitiveness of the intermediate goods market, bargaining power of intermediate sector unions and the relative sectoral wage z.

Remember that the relative wage is an endogenous variable and is given by the following equation:[15]

$$\tilde{z} = \underbrace{\frac{\gamma}{(1-\gamma)\cdot\alpha+\gamma}\cdot\tilde{\alpha} - \frac{(1-\alpha)\cdot\gamma}{(1-\gamma)\cdot\alpha+\gamma}\cdot\tilde{\gamma}}_{-\tilde{\phi}_x} + \underbrace{\frac{(1-\lambda)\cdot\mu}{(1-\mu)\cdot\lambda+\mu}\cdot\tilde{\mu}}_{\tilde{\phi}_n}. \tag{13.41}$$

First of all consider a change in the competitiveness in the intermediate goods market. A higher α has two direct effects. On the one hand the price setting curve will shift upwards implying a reallocation of labour towards the intermediate sector. This is because with a higher α intermediate goods are better substitutes and hence, monopoly profits of intermediate sector firms decrease. But this decrease implies that the demand for blueprints decreases too with the consequence that the price for blueprints declines. Therefore, labour demand in the research sector will decrease compared to that of the intermediate sector. On the other hand the wage setting curve will shift outwards, because with a higher α the bargained wage in the intermediate sector declines since the monopoly profits the union can capture are lower than before. But this also implies that the outside opportunities in the research sector decline. So the bargained wage in that sector will decreases, too.

In addition to these direct effects, the change in α also affects the relative sectoral wage z. The overall coefficients governing the effect of α changes on unemployment in the economy is given by:

$$-d_1 + \frac{\gamma}{(1-\gamma)\cdot\alpha+\gamma}\cdot d_3 \lesseqgtr 0. \tag{13.42}$$

Because of the several, partly countervailing effects, the sign of this coefficient is ambiguous. Nevertheless the following can be shown: if z exceeds one (hence, the wage in the research sector is higher than in the intermediate sector)

[15] We assume the production function in the research sector as being constant, hence, we do not consider changes of λ in the analysis.

and is high enough, it is more likely that a higher α will lead to declining unemployment.

If z is exceeds one, the coefficient $-d_1$ showing the direct effect of a change in α is unambiguously negative. The rationale behind this is the following. Due to the outward shift of the wage setting curve unemployment will unambiguously decline. There is only a countervailing effect to this unemployment dampening effect if the change in the relative labour demand causes a reallocation towards the more unionised sector. As the change in the labour demand shifts resources into the intermediate sector, the direct effect will dampen unemployment only if the labour market in this sector is more competitive. This is the case when z exceeds one. The indirect effect of a change in α on unemployment via the change in z is ambiguous. If z is very low a change in z will cause unemployment to increase. This is due to the following. Inspecting equations (13.19) and (13.34) shows that a higher z will shift the price setting curve upwards (because relative labour demand in the intermediate sector increases) but will shift the wage setting curve inwards. Therefore, only if z exceeds one, the direct effect will dampen unemployment and if z is high the countervailing indirect effect will be small and it is more likely that the overall effect lowers unemployment.

Altering bargaining power of unions in the intermediate sector has also ambiguous effects. Again we have direct effects and effects via a change in the relative wage. The overall impact is depicted by the following equation:

$$d_2 - \frac{(1-\alpha)\cdot\gamma}{(1-\gamma)\cdot\alpha+\gamma}\cdot d_3 \lesseqgtr 0. \qquad (13.43)$$

The sign of this coefficient is indeterminate and hence, the overall employment effects are ambiguous. The economic intuition is a bit sophisticated so we will argue in two steeps. First of all note that with a lower γ c.p. the low-skilled wage in the intermediate sector will decrease and employment will increase. But with this, the bargained wage in the research sector will increase *and* low-skilled labour demand will decrease, because with lower intermediate sector production the price of blueprints will decline. In the new equilibrium, low-skilled employment in the intermediate sector will be higher and employment in the research sector lower than in the old equilibrium (see equations (13.36) and (13.37)). Hence, the effect on overall employment is ambiguous.

Very similar arguments hold true for a change in the bargaining power in the research sector. A decline in μ results c.p. in higher low-skilled employment in the research sector. With this the bargained wage in the intermediate sector increases and employment decreases. The overall effect is again ambiguous.

13.4 Growth Effects of the Wage Bargain

In this section we analyse the impact of unionisation on the (steady state) rate of growth of the economy. We have seen that the rate of growth is determined by the rate of the evolution of new intermediate good varieties. But the growth rate of intermediate good varieties is a function of resources (low-skilled labour and high-skilled labour) devoted to the research sector. Since the supply of high-skilled is perfectly inelastic, high-skilled labour is always full-employed. Hence, unionisation affects the rate of growth only via changes in research sector low-skilled employment.

In the last section we have already analysed the overall employment effects of union wage bargaining. In the following we focus on the effects on research sector employment. Moreover, we want to compare the rate of growth in the unionised case with that of the competitive case. This implies that we analyse how parameters change the rate of growth in the union case, but also how parameters change the growth differential between the unionised and the non-unionised economy. We define the growth differential as the growth rate in the non-union case over the growth rate in the union case. So we can use the difference between equations (13.19) and (13.36) to analyse the impact of parameters on the growth differential. The interesting point is that we can analyse the relative impact of parameter changes, hence, whether parameter changes improve or worsen the situation of the economy compared to the benchmark case of competitive labour markets. This is especially interesting when analysing parameter that change both the growth rate of an economy with competitive as well as with unionised labour markets.

First of all we analyse the effects of parameters that only affect research employment in the unionised case (to distinguish effects on the rate of growth and the growth differential). Inspecting equations (13.19) and (13.36) it can be seen that these are only the replacement ratio b, union bargaining power in the intermediate sector γ and changes of the relative wage (where we focus on the effect of changes of the bargaining power of research sector unions and changes of α). A higher replacement ratio and/or greater bargaining power of research sector unions will unambiguously dampen employment in the research sector. This is straightforward as this will lead to higher bargained wages in this sector. This causes a reallocation of the labour pool to unemployment (in the case of a higher b) or to the intermediate goods sector (in the case of a higher μ). An interesting point is the impact of higher union bargaining power in the intermediate sector (hence, a rise in γ). The effect of higher γ on research sector employment is twofold. With higher γ the wage in the intermediate sector will increase and c.p. the value of being unemployed increases, too. So agents will find it optimal to move from the research sector into unemployed, because they hope to find a better paid job in the intermediate sector. Therefore, employment in the research sector will decrease; this first effect is growth dampening. The second effect is that relative labour demand in the research sector increases. But with this more people will find a job in the research sector and c.p. research sector employment increases; this second effect is growth enhancing. Thus, we can observe a "good" and a "bad" union effect. We can determine the overall effect account, the overall effect of a higher γ on research sector employment is (using equation (13.36) and (13.41)) given by:

$$-c_2 + (c_4 + 1) \cdot \left(\frac{(1-\alpha) \cdot \gamma}{(1-\gamma) \cdot \alpha + \gamma} \right). \tag{13.44}$$

If this coefficient exceeds zero, an increase in the bargaining power of intermediate sector union power will result in higher research sector employment and hence, in a higher rate of growth. Using the definition of c_2 and c_4 given in the appendix we get the following condition that must be satisfied for research employment to increase with γ:

$$-\bar{L} + \frac{1}{\phi_n} \cdot L_n + (1-b) \cdot L_x > 0. \tag{13.45}$$

As (13.45) reveals, this condition will never be satisfied because both $\frac{1}{\phi_n}$ and $(1-b)$ are smaller than one and with the resource constraint $L_n + L_x$ cannot exceed $\bar{L}$. So unionisation of the intermediate sector labour market will unambiguously dampen the rate of growth. But nevertheless the decline of the rate of growth will be lower with a high mark-up in the research sector and a low replacement ratio. The economic intuition for these properties is the following. With a lower replacement ratio and a higher mark-up in the research sector, less agents will find it optimal to move from the research sector into unemployment to find a job in the intermediate sector; since the incentive for "migration" decreases, the employment loss in the research sector will be small and hence, the decrease in the rate of growth will be small, too.

Another interesting parameter is the change in the price elasticity of the demand of intermediate goods, α. An increase in α has several effects on low-skilled employment in the research sector. Firstly, labour demand in the intermediate sector decreases and therewith production. But this implies that low-skilled labour demand in the research sector decrease, too.[16] This is the effect which is also present in growth models with perfectly competitive labour markets. But moreover a higher α also changes the wage setting relation in the economy. Since, with a higher α monopoly profits that could be captured by the union decline, the bargained wage in the intermediate sector c.p. declines, too. Hence, the wage and employment (remember that the low-skilled labour demand curve in the intermediate sector shifts inwards) decline, the value of being unemployed declines. Therewith, the bargained wage in the research sector declines, too.

The coefficient determining the overall effect of a change in α on research sector employment is (using (13.36) and (13.41)) given by:

$$c_3 - \frac{b_2}{1-\alpha} - (c_4 + 1) \cdot \frac{\alpha}{(1-\gamma) \cdot \alpha + \gamma} \lesseqgtr 0. \tag{13.46}$$

[16] The argument goes again as follows. A higher α implies lower monopoly profits in the intermediate goods sector. Hence, there are fewer entrepreneurs entering the intermediate goods market with the consequence that blueprint demand decreases. This dampens blueprint prices.

The sign of this coefficient is indeterminate, as the preceding analysis already suggested.

After having analysed the absolute impact of union wage bargaining on research sector employment, we will also analyse how the parameters that determine research sector employment in both the unionised and the competitive case, affect the growth differential, defined as research sector employment in the competitive case over research employment when unions bargain the wage. Using equations (13.36) and (13.19) and assuming that the change in all parameters that only affect research employment in the competitive or in the union case are zero ($\tilde{b} = \tilde{\mu} = \tilde{\gamma} = 0$), we get the linearised growth differential ($\tilde{\Delta g}$) as:

$$\tilde{\Delta g} = e_1 \cdot \tilde{\bar{L}} + e_2 \cdot \tilde{\bar{H}}_n - e_3 \cdot \tilde{\rho} + e_4 \cdot \tilde{\alpha}. \tag{13.47}$$

where the coefficients e_1, e_2, e_3 and e_4 are given in the appendix. Equation (13.47) reveals that changes of the stock of high-skilled labour will narrow the growth differential as long as c_5 is smaller than $\frac{L_n}{L-L_n}$. This is true as long as z is smaller than one, i.e., unionisation in the research sector is "weaker" than in the intermediate sector. The intuition for this property is that in both cases (when labour markets are competitive and when they are unionised) research employment will increase, because marginal productivity of labour increases. But in the unionised case there will in addition be the effect that unions in the intermediate sector will bargain higher wages (since c.p. the value of being unemployed has increased) with the consequence that more low-skilled labour will become unemployed. If research sector unionisation is weaker than that in the intermediate sector more people will then again find a job in the research sector. As such, there will be a reallocation of the labour pool towards the research sector. So the impact of a changing stock of high-skilled labour on the rate of growth of the economy will be more severe in the unionised economy as long as z is smaller than one. Very similar arguments hold true when analysing the effect of a change in the rate of time preference on the growth differential. If z is smaller than one, a decline of the rate of time preference of agents implies a bigger increase in research sector employment in the unionised than in the competitive case. Hence, the growth differential will decrease. Speaking in graphical terms, the wage setting curve is flatter than the resource restriction (in L_x-L_n-space). Therefore, any shift of the price setting curve will have a stronger effect on research sector employment.

The coefficient showing the impact of a change in the low-skilled labour pool on the growth differential is positive as long as the following holds:

$$\frac{\bar{L}}{\bar{L} - L_n} \cdot \frac{1}{c_1} - \frac{1 - \lambda + \lambda \cdot b_1 + \frac{L_n}{\bar{L}-L_n}}{1 - \lambda + \lambda \cdot b_1 + c_5} > 0. \tag{13.48}$$

It can be shown (using the definition of c_1) that the first term of equation (13.48) always exceeds one. So as long as the second term is unambiguously smaller than one, the coefficient will be positive. This will be the case as long as z exceeds one (and so the mark-up in the research sector is bigger than that in the intermediate sector).[17] With a positive coefficient the growth differential will rise if the stock of labour rises. Thus, the increase in research employment will be bigger in the competitive case than in the unionised case. The intuition is that the allocation of the larger resource pool between the two sectors of the economy will be biased in the unionised economy, since labour demand will be higher in the sector where the relative wage is lower.

The sign of the coefficient depicting the impact of α on the growth differential is indeterminate. This is because the effect of changes of α on research employment in the unionised case is indeterminate (as was already analysed in the preceding part), whereas in the competitive case a higher α will always lead to lower research sector employment.

Summarising, we can say that in the model with simultaneous wage bargaining there will be unemployment, because unions bargain wages that exceed the competitive ones. Moreover there will be a wage differential between the two sectors of the economy.

First of all the impact of unionisation on unemployment has been analysed. It was shown that a bigger stock of low-skilled labour will raise employment in both sectors of the economy. An interesting point is that although overall employment increases, it is possible that the unemployment rate will increase. The employment effects of a bigger stock of high-skilled labour and a lower rate of time preference are ambiguous and depend on the relative wage z. If z is lower than one a larger stock of human capital or a lower rate of time preference implies a reallocation of low-skilled labour towards the research sector. Since this is less unionised if z is lower than one, overall employment will increase, too. It was also shown that the employment effects of higher union bargaining power is ambiguous and crucially hinges on the wage differential. Another interesting point is that lower intermediate sector competitiveness will not necessarily lead to either higher employment in the unionised economy or to a lower rate of growth (as is sometimes suggested in the standard labour and growth literature (see, e.g., Aghion and Howitt (1999) or Layard et al. (1991)).

Moreover we have analysed the impact of unionisation on the rate of growth of the economy. Not surprisingly, unionisation of the research sector labour market is unambiguously bad for the rate of growth. Higher bargaining power in the research sector will dampen research sector employment and hence, the rate of growth. The effect of the unionisation of the intermediate goods sector is growth dampening, too. Although in this case there are two countervailing effects: higher bargaining power increases the rationing effect of the union, but there is also a reallocation effect, because the relative labour

[17] It is true that the coefficient will be positive if z exceeds one. But it is obviously not true that the coefficient will be negative if z is smaller than one. There will be an intermediate case with z smaller than one but a positive coefficient. We will not consider this intermediate case.

demand in the research sector increases. It can be shown that the rate of growth will always decline.

Eventually, the impact of parameter changes on the growth differential, defined as research employment in the competitive case over research employment in the unionised case have been analysed. It was shown that these parameter changes (e.g., changes in the stock of human capital, the labour pool or the rate of time preference and the competitiveness parameter α) affect the rate of growth in the two cases asymmetrically. It could be shown that the impact of parameter changes is more severe in the unionised economy as long as z is smaller than one and hence, unionisation in the research sector is weaker than in the intermediate sector.

Comparing the one-sector and two-sector bargaining models of this part, we can state that for analysing the impact of union wage bargaining on the rate of growth, it is of crucial importance which production and bargaining structure is assumed. In the one sector bargaining model we only focused on the reallocation effect of the wage bargain. The union did not ration resources in the research sector. In the model with simultaneous bargaining we suppressed the indirect allocation effect and concentrated on the direct "scale" effect. It was shown that in this case the rate of growth will unambiguously decline. Hence, in a more general 2×2 model of economic growth both of these effects would be present. This implies that the condition that the union would foster economic growth would become even more restrictive.

13.5 Appendix

13.5.1 The Bargained Wage in the Intermediate Goods Sector

Maximising the Nash product given by equation (13.24) subject to the labour demand curve in the intermediate goods sector yields the following first order condition (remember that the wage elasticity of the intermediate goods sector labour demand is identical to the price elasticity of the intermediate goods demand, because of the linear production function):

$$\gamma \cdot \left(\frac{1}{\alpha - 1} + \underbrace{\frac{1}{\rho - g_Y + a \cdot (1 + g_Y)}}_{\frac{dV_t^{x(i)}}{dw_{x(i)}^L}} \cdot \frac{w_{x(i)}^L}{V_t^{x(i)} - V_t^U} \right) - (1 - \gamma) \cdot \frac{\alpha}{1 - \alpha} = 0. \quad \text{(A1)}$$

From equation (13.20) we know that in a steady state the following holds:

$$(\rho - g_Y + a \cdot (1 + g_Y)) \cdot V_t^{x(i)} = w_{x(i)}^L + D_t + a \cdot (1 + g_Y) \cdot V_t^U. \quad \text{(A2)}$$

Manipulation of (A2) shows that along the steady state the following will hold:

$$(\rho - g_Y + a \cdot (1 + g_Y)) \cdot \left(V_t^{x(i)} - V_t^U\right) = w_{x(i)}^L + D_t - (\rho - g_Y) \cdot V_t^U. \quad \text{(A3)}$$

Plugging (A3) into (A1) and collecting terms yields the wage equation stated in the text.

13.5.2 The Bargained Wage in the Research Sector

Maximising the Nash product given in equation (13.26) with respect to the wage and subject to the labour demand curve in the research sector (given by equation (13.8)) this gives the following relation:

$$\frac{\mu}{\rho - g_Y + e \cdot (1 + g_Y)} \cdot \frac{w_n^L}{V_t^n - V_t^U} = \frac{(1 - \mu) \cdot \lambda\mu}{1 - \lambda}. \quad \text{(A4)}$$

From equation (13.21) we know that the following holds:

$$(\rho - g_Y + e \cdot (1 + g_Y)) \cdot (V_t^n - V_t^U) = w_n^L + D_t - (\rho - g_Y) \cdot V_t^U. \quad \text{(A5)}$$

Plugging (A5) into (A4) we can solve for the bargained wage in the research sector as given in the text.

13.5.3 Coefficients of the Linearised Equilibrium Conditions

b_1	$0 < \frac{g_n \cdot \frac{1-\alpha}{\alpha}}{g_n \cdot \frac{1-\alpha}{\alpha} + \rho} < 1$
b_2	$0\text{¡} \frac{\rho}{g_n \cdot \frac{1-\alpha}{\alpha} + \rho} < 1$
c_1	$0 < \frac{\bar{L} \cdot \left(\frac{\alpha}{(1-\gamma)\cdot\alpha+\gamma} - b \right) \cdot (1-b)^{-1}}{L_x} > 1$
c_2	$\frac{\bar{L} \cdot \frac{\gamma\cdot\alpha\cdot(1-\alpha)}{((1-\gamma)\cdot\alpha+\gamma)^2} \cdot (1-b)^{-1}}{L_x} > 0$
c_3	$\frac{\frac{L\cdot\gamma\cdot\alpha}{((1-\gamma)\cdot\alpha+\gamma)^2} \cdot (1-b)^{-1}}{L_x} > 0$
c_4	$\frac{z \cdot L_n}{(1-b)\cdot L_x} > 0$
c_5	$\frac{\frac{z-b}{1-b} \cdot L_n}{L_x} > 0$
d_1	$\left(\frac{L_n}{U} \cdot (c_3 - \frac{b_2}{1-\alpha}) + \frac{L_x}{U} \cdot (c_3 + c_5 \cdot \frac{b_2}{1-\alpha}) \right)$
d_2	$c_2 \cdot \left(\frac{\bar{L}-U}{U} \cdot (1 - \lambda \cdot b_2) \right) > 0$
d_3	$\left(\frac{L_n}{U} \cdot (c_4 + 1) + \frac{L_x}{U} \cdot (c_4 \cdot (1 - \lambda \cdot b_2) - c_5) \right)$
d_4	$b_2 \cdot \left(\frac{L_n}{U} - \frac{L_x}{U} \cdot c_5 \right)$
d_5	$c_1 \cdot \left(\frac{L_n}{U} + \frac{L_x}{U} \cdot (1 - \lambda \cdot b_2) \right)$
d_6	$\frac{d_5}{c_1}$
d_7	$(1-\lambda) \cdot b_2 \cdot \left(\frac{L_x}{U} \cdot c_5 - \frac{L_n}{U} \right)$
e_1	$\left(\frac{\bar{L}}{L-L_n} \cdot \frac{1}{1-\lambda+\lambda\cdot b_1 + \frac{L_n}{L-L_n}} \right)$
e_2	$(1-\lambda) \cdot b_1 \cdot \left(\frac{1}{1-\lambda+\lambda\cdot b_1 + \frac{L_n}{L-L_n}} - \frac{1}{1-\lambda+\lambda\cdot b_1 + c_5} \right)$
e_3	$b_2 \left(\frac{1}{1-\lambda+\lambda\cdot b_1 + \frac{L_n}{L-L_n}} - \frac{1}{1-\lambda+\lambda\cdot b_1 + c_5} \right)$
e_4	$\left(-\frac{b_2}{1-\alpha} \cdot \frac{1}{1-\lambda+\lambda\cdot b_1 + \frac{L_n}{L_n - L_x}} - c_3 \cdot \frac{1}{1-\lambda+\lambda\cdot b_1+c_5} + \frac{b_2}{1-\alpha} \cdot \frac{1}{1-\lambda+\lambda\cdot b_1+c_5} + \frac{(c_4+1)}{1-\lambda+\lambda\cdot b_1+c_5} \cdot \frac{\alpha}{(1-\gamma)} \cdot \alpha + \gamma \right)$

Part VI

Unions, Labour Productivity and Dual Labour Markets

Union, Labour Productivity and Dual Labour Markets

In the preceding parts, we have analysed the effects of union wage bargaining in models where growth was endogenous and driven by the evolution of more efficient products or by the invention of new product varieties which then in turn caused a deeper division of labour. In both cases the economy could produce more consumption goods without any change in the primary resource base. Furthermore we have assumed that the factor that was covered by union wage bargaining was only employed in one sector of the economy or that when it was employed in both sectors there was also simultaneous bargaining in two sectors.

In this section we firstly, take a different approach to model the determinants of economic growth. We assume that R&D will directly change the productivity of labour, because, e.g., the research sector develops new production methods.

Secondly and more importantly, when modelling the labour market we take up the notion of duality. Duality implies that good and bad jobs exist in the labour market. Good jobs are in the sectors of the economy, where rents are generated that could be shared between workers and firms. In these sectors there will be wage bargaining. The other sectors (the traditional or service sectors) in the economy have competitive labour markets. So unemployed union members could be sure to get a job in the secondary sector. Nevertheless there will be unemployed, i.e. unemployed union members *choose* to stay unemployed. Remember that in the preceding part with simultaneous wage bargaining the unemployed were not able to switch sectors, because the union rationed labour in *both* sectors. In the following models unemployment arises from an optimal decision of unemployed, because when they take up a job in the competitive sector the probability of finding a job in the unionised sector declines. Therefore, to some extend it is rational not to move into the competitive sector. So there will be "wait" unemployment and there will be a sustained wage differential.

This wait unemployment relies crucially on the assumption that frictions exist which prevent workers in the competitive sector from finding a job in the unionised sector as easily as the unemployed.[18]

The first model in this spirit we will present is an OLG model based on Quang and Vousden (1999). They model the labour market in the tradition of Harris and Todaro (1970) and assume that switching costs between sectors (ex-post) are prohibitively high. So once workers have decided in which sector to work they are not able to switch into the other sector. The second model is an infinite horizon model of Groot (2000). The infinite horizon structure of this model allows more realistic assumptions about the flows of labour. The flow-friction in this model does not rest on the assumption that switching is prohibitively high, but that no on-the-job search is possible (or that the probability of finding a job is bigger when unemployed).

The growth effect of union bargaining is that employment in the rent generating sector declines. Since this is the high-tech sector of the economy, the demand for research will decline. When research sector employment declines, the growth rate of labour productivity will decline, too and so will the rate of growth of the economy.

[18] The legitimation for this assumption could be again that agents face time constraints and hence, only the unemployed can spare to time to search for new jobs.

14

An OLG Model with Growing Labour Productivity

In this chapter we will present an overlapping generations model which is based on Quang and Vousden (1999). In this model the economy consists of old and young workers. Only young workers are covered by the wage bargain of the union and it will be shown that this labour market friction will lead to a decrease in the rate of growth.

14.1 The Basic Model

14.1.1 Production

The consumption good is produced using a traditional good Y_t and a high-tech good X_t. The production function of the consumption good sector reads:

$$C_t = {Y_t^C}^{1-\beta} \cdot {X_t^C}^{\beta}, \tag{14.1}$$

where Y_t^C and X_t^C is the amount of the traditional and the high-tech, respectively, employed in the consumption sector. This sector is perfectly competitive and by profit maximisation the factor demand functions are given by[1]:

$$P_{Y_t} = (1-\beta) \cdot (Y_t^C)^{-\beta} \cdot (X_t^C)^{\beta}, \tag{14.2}$$

$$P_{X_t} = \beta \cdot (Y_t^C)^{1-\beta} \cdot (X_t^C)^{\beta-1}. \tag{14.3}$$

The traditional good Y_t is produced using labour, L_t^Y. The production function is given by:

$$Y_t = A_{t-1} \cdot L_t^Y. \tag{14.4}$$

[1] Note that we assume the consumption good to be the numéraire of the economy and hence, the price of this good is equal to one.

Equation (14.4) shows that the production technology of the traditional sector is outdated because this sector can only use last period's labour productivity A_{t-1}. The traditional goods sector is perfectly competitive. The high-tech sector also employs labour, L_t^X, but has access to the state-of-the-art production technology. Thus, labour productivity is given by A_t. So the production function of the high-tech sector is:

$$X_t = A_t \cdot L_t^X. \tag{14.5}$$

In contrast to the traditional good, the high-tech good is sold monopolistically to the consumption good sector.

The last sector of the economy is the research and development sector in which new production technologies are invented. The R&D sector uses the traditional and the high-tech good to produce these new technology vintages. The R&D production function is given by:

$$A_{t+1} - A_t = B \cdot (Y_t^{R\&D})^{1-\beta} \cdot (X_t^{R\&D})^{\beta}, \tag{14.6}$$

where B is a productivity parameter.

We assume that only one firm in the research sector performs R&D in the equilibrium, but that the risk of outside competitors drives profits down to zero. In the next period this research firm will be the new monopolist. Hence, the revenue of performing R&D is the discounted monopoly profits of next period.

To finance the venture of R&D in the meantime, when there is no flow of revenue, the research firm demands savings. An important point is that the overall amount of savings determines the absolute size of the research firm. We will later on see that this drives the growth effect of union wage bargaining.

The demand functions in the high-tech sector are very similar to the functions in the consumption good sector and are given by:

$$\frac{P_{Y_t}}{P^{R\&D}} = B \cdot (1-\beta) \cdot (Y_t^{R\&D})^{-\beta} \cdot (X_t^{R\&D})^{\beta}, \tag{14.7}$$

$$\frac{P_{X_t}}{P^{R\&D}} = \beta \cdot B \cdot (Y_t^{R\&D})^{1-\beta} \cdot (X_t^{R\&D})^{\beta-1}. \tag{14.8}$$

14.1.2 Households

Agents in the economy live for two periods. When they are young they supply inelastically labour and get wage income. The income will be consumed and saved. The old households' income, which is given by the interest on their savings, will be completely consumed. The utility function of a household is given by:

$$U_t = (C_t^{young})^{\alpha} \cdot (C_{t+1}^{old})^{1-\alpha}. \tag{14.9}$$

Households maximise equation (14.9) subject to the intertemporal budget constraint $w_t^X \cdot L_t^X + w_t^Y \cdot L_t^Y = C_t^{young} + \frac{1}{1+r} \cdot C_{t+1}^{old}$ (where w_t^i is the wage at time t in sector i and r is the rate of interest). Since N is the exogenously given amount of young in the economy, the resource constraint reads $L_t^X + L_t^Y = N$. The Lagrangian of this problem is given by:

$$\mathcal{L} = (C_t^{young})^\alpha \cdot (C_{t+1}^{old})^{1-\alpha} + \lambda \cdot \left(w_t^X \cdot L_t^X + w_t^Y \cdot L_t^Y - C_t^{young} - \frac{1}{1+r} \cdot C_{t+1}^{old} \right). \tag{14.10}$$

With this, the first order conditions are:

$$\frac{\partial \mathcal{L}}{\partial C_t^{young}} = \alpha \cdot (C_t^{young})^{\alpha-1} \cdot (C_{t+1}^{old})^{1-\alpha} - \lambda = 0, \tag{14.11}$$

$$\frac{\partial \mathcal{L}}{\partial C_{t+1}^{old}} = (1-\alpha) \cdot (C_t^{young})^{\alpha} \cdot (C_{t+1}^{old})^{-\alpha} - \frac{\lambda}{1+r} = 0, \tag{14.12}$$

$$\frac{\partial \mathcal{L}}{\partial \lambda} = w_t^X \cdot L_t^X + w_t^Y \cdot L_t^Y - C_t^{young} - \frac{1}{1+r} \cdot C_{t+1}^{old} = 0. \tag{14.13}$$

Using these first order conditions, we can determine the utility maximising consumption path of the young and therewith the savings function in the economy. Because savings are income minus consumption when young, the savings function is given by:

$$S_t = (1-\alpha) \cdot \left(w_t^X \cdot L_t^X + w_t^Y \cdot L_t^Y \right). \tag{14.14}$$

Due to the Cobb-Douglas specification of the utility function, savings are interest rate inelastic.

14.1.3 Equilibrium

In this section we will determine the equilibrium solution of the model. First of all let us derive the economy wide demand for the traditional and the high-tech good. Using equations (14.2) and (14.7) we can derive the economy wide demand for the traditional good ($Y_t = Y_t^C + Y_t^{R\&D}$). This is given by:

$$Y_t = (P_{Y_t})^{-\frac{1}{\beta}} \cdot (1-\beta)^{\frac{1}{\beta}} \cdot X_t \cdot \left(\theta_X + (1-\theta_X) \cdot (B \cdot P^{R\&D})^{\frac{1}{\beta}} \right), \tag{14.15}$$

where $\theta_X = \frac{X_t^C}{X_t}$ is the fraction of the economy wide high-tech production used in the consumption goods sector. Using equations (14.3) and (14.8) we can derive the economy wide demand for the high-tech good ($X_t = X_t^C + X_t^{R\&D}$) as:

$$X_t = (P_{X_t})^{\frac{1}{\beta-1}} \cdot (1-\beta)^{\frac{1}{1-\beta}} \cdot Y_t \cdot \left(\theta_Y + (1-\theta_Y) \cdot (B \cdot P^{R\&D})^{\frac{1}{\beta-1}} \right). \tag{14.16}$$

with $\theta_Y = \frac{Y_t^C}{Y_t}$ being the fraction of the traditional good employed in the consumption sector.

Using again the sectoral demand functions, we can derive a relationship between θ_X and θ_Y. Dividing equation (14.2) by (14.7) and equation (14.3) by (14.8), we get the following two equations showing the relative demand functions in the consumption and the research sector of the economy:

$$1 = \left(\frac{Y_t^{R\&D}}{Y_t^C}\right)^{-\beta} \cdot P^{R\&D} \cdot B \cdot \left(\frac{X_t^{R\&D}}{X_t^C}\right)^{\beta}, \tag{14.17}$$

$$1 = \left(\frac{Y_t^{R\&D}}{Y_t^C}\right)^{1-\beta} \cdot P^{R\&D} \cdot B \cdot \left(\frac{X_t^{R\&D}}{X_t^C}\right)^{\beta-1}. \tag{14.18}$$

Equalising these two equations and keeping in mind that by definition $\frac{Y_t^{R\&D}}{Y_t^C} = \frac{1-\theta_Y}{\theta_Y}$ and $\frac{X_t^{R\&D}}{X_t^C} = \frac{1-\theta_X}{\theta_X}$, it is easy to show that θ_X is equal to θ_Y. This is obvious, because the production functions in both sectors are the same. Using this and, e.g., equation (14.17) it is also easy to show that in an equilibrium $P^{R\&D}$ must be equal to $\frac{1}{B}$. If this condition was hurt, one could arbitrage and use the consumption good as an input in the research sector. Using these equilibrium conditions, the overall demand for high-tech and traditional goods can be simplified to:

$$Y_t = (P_{Y_t})^{-\frac{1}{\beta}} \cdot (1-\beta)^{\frac{1}{\beta}} \cdot X_t, \tag{14.19}$$

$$X_t = (P_{X_t})^{\frac{1}{\beta-1}} \cdot (1-\beta)^{\frac{1}{1-\beta}} \cdot Y_t. \tag{14.20}$$

Now we can derive the labour demand functions of the traditional and the high-tech sector. When deriving the labour demand of the high-tech sector, one has to keep in mind that this good is sold monopolistically, i.e., that the producer can set the price. By profit maximisation, labour demand in the two sectors is given by:

$$w_t^Y = A_{t-1} \cdot P_{Y_t}, \tag{14.21}$$

$$w_t^X = \beta \cdot A_t \cdot P_{X_t}. \tag{14.22}$$

We know that savings in the economy determine the size of the research sector, because all expenditures in the research sector must be financed in period t. So the following condition must hold:

$$(1-\alpha) \cdot (w_t^Y \cdot L_t^Y + w_t^X \cdot L_t^X) = P_{X_t} \cdot (1-\theta) \cdot X_t + P_{Y_t} \cdot (1-\theta) \cdot Y_t, \tag{14.23}$$

where $\theta = \theta_X = \theta_Y$. The lhs of equation (14.23) is the amount of savings done by the young households in the economy. The rhs depicts the expenditures of the research sector. Plugging in the wage which is given by the labour demand functions, the capital market equilibrium condition (equation (14.23)) modifies to:

$$(1-\alpha) \cdot (P_{Y_t} \cdot Y_t + P_{X_t} \cdot X_t \cdot \beta) = P_{X_t} \cdot (1-\theta) \cdot X_t + P_{Y_t} \cdot (1-\theta) \cdot Y_t. \tag{14.24}$$

Using the fact that due to outside competitors' profits in the research sector must be zero, thus, $P^{R\&D} \cdot B \cdot (Y_t^{R\&D})^{1-\beta} \cdot (X_t^{R\&D})^{\beta} = P_{X_t} \cdot (1-\theta) \cdot X_t +$

$P_{Y_t} \cdot (1-\theta) \cdot Y_t$ and use equations (14.19) and (14.20), we get after some straightforward algebraic manipulations the equilibrium amount of the high-tech and the traditional goods production used in the consumption sector:

$$\theta^* = (1-\alpha) \cdot \left((1-\beta) + \beta^2\right). \tag{14.25}$$

The amount of resources devoted to the consumption sector will be high, when the rate of time preference, α, is low. The economic intuition for this property is that when the rate of time preference is high (measured by the current consumption elasticity of the utility function) savings will be low, so the research sector is by definition small. But this implies via the resource constraint that a lot of resources are employed in the consumption sector.

The effects of β are ambiguous, because we observe two countervailing effects. One the one hand, wage income in the research sector increases, because with higher β resources are shifted to the high-tech sector *and* the rents in this sector increase. On the other hand income in the traditional sector decreases as demand shifts away from this sector. When the first effect dominates the second, the income increase in the high-tech sector outweighs the income loss in the traditional and hence, income of the young and therewith savings will increase.

To determine the growth rate of the economy we must, besides the determination of the part of resources used in the research sector, determine overall production in the high-tech and the traditional sector. Because we assume perfect mobility, the wage must be equal across sectors of the economy, hence, $w_t^Y = w_t^X$. Using this condition and plugging in the price of the traditional and the high-tech good of the economy, we get the following relative labour demand equation:

$$\frac{X_t}{Y_t} \cdot \frac{1-\beta}{\beta} = \beta \cdot \frac{A_t}{A_{t-1}}. \tag{14.26}$$

Plugging the production functions into equation (14.26) and using the resource constraint of the economy we get the equilibrium employment in the traditional and the high-tech sector of the economy:

$$(L_t^X)^* = \frac{\beta^2}{1-\beta+\beta^2} \cdot N, \tag{14.27}$$

$$(L_t^Y)^* = \frac{1-\beta}{1-\beta+\beta^2} \cdot N. \tag{14.28}$$

Using equilibrium employment and the equilibrium part of the traditional and the high-tech good used in the research sector, we get for the equilibrium rate of growth:

$$g_t^* = ((1-\alpha)\cdot((1-\beta)+\beta^2)\cdot B \cdot N \cdot \frac{1}{1-\beta+\beta^2} \cdot (\beta^2)^\beta \cdot (1-\beta)^{1-\beta} \cdot \left(\frac{1}{1+g_{t-1}^*}\right)^{1-\beta}. \tag{14.29}$$

Equation (14.29) determines a first order difference equation in the equilibrium rate of growth. A steady state exists, because $\frac{dg_t^*}{dg_{t-1}^*} < 0$. So we could, by solving the difference equation, determine the steady state rate of growth of the economy with competitive labour markets.

The economic intuition for the path dependency of the rate of growth of the economy is straightforward. When the rate of growth yesterday was very high, labour productivity of the traditional goods sector is high today, because traditional firms employ last period's production process. So c.p. more traditional goods will be produced (the relative labour demand will be biased towards L_t^Y). Hence, c.p. employment in the high-tech sector and therewith profits will be low. This discourages the research sector firm which employ less resources, implying a lower rate of growth today.

A high savings rate will be growth enhancing, because more resources can be employed in the research sector. Moreover the rate of growth will be high when the workforce is large. This scale effect is due to the fact that firstly more traditional and high-tech goods will be produced and secondly that savings will increase as the number of young in the economy rises. Both will lead to a higher rate of growth.

14.2 Union Wage Bargaining

In the preceding section we have determined the rate of growth of the OLG model for the case that labour markets were perfectly competitive. In this section we will incorporate union wage bargaining into the model and analyse the effect of this imperfection on the rate of growth.

We assume that a union at time t bargains the wage in the high-tech sector. For the outcome of the wage bargain the sequence of decisions is crucial. We assume that young workers have to decide ex-ante, based on their expectations, in which sector they would like to work. After this decision of young workers, the union will bargain the wage. The workers who will be unemployed ex-post have not the option to go back into the traditional sector, because, e.g., moving costs are prohibitively high. The allocation of the young is driven by the equality of the expected income. So workers take into account that they may be unemployed when choosing the high-tech sector, but they accept this threat, because the wage in the high-tech sector will be higher than in the traditional sector.

The utility function of the union is given by the following function:

$$U = (w_t^X - w_t^Y) \cdot L_t^X . \tag{14.30}$$

So the union wants to maximise the wage of high-tech workers over the wage that could have been earned when working in the traditional goods sector. We can determine the bargained wage by the Nash bargaining solution:

$$\Omega = (U_t - \bar{U}_t)^{\gamma} \cdot (\Pi_{X_t} - \bar{\Pi}_{X_t})^{1-\gamma} . \tag{14.31}$$

The utility the union members obtain when no agreement is reached, $\bar{U}_t$ is zero, because they have themselves committed to the high-tech sector and cannot move back into the traditional sector. The profit of the high-tech good monopolist when the bargain fails, $\bar{\Pi}_{X_t}$ is zero, because he cannot produce anything without labour. The bargained wage in this situation is given by (see the appendix for details):

$$w_t^X = \phi_X \cdot w_t^Y, \tag{14.32}$$

with $\phi_x \equiv \frac{1-\beta}{1-\beta-\gamma} > 1$. So the bargained wage is a mark-up over the wage in the traditional sector of the economy. The mark-up rises, when bargaining power of unions increases and when the wage elasticity decreases.

The decision of the young in which sector to allocate is driven by the equality of expected incomes.[2] So in an equilibrium, the following relation must hold:

$$w_t^Y = (1-u) \cdot w_t^X, \tag{14.33}$$

where u is the unemployment rate and $(1-u)$ is the probability of getting a job when the union bargains the wage. The interesting point is that the young will want to go into the high-tech sector to take advantage of the higher wage, although they know that they may not find a job and will have to stay in the high-tech sector even if they are unemployed.[3] Combining the wage equation (14.32) and the ex-ante no-arbitrage condition of young, we get the equilibrium rate of unemployment as:

$$u^* = \frac{\phi_X - 1}{\phi_X}. \tag{14.34}$$

Equation (14.34) depicts that the equilibrium rate of unemployment in the model is solely determined by the union mark-up.

With the equilibrium rate of unemployment at hands, we can finally show the effect of union wage bargaining on the rate of growth of the economy. When determining the equilibrium rate of growth, we use the same approach as in the preceding section, i.e., determining the size of the R&D sector via the savings of the economy and then determining the equilibrium allocation of resources between the high-tech and the traditional goods sector.

The size of the R&D sector is given by the same equation as in the economy without union wage bargaining. An interesting point is that the relative size of the research sector in an equilibrium is not affected by the union, hence $\theta^* = (1-\alpha) \cdot ((1-\beta)+\beta^2)$. The economic intuition for this point is that, due to the symmetry of the research and the consumption good sector, the union wage bargain will affect both sectors in the same way. So the relative size of neither the research nor the consumption sector will change.

---

[2] For simplicity we assume risk neutral individuals.

[3] A very similar argumentation, though in a different context, is applied in the famous article by Harris and Todaro (1970), in which the unemployed cannot move into the other sector, because of its different geographical location.

To determine the absolute size of the research sector and hence, the rate of growth of the economy, we use again the two labour demand equations (14.22) and (14.21). Using the wage equation (14.32), we can determine a relation between unemployment in the high-tech and the traditional sector of the economy:

$$\frac{\beta}{\phi x} = \frac{L_t^X}{L_t^Y}. \tag{14.35}$$

With the modified resource constraint, extended to account for unemployment $N = L_t^X + L_t^Y + U$, we get equilibrium employment in both sectors as:

$$L_t^X = \frac{1}{(\phi x)^2 + \beta \cdot \phi x} \cdot N, \tag{14.36}$$

$$L_t^Y = \frac{1}{\beta + \phi x} \cdot N. \tag{14.37}$$

Equations (14.36) and (14.37) show that both, employment in the high-tech sector as well as in the traditional sector will decline. This is due to the fact that unemployment occurs in the high-tech sector and that young worker move into the high-tech sector hoping for a better paid job.

Using equilibrium employment and the equilibrium size of the research sector, the equilibrium rate of growth of the unionised economy can be derived as:

$$g_t^{U*} = ((1-\alpha) \cdot ((1-\beta) + \beta^2)) \cdot B \cdot N \cdot \left(\frac{1}{1 + g_{t-1}^{U}{}^*}\right) \cdot \left(\frac{1}{(\phi x)^2 + \beta \cdot \phi x}\right)^{\beta} \cdot \left(\frac{1}{\beta + \phi x}\right)^{1-\beta}. \tag{14.38}$$

Equation (14.38) depicts that the equilibrium will decline if there is union wage bargaining in the economy or if, e.g., the bargaining power of unions increases. The union will cause unemployment, because the bargained wage will be too high. So production of secondary inputs (the high-tech good and the traditional goods) will decline. But if there are less secondary inputs, the research as well as the consumption goods will contract. So the rate of growth will decline. An interesting point in this model is that there is no reallocation effect in addition to the above mentioned "scale" effect. This is because of the symmetric structure of the economy and because savings (and hence, the size of the research sector) is not a function of the rate of interest.

14.3 Appendix

Plugging in and maximising equation (14.31) subject to the labour demand curve in the high-tech sector (given by equation (14.22)), we get the following equation:

$$\gamma \cdot \left((w_t^X - w_t^Y) \cdot L_t^X \right)^{\gamma - 1} \cdot \left(\frac{\partial L_t^X}{\partial w_t^X} \cdot (w_t^X - w_t^Y) + L_t^X \right) \cdot (\Pi_{X_t})^{1-\gamma} + (1-\gamma) \cdot (\Pi_{X_t})^{-\gamma} \cdot \frac{\partial \Pi_{X_t}}{\partial w_t^X} \cdot \left((w_t^X - w_t^Y) \cdot L_t^X \right)^{\gamma} = 0. \tag{A1}$$

Simplifying equation (A1) and multiplying both sides by the wage w_t^X, we get the following equation.

$$\gamma \cdot \left(\frac{\partial L_t^X}{\partial w_t^X} \cdot \frac{w_t^X}{L_t^X} + \frac{w_t^X}{w_t^X - w_t^Y} \right) + (1-\gamma) \cdot \frac{\partial \Pi X_t}{\partial w_t^X} \cdot \frac{w_t^X}{\Pi_{X_t}} = 0. \tag{A2}$$

Remembering firstly, that the wage elasticity of the labour demand curve is equal to the price elasticity of the high-tech good demand curve, because of the linear production technology. Secondly, that by the envelope theorem $\frac{\partial \Pi_{X_t}}{\partial w_t^X} = -L_t^X$ and that thirdly, labour's share of profits in the high-tech sector in an equilibrium is $(1-\beta)$, we can simplify equation (A3) to:

$$-\gamma \cdot (1-\beta) + \gamma \cdot \frac{w_t^X}{w_t^X - w_t^Y} - (1-\gamma) \cdot (1-\beta) = 0. \tag{A3}$$

Rearranging equation (A3) gives the wage stated in the text.

15

An Infinite Horizon Model with Growing Labour Productivity

In the preceding section, we have analysed the impact of union wage bargaining on the rate of growth in an OLG model with dual labour markets. The main drawback of this model was that after choosing a sector where to work, the workers had to stay in this sector without having the chance of moving into another sector of the economy when finding themselves unemployed. The assumption of such an artificial mobility constraint was necessary, because of the two-period structure of the model. The consequence of dropping this assumption would be that unemployed workers could move from the high-tech into the traditional sector ex-post. As such, with more realistic assumptions about worker mobility there would be no unemployment and no union growth effect in the model. Therefore the two-period structure of the model does not seem to be appropriate to analyse a dynamic economic with a dual labour market.

To avoid this assumption of the mobility constraint, we will in the following present a model with infinitely lived agents in which workers can move between the unionised and the non-unionised sector. The only restriction on intersectoral mobility is that no on the job search is possible. Thus, when switching a job, workers face the risk of being unemployed for some period of time.[1]

Nevertheless, some workers will prefer to be unemployed to get the chance of finding a job in the better paid unionised sector. So part of the unemployment will be "wait" unemployment. Workers will queue for better jobs.

The following model in which we analyse the impact of union wage bargaining and this dual labour market on the rate of growth is a modified version of Groot (2001). We will firstly present the basic model and then introduce the labour market imperfection.

[1] This assumption is not crucial for the outcome. The only important point is that the probability of finding a job when unemployed is higher than when being employed in the secondary sector (see, e.g., Groot (2001) and (2000)). But the assumption of no on the job search simplifies matters a lot.

15.1 The Basic Model

Consider an economy in which the consumption good is produced using a traditional good Y and a bundle of high-tech goods X.[2] This high-tech good bundle consists of n different high-tech good varieties. Hence, $X = (\sum_{i=1}^{n} x_i^{\alpha})^{\frac{1}{\alpha}}$. The production function of the consumption good sector reads:

$$C = Y^{1-\beta} \cdot X^{\beta}. \tag{15.1}$$

Agents only derive utility from consuming this good. Moreover it is the numéraire in the economy, hence, $P_C = 1$. Maximising the profit function $\Pi^C = C - P_Y \cdot Y - P_X \cdot X$ yields the demand for the traditional good and for a variety of the high-tech good:

$$P_Y = (1-\beta) \cdot Y^{-\beta} \cdot X^{\beta}, \tag{15.2}$$

$$P_{x_i} = \beta \cdot X^{\beta-\alpha} \cdot x_i^{\alpha-1} \cdot Y^{1-\beta}. \tag{15.3}$$

The traditional good is produced using labour. The production function is linear and reads:

$$Y = L_Y. \tag{15.4}$$

A variety of the high-tech good is also produced using labour:

$$x_i = A_i \cdot L_{X_i}, \tag{15.5}$$

where A_i is productivity of labour in a high-tech firm i. But the high-tech firms do not only produce goods, but also have a research department. This allows the high-tech firms to produce, using increasing labour productivity in the future. Labour productivity evolves according to the following function:

$$\dot{A}_i = B \cdot A_i \cdot L_{r_i}, \tag{15.6}$$

where B is the efficiency parameter of the research production process and L_{r_i} is the amount of labour employed in the research department of firm i. Furthermore, it is assumed that the amount of labour used in the research department of firm i is a fixed fraction ψ of the amount of labour used in the production process, hence, $L_{r_i} = \psi \cdot L_{x_i}$.[3]

The equilibrium allocation of the exogenously given labour pool N to the traditional goods and the high-tech good sector of the economy determines the equilibrium rate of growth of the economy. This is because with the equilibrium allocation, employment in the high-tech sector is determined and with this the size of the research departments.

[2] For notational convenience we omit time indices when variables refer to the same point of time.

[3] This assumption is the main drawback of the model. It would be much better to assume that firms choose the fraction ψ by intertemporal optimisation.

Since we assume perfect mobility between sectors, the allocation is driven by the no-arbitrage condition that the wage must be equal in both sectors.

By profit maximisation, labour demand in the two sectors of the economy is given by:[4]

$$P_Y = w_Y, \tag{15.7}$$

$$w_{x_i} = \frac{1}{(\psi+1)} \cdot A_i \cdot \alpha \cdot P_{x_i}. \tag{15.8}$$

Assuming symmetry over all high-tech good firms ($x_i = x$, $A_i = A$ and $P_{x_i} = P_x$) and plugging equations (15.2) and (15.3) into the labour demand equations, we get:

$$w_Y = (1-\beta) \cdot {L_Y}^{-\beta} \cdot n^{\frac{\beta}{\alpha}} \cdot A^{\beta} \cdot {L_x}^{\beta}, \tag{15.9}$$

$$w_x = \frac{1}{(\psi+1)} \cdot A \cdot \alpha \cdot \beta \cdot n^{\frac{\beta-\alpha}{\alpha}} \cdot A^{\beta-1} \cdot {L_x}^{\beta-1} \cdot {L_Y}^{1-\beta}. \tag{15.10}$$

With the no-arbitrage assumption and the resource constraint, we can determine equilibrium employment in both sectors of the economy using equations (15.9) and (15.10). With this equilibrium employment is given by:

$$L_Y^* = N \cdot \left(\frac{(1+\psi) \cdot (1-\beta)}{(1+\psi) \cdot (1-\beta) + \alpha \cdot \beta} \right), \tag{15.11}$$

$$n \cdot L_x \equiv L_X^* = N \cdot \left(\frac{\alpha \cdot \beta}{(1+\psi) \cdot (1-\beta) + \alpha \cdot \beta} \right). \tag{15.12}$$

Using these equations, we can determine the steady state rate of growth. In a steady state the allocation of the labour force is constant. Hence, L_Y and L_X are constant. So the rate of growth of the consumption good sector (which is equal to the rate of growth of the economy) is given by: $g_C = \beta \cdot \frac{\dot{A}}{A}$. Using the production function of the research sector and equation (15.12) the steady state rate of growth turns out to be:

$$g_C{}^* = \beta \cdot B \cdot \psi \cdot N \cdot \left(\frac{\alpha \cdot \beta}{(1+\psi) \cdot (1-\beta) + \alpha \cdot \beta} \right). \tag{15.13}$$

Equation (15.13) depicts that the steady state rate of growth increases when the research sector will be more efficient, when the labour pool increases (resource effect), when β increases and when α decreases. The economic intuition for these properties is straightforward. With a larger resource pool, production in all sectors of the economy will increase. A higher α implies that high-tech intermediate good varieties are better substitutes. With this the price

[4] When deriving the labour demand curve of a high-tech firm, we assume that the decision of one monopolistic firm will not change prices or production of the other high-tech firms (large group assumption).

which the consumption sector is willing to pay for an intermediate good variety decreases. This in turn dampens production in the high-tech sector and therewith research department employment. Higher β has the opposite effects. Inspecting the consumption good production function (15.1) it is easy to see that higher β implies a higher production elasticity of high-tech goods. With this demand and the price for an intermediate good variety increases. Hence, production and research sector employment increases.

15.2 Union Wage Bargaining

In this section we analyse the macroeconomic consequences of union wage bargaining. We assume that a union operates in every high-tech firm. A further assumption is that the bargain will be at the firm-level, i.e., all macroeconomic variables are taken as constant during the bargain.

The union wants to maximise the present value of life-time utility of all its members m, where membership is exogenous to the union. Hence, the utility function reads:

$$U = L_{x_i} \cdot V_t^{x(i)} + (m - L_{x_i}) \cdot V_t^U, \tag{15.14}$$

where $V_t^{x(i)}$ is the life-time utility of working in a high-tech firm i and V_t^U is the value of being unemployed.[5] We assume that the values of working in a high-tech firm i and of being unemployed can be described by the following continuous time Bellman's equations (see, e.g., Dixit and Pindyck (1994) or for a similar problem the appendix of part IV "Unions and Creative Destruction".):

$$\rho \cdot V_t^{x(i)} = w_t^{x_i} + a \cdot \left(V_t^U - V_t^{x(i)}\right) + \dot{V}_t^{x(i)}, \tag{15.15}$$

$$\rho \cdot V_t^U = \dot{V}_t^U + b \cdot \left(V_t^X - V_t^U\right) + c \cdot \left(V_t^Y - V_t^U\right), \tag{15.16}$$

where a is the exogenously given probability of loosing a job when employed in the high-tech sector and finding oneself unemployed and b and c are the probabilities of finding a job in the high-tech sector and the traditional sector, respectively, once unemployed. V_t^Y is the value of being employed in the traditional sector and V_t^X is the value of being employed in the high-tech sector. Because we are only interested in the steady state effects of the wage bargain, we focus on steady states. We know that in a steady state the following holds: $\frac{\dot{V}_t^U}{V_t^U} = \frac{\dot{V}_t^{x(i)}}{V_t^{x(i)}} = g_h$.

[5] Note that we assume the union only to maximise the life-value of high-tech sector workers who are employed in the production department. It will turn out that the bargained wage is a mark-up over the value of being unemployed and that the mark-up is a function of the wage elasticity of the labour demand curve and of the bargaining power of unions. As long as ψ does not change the latter variables, the applied formulation coincides with the one where the union cares for all workers in the high-tech sector.

The bargained wage is determined by the maximisation of the following Nash product:

$$\Omega = \left(U - \bar{U}\right)^{\gamma} \cdot \left(\Pi - \bar{\Pi}\right)^{1-\gamma}, \tag{15.17}$$

where $\bar{U}$ denotes the utility of the union when no agreement is reached. This is given by $m \cdot V_t^U$. Π is the profit of the firm in case an agreement is reached and $\bar{\Pi}$ is the profit when the bargain fails. We assume the latter to be zero, thus, when no agreement is reached nothing can be produced. Maximising the Nash product subject to the labour demand curve, we get the following bargained wage (for details see the appendix):

$$w_{x_i} = \phi_x \cdot (\rho - g_h) \cdot V_t^U, \tag{15.18}$$

where $\phi_x \equiv \frac{\alpha + (1-\alpha)\cdot\gamma}{\alpha}$. So the bargained wage at the firm-level is a mark-up over the (present) value of being unemployed. It is easy to see that the mark-up increases, when bargaining power of unions increases and when the price elasticity of the high-tech goods demand curve decreases. The labour demand curve of firm i will be steep in the latter case. Hence, the union can bargain a high wage without loosing too much employment.

Up to this point we have only determined the bargained wage at the firm-level. Assuming symmetry across firms we can determine the aggregate wage level in the economy. With symmetry the following holds $w_{x_i} = w_x$. Furthermore we have to determine the aggregate steady state value of being unemployed. To do this we need, besides equations (15.15) and (15.16), an equation for the value of working in the traditional sector of the economy. We do not assume exogenous job splits as, e.g., in the high-tech sector, but we assume that workers switch between the traditional sector and being unemployed, hoping to find a job in the high-tech sector.[6] We assume the probability to switch from the traditional sector to unemployment to be a fraction of the probability of loosing a job in the high-tech sector. Hence, the value of being employed in the traditional sector is given by the following Bellman's equation:

$$\rho \cdot V_t^Y = w^Y + \dot{V}_t^Y + \varphi \cdot a \cdot (V_t^U - V_t^Y), \tag{15.19}$$

with $\varphi < 1$. The steady state rate of growth of the value of being employed in the traditional sector is given by g_h.[7] Using equations (15.15), (15.16) and (15.19), we can determine the steady state value of being unemployed. This is given by the following equation:

[6] If we would not assume this kind of switching process, we would get what is sometimes called "bang-bang" solutions, i.e., that either no one would be unemployed or nobody would be employed in the traditional sector.

[7] This is because in a steady state, the wage paid in the traditional sector increases, because the relative price of the traditional good increases. The rate of this price increase is given by the growth rate of labour productivity in the high-tech sector.

$$
\begin{aligned}
(\rho - g_h) \cdot V_t^U = & \frac{b}{\rho - g_h + a} \cdot w_x + \frac{c}{\rho - g_y + \varphi \cdot a} \cdot w_Y + \\
& \left(\frac{g_h - \rho}{\rho - g_h + a} \cdot b + \frac{g_h - \rho}{\rho - g_h + \varphi \cdot a} \cdot c \right) \cdot V_t^U .
\end{aligned} \tag{15.20}
$$

To simplify the analysis, we assume that the rate of time preference approaches the growth rate of labour productivity. Furthermore, we assume a steady state on the labour market, i.e., $\dot{U} = \dot{L}_X = \dot{L}_Y = 0$.[8] With this we get for the value of being unemployed:

$$
\lim_{\rho \to g_h} (\rho - g_h) \cdot V_t^U = \frac{(1+\psi) \cdot L_X}{U} \cdot w_x + \frac{L_Y}{U} \cdot w_Y . \tag{15.21}
$$

Equation (15.21) nicely depicts that in the limit, the value of being unemployed is a weighted average of the wage in the traditional and in the high-tech sector, where the weights reflect the steady state transition probabilities from unemployment to employment. Plugging equation (15.21) into the wage equation, we get:

$$
w_x = \phi_x \cdot \left(\frac{(1+\psi) \cdot L_X}{U} \cdot w_x + \frac{L_Y}{U} \cdot w_Y \right) . \tag{15.22}
$$

Extracting w_x from the right hand side of equation (15.22) and rearranging yields:

$$
1 = \phi_x \cdot \left(\frac{(1+\varphi) \cdot L_X}{U} + z \cdot \frac{L_Y}{U} \right) , \tag{15.23}
$$

where z is the wage in the traditional sector relative to that of the high-tech sector, hence, $z = \frac{w_Y}{w_x}$. Using equations (15.10) and (15.9), we get the following relative demand equation:

$$
z = \frac{1-\beta}{\alpha} \cdot (1+\psi) \cdot \frac{L_X}{L_Y} . \tag{15.24}
$$

Note that an equilibrium implies that the wage in the traditional sector is equal to the value of being unemployed $w_Y = (\rho - g_h) \cdot V_t^U$.[9] Hence, the relative wage z is just the reciprocal of the mark-up. Finally, using the resource constraint $N = (1+\psi) \cdot L_X + L_Y + U$, equations (15.24) and (15.23) determine equilibrium unemployment in the unionised economy.

Due to the structure of the model, we cannot analytically solve for the equilibrium *levels* of employment, but for relative changes. Log-linearising

[8] For simplicity we assume the exogenous relation between employment in the research department and in the production department to be constant over time.

[9] If this condition was violated, unemployed workers would switch into the competitive traditional goods sector, because the current value there would exceed the current value of being unemployed.

equations (15.24), (15.22) and the resource constraint and denoting a relative change by a tilde, we get the following system of equations[10]:

$$\begin{pmatrix} 1 & -e_1 & (e_1 - 1) \\ 0 & -1 & 1 \\ r_U & r_X & r_Y \end{pmatrix} \cdot \begin{pmatrix} \tilde{U} \\ \tilde{L}_X \\ \tilde{L}_Y \end{pmatrix} = \begin{pmatrix} e_1 \cdot \frac{\psi}{1+\psi} \cdot \tilde{\psi} + e_1 \cdot \tilde{\phi}_x \\ \tilde{\phi}_x + \frac{\psi}{1+\psi} \cdot \tilde{\psi} \\ \tilde{N} - r_X \cdot \frac{\psi}{1+\psi} \cdot \tilde{\psi} \end{pmatrix}, \tag{15.25}$$

where $e_1 \equiv \frac{\phi_x \cdot (L_X \cdot (1+\psi))}{\phi_x \cdot (L_X \cdot (1+\psi)) + (L_Y)} < 1$ and r_i is the ratio of the labour force N employed in "sector" i, e.g., $r_U = \frac{U}{N}$. Using Cramer's rule we get the solution of the system (15.25):[11]

$$\tilde{U} = \left(r_X \cdot \tilde{\phi}_X + \tilde{N} \right), \tag{15.26}$$

$$\tilde{L}_X = \left(\tilde{N} - (1 - r_X) \cdot \tilde{\phi}_X - \frac{\psi}{1+\psi} \cdot \tilde{\psi} \right), \tag{15.27}$$

$$\tilde{L}_Y = \left(\tilde{N} + r_X \cdot \tilde{\phi}_X \right). \tag{15.28}$$

Equations (15.26), (15.27) and (15.28) show that employment in both sectors will increase when the stock of labour increases. Furthermore unemployment will also increase. Hence, the increased resource base will be allocated evenly to the economy.

A higher mark-up (e.g., due to higher bargaining power of unions)[12] raises unemployment and dampens employment in the high-tech sector.[13] Employment in the traditional sector would increase with a higher union mark-up. The economic intuition for the employment decrease in the high-tech sector is that unions bargain higher wages with the result that employment decreases. The reason for the employment increase in the traditional sector is more subtle. Note, that the impact of the exogenous parameters on traditional employment and on unemployment is symmetric. This is because of the no-arbitrage condition. With a higher mark-up, unemployment increases, which implies that the value of being unemployed decreases. So more agents will find it optimal to work in the traditional sector instead of waiting in the unemployment pool. This is because chances of getting a better paid traditional job decline. Hence, employment in the traditional sector increases. With a higher mark-up we witness a reallocation of resources towards the traditional sector,

---

[10] When log-linearising the equations, we have assumed that the production technology in the economy will not change, hence, $\tilde{\beta} = \tilde{\alpha} = 0$.

[11] Note that the determinant of the coefficient matrix is given by -1.

[12] Note that the mark-up is an endogenous variable. So we would have to plug in the linearised mark-up in the system of equations. We abandon from this for notational convenience.

[13] Inspecting equation (15.27) this will be the case when the unemployment rate is smaller than the employment rate in the high-tech sector. We assume this property to hold.

but the employment increase does not outweigh the employment decrease in the high-tech sector.

The last parameter influencing the equilibrium allocation in the union case is ψ, the part of production employment in the high-tech sector working in the research department. When this increases, employment in the production department in the high-tech sector will decrease. The intuition for this is the same as in the case with competitive labour markets: an increase in ψ acts like an increase in marginal costs. This will dampen labour demand and hence, production employment will decrease. An interesting point is that a change in ψ is neutral with respect to unemployment and to traditional sector employment. As such, there will only be a reallocation *within* the high-tech sector. The rational for this is the following: firstly note, that *production* employment in the high-tech sector decreases, but that overall employment in the high-tech sector does not need to change since ψ increased. So unemployment need not to increase. Secondly, these effects are neutral with respect to traditional sector employment, because a change in ψ does not change the value of being unemployed since L_X and ψ change. With an unchanged value of being unemployed there is no incentive for the traditional sector workers to move into unemployment. Hence, both will be constant.

Because the rate of growth is implicitly a function of L_X, due to the assumption that the ratio between production and research labour in the high-tech sector must be constant (see equation (15.6)), the growth effects of unionisation are very straightforward. We have already seen that unionisation of high-tech labour will dampen L_X. But this in turn dampens research employment. Therefore, the rate of growth in a unionised economy will decrease.

15.3 Appendix

Maximising equation (15.17) gives the following:

$$\gamma \cdot \left(L_{x_i} \cdot \left(V_t^{x(i)} - V_t^U\right)\right)^{-1} \cdot \left(\frac{\partial L_{x(i)}}{\partial w_{x_i}} \cdot \left(V_t^{x(i)} - V_t^U\right) + L_{x(i)} \cdot \frac{\partial V_t^{x(i)}}{\partial w_{x_i}}\right) \cdot (\Pi) + (1-\gamma) \cdot \left(L_{x_i} \cdot \frac{\partial \Pi}{\partial w_{x_i}}\right) = 0. \tag{A1}$$

Multiplying both sides by w_{x_i} and remembering that the wage elasticity of the labour demand curve is equal to the price elasticity of the high-tech goods demand curve, the derivative of the profit function with respect to the wage is equal to $-L_{x(i)} \cdot (1+\psi)$ (by the envelope theorem) and that the derivative of the value of being employed in firm i with respect to the wage can be derived from equation (15.15). With this (A1) modifies to:

$$\gamma \cdot \left(\frac{1}{(\alpha - 1)} + \frac{w_{x_i}}{(\rho - g_h) \cdot V_t^U - w_{x_i}}\right) - (1-\gamma) \cdot \frac{L_{x(i)} \cdot (1+\psi) \cdot w_{x_i}}{\Pi} = 0. \tag{A2}$$

Using equation (15.8) and noting that the profit of a high-tech firm is given by $\Pi = P_{x_i} \cdot x_i - (1+\psi) \cdot w_{x_i} \cdot L_{x(i)}$, equation (A2) modifies to:

$$\gamma \cdot \frac{1}{\alpha - 1} + \gamma \cdot \frac{w_{x_i}}{w_{x_i} - (\rho - g_h) \cdot V_t^U} - (1-\gamma) \cdot \frac{\alpha}{1-\alpha} = 0. \qquad \text{(A3)}$$

Rearranging (A3) gives the wage stated in the text.

Part VII

Summary and Conclusion

Summary and Conclusion

In this work we have analysed the impact of union wage bargaining on the rate of growth within a broad variety of growth models. We have focused the analysis on the effects of union wage bargaining on the two primary and most important sources of economic growth: the accumulation of capital and the investment into R&D.

As such, the first part of this work dealt with the impact of unionised labour markets within various models of capital accumulation. Capital accumulation is always done via investment, so it seems natural as a first step to analyse in which way unions will affect the investment behaviour of firms if capital adjustment is costly. We have presented that in this case the union's wage strategy is time inconsistent. The union would like to set low wages to stimulate investment, but once investment is done they will press for high wages to extract some of the quasi-rents generated by the additional stock of capital. The problem is that the firm can anticipate this behaviour of the union and hence, investment will be too low in the first place. The intuition for this point was shown in a very simple two-period textbook model. After the basic point was made, we have presented a generalised infinite horizon version of this model based on Ploeg (1987). The interesting feature of the infinite horizon model compared to the two period case is that, e.g., reputation mechanism can be implemented which can partly solve the problem of time-inconsistency.

In a second step we analysed union wage bargaining in neoclassical growth models. On the one hand, we have delineated a Solow-Swan growth model with collective bargaining and on the other hand a Diamond type OLG model. The interesting point of the Solow model with an imperfect labour market (based on Kemp and Van Long (1987)) was that there exist two polar cases when the union bargains the wage. We have either a situation in which the union sets the competitive wage and there will be no unemployment or the wage will be so high that there exists no steady state and the stock of capital is run down to zero. The intuition for this point was that the union wanted to maximise the present value of the stream of wage bills. But with this the union faces an intertemporal trade-off: increasing the wage today implying that capital accumulation declines and hence, the feasible wages in the future or setting a low wage to foster capital accumulation. It is obvious that the question which strategy is optimal depends on the rate of time preference. If this exceeds some threshold, the union will set a wage that is too high to ensure steady state growth. Besides this standard model, we analysed what would happen if, e.g., the production technology changed. This was done in a model by Palokangas (1989) in which a convex-concave production technology is applied. The result of this modified Solow growth model is that the existence of intermediate cases is possible. These intermediate cases are characterised by unemployment without the capital stock being run down to zero. Thus, the results derived in the standard model react very sensitive to changes in the assumptions.

To complete the picture on the impact of collective bargaining in neoclassical growth models, we have presented a Diamond OLG model with unionised labour markets. The crucial difference is that in the OLG model there exists a steady state with unemployment even in the standard case. The intuition as to why the results stands in contrast to that of the Solow model is that in the Diamond model it was assumed that the union only covers one generation of young. With this the bargaining problem is inherently static (see, e.g., Devereux and Lockwood (1991)). Hence, the union does not face this intertemporal trade-off and this instability problem does not arise. The effect of union wage bargaining in this model is that because the union rations labour, the marginal product of capital and as such, the interest rate will decline. This dampens savings and the steady state stock of capital will be lower than in the competitive case.

In the last section of this part we have integrated collective bargaining into a simple endogenous growth model with capital accumulation, namely the AK model. This model is a variant of Daveri and Tabellini (2000) and assumes that the accumulation of capital does not only increase the stock of capital, but also, via a learning-by-doing research spill-over, total factor productivity. So in this model the economy can grow unboundedly only by the accumulation of capital. The effects of the union are very much the same as in the Diamond model with the exception that the decrease of savings does not only lower the stock of capital, but also the rate of growth.

Summarising we can state that it was shown that the steady state stock of capital will decline when unions bargain the wage, except in the case where the union has an infinite planning horizon, because in this case it faces an intertemporal trade-off. The general economic intuition for this decline is that:

1. the wage policy of the union is time inconsistent which is anticipated by the firm,
2. the union extracts income from capital income earners and hence, decreases savings,

3. and the union rations labour with the consequence that the interest rate and hence, savings decline.

This decline is more pronounced the more short sighted the union is (the higher is its rate of time preference) and the shorter the period for which wage contracts last, because with this the problem of time-inconsistency is more severe.

The following parts of the work dealt with the effect of union wage bargaining in models in which there is endogenous growth caused by R&D.

The first model which has been analysed was an extended version of the seminal growth model by Aghion and Howitt (1992). The main idea of this growth model is that a monopolist sells an intermediate good to the consumption good sector. Furthermore, there is a research sector in which research firms employ resources to invent more efficient intermediate goods and become the new monopolist, therefore, growth is due to creative destruction. It is assumed that there are two factors of production: high-skilled and low-skilled labour. Both are employed in the intermediate sector whereas only high-skilled labour is employed in the research sector. The union bargains the low-skilled wage and causes low-skilled unemployment. In which way this affects high-skilled employment in the research sector is ambiguous. The demand for high-skilled in the intermediate as well as in the research sector will decline if the union bargains the low-skilled wage. So the growth effect depends on whether these shifts are symmetric or not. It was shown that this crucially hinges on the assumption about the production function in the intermediate sector. In the Cobb-Douglas case both high-skilled demand curve will decline symmetrically implying that the rate of growth will not change. If high-skilled and low-skilled labour are bad (good) substitutes, $\sigma < (>) 1$, the decrease in high-skill labour demand in the intermediate sector is stronger (weaker) than that in the research sector implying that resources are shifted into the research (intermediate) sector. With this, the rate of growth will increase (decline). So union wage bargaining might foster economic growth.

To check for robustness of this result we have integrated collective bargaining into the second standard R&D growth model, namely into a model with expanding product variety. In this case, growth is not driven by creative destruction, but by the fact that a research sector introduces new varieties of an intermediate good and that with this the division of labour gets deeper. An interesting point is that the results on the impact of union wage bargaining that were derived in the chapter on unions and creative destruction, also hold in the growth model with expanding product varieties.

An appealing feature of the model is that it is quite easy to handle. Therefore, we took up the opportunity to integrate taxation into the model. This has the advantage that firstly we take a general equilibrium view and that secondly we can analyse the effects of revenue neutral tax policies on unemployment and growth. It was shown that the considered taxes have no direct effects on the rate of growth, but that they alter low-skilled employment and hence, influence the rate of growth indirectly. Alas, the impact of taxation is ambiguous, because the impact of a change in low-skilled labour is ambiguous. Furthermore we have analysed tax switches that keep the governmental budget unchanged. The problem was that the impact of these tax switches is very complex and as such, we were not able to derive clear cut results.

The last variant of the expanding product variety model which we considered, was a model with a slightly changed assumption about the production structure in the economy. In contrast to the basic model, we assumed that low-skilled labour is employed in the intermediate and in the research sector and that high-skilled labour is only employed in the research sector. The reason for changing this assumption was firstly, that up to that point we had focused very much on models in which the union had no direct effects on research sector employment. In these models, the union only changed the allocation of the high-skilled labour pool. It did not ration resources that were directly employed in the research sector. Hence, this analysis of union behaviour was quite optimistic. In this model we wanted to analyse the direct effects of collective bargaining and wanted to check if the result that the union might be growth enhancing is robust or whether it is due to this very special assumption about the production structure of the economies in the preceding part. Secondly, simultaneous bargaining seems to be a real world feature which we wanted to integrate in the analysis.

The interesting point of this model is that in this case the union will unambiguously dampen the rate of growth and that this decrease in the rate of growth will be more fierce when union bargaining power in the research sector is stronger than in the intermediate sector. The reason why the result is different from that of the basic model is that we did not consider the possible growth enhancing effect of high-skilled labour migration from the intermediate into the research sector, because high-skilled labour is only employed in the research sector. Hence, only the growth dampening effect of a smaller resource base survives. Thus the result that the union may foster growth could be too optimistic and misleading.

Summarising, we can conclude that the effect of union wage bargaining in the two standard models of growth through R&D, expanding product variety and creative destruction, is ambiguous. Collective bargaining decreases the available resource base, but might also cause a reallocation of resources. Whether the union will be growth dampening, enhancing or neutral crucially depends on the assumed production functions and on the structure of production, i.e., which resources are employed in which sector of the economy.

The last part eventually analysed models in which the notion of dual labour markets is integrated. Dual labour markets imply that a unionised sector with high paid jobs coexist with a competitive sector with low paid jobs. In these models it is assumed that the high-tech sector is unionised and the traditional sector is characterised by competitive labour markets. When the union bargains the wage in the high-tech sector, production in this sector will decline, implying that the incentive for R&D declines, too. Hence, collective bargaining is growth dampening.

Concluding, the analysis suggests three main points:

1. Union wage bargaining affects the rate of growth of an economy. Growth models with perfectly competitive labour markets can lead to wrong conclusions.
2. In the majority of models, the rate of growth or the steady state will decline. Hence, unions can have negative static and dynamic effects.
3. Nevertheless, depending on the specification of the production side of the economy unions might also foster economic growth.

So it seems to be important to integrate union wage bargaining into growth models and future research (theoretical as well as empirical) should take up this point.

References

1. Aghion, Philippe and Peter Howitt (1992). *A Model of Growth through Creative Destruction*. Econometrica 60: PP 323-351.
2. Aghion, Philippe and Peter Howitt (1994). *Growth and Unemployment*. Review of Economic Studies 61: PP 477-494.
3. Aghion, Philippe and Peter Howitt (1999). *Endogenous Growth*. MIT Press.
4. Arrow, Kenneth J. (1962). *The Economic Implications of Learning-By-Doing*. Review of Economic Studies 29: PP 155-173.
5. Atkinson, Anthony B. and Stiglitz Joseph E. (1980). *Lectures in Public Economics*. MacGraw Hill.
6. Barro, Robert J., (1990). *Government Spending in a Simple Model of Endogenous Growth*. Journal of Political Economy 98: PP S103-S125.
7. Barro, Robert J. and Xavier Sala-i-Martin, (1995). *Economic Growth*. McGraw-Hill.
8. Bean, Charles and Christopher Pissarides (1993). *Unemployment, Consumption, and Growth*. European Economic Review 37: PP 837-859.
9. Binmore, Ken (1987). *Nash Bargaining Theory II*. The Economics of Bargaining (Ken Binmore and Partha Dasgupta, eds): PP 61-76. Cambridge University Press.
10. Binmore, Ken, Rubinstein, Ariel and Asher Wolinsky (1986). *The Nash Bargaining in Economic Modelling*. Rand Journal of Economics 17: PP 176-188.
11. Binmore, Ken; Avner Shaked and John Sutton. *An Outside Option Experiment*. Quarterly Journal of Economics 104: PP 753-70.
12. Birk, Angela and Jochen Michaelis (2002). *Employment and Growth Effects of Tax Reforms*. Working Paper Nr. 37/02, University of Kassel.
13. Blanchard, Olivier and Stanley Fischer (1989). *Lectures in Macroeconomics*. MIT Press.
14. Blanchard, Olivier and Justin Wolfers (2000). *The Role of Shocks and Institutions in the Rise of European Unemployment: The Aggregate Evidence*. The Economic Journal 110: PP C1-33.
15. Booth, Alison, (1996). *The Economics of the Trade Union*. Cambridge University Press.

16. BRÄUNINGER, MICHAEL (2000). *Wage Bargaining, Unemployment and Growth.* Journal of Institutional and Theoretical Economics (JITE) 156: PP 646-660.
17. BULOW, JEREMY I. AND LAWRENCE H. SUMMERS (1986). *A Theory of Dual Labor Markets with Application to Industrial Policy, Discrimination, and Keynsian Unemployment.* Journal of Labor Economics 4: PP 376-414.
18. BURDA, MICHAEL (1988). *"Wait Unemployment" in Europe.* Economic Policy 7: PP 391-425.
19. CABALLERO, RICARDO (1999). *Aggregate Investment.* The Handbook of Macroeconomics (John B. Taylor and Michael Woodford, eds): Ch. 12, PP 813-862. Elsvier.
20. CARLIN, WENDY AND DAVID SOSKICE (1990).*Macroeconomics and the Wage Bargain: A Modern Approach to Employment, Inflation and the Exchange Rate.* Oxford University Press.
21. CESIFO DICE. http://www.ifo.de/pls/diceguest/
22. CLARK, KIM B. AND LAWRENCE H. SUMMERS (1979). *Labor Market Dynamics and Unemployment: A Reconsideration.* Brookings Papers on Economic Activity 79: PP 13-60.
23. COLES, MELVYN G. AND ABHINAY MUTHOO (2003). *Bargaining in a Non-Stationary Environment.* Journal of Economic Theory, 109: PP 70-89.
24. COTO-MILÁN, PABLO (1999). *Utility and Production.* Springer.
25. DAVERI FRANCESCO AND GUIDO TABELLINI (2000). *Unemployment, Growth and Taxation in Industrial Countries.* Economic Policy 30: PP 49-104.
26. DEVEREUX, MICHAEL B. AND BEN LOCKWOOD (1991). *Trade Unions, Non-Binding Wage Aggrements, and Capital Accumulation.* European Economic Review 35: 1411-1426.
27. DIAMOND, PETER A. (1965). *National Debt in a Neoclassical Growth Model.* American Economic Review 55: PP 1126-1150.
28. DIXIT, AVINASH K. (1990). *Optimization in Economic Theory.* 2nd edition, Oxford University Press.
29. DIXIT, AVINASH K. AND ROBERT S. PINDYCK (1994). *Invetsment under Uncertainty.* Princeton University Press.
30. EASTERLY, WILLIAM AND SERGIO REBELO (1993). *Fiscal Policy and Economic Growth: An Empirical Investigation.* Journal of Monetary Economics 32: 417-458.
31. EDIN, PERS-ANDERS AND JOHNNY ZETTERBERG (1992). *Interindustry Wage Differentials: Evidence from Sweden and a Comparison with the United States.* American Economic Review 82: PP 1341-1349.
32. ETHIER, WILFRED (1982). *National and International Returns to Scale in the Modern Theory of International Trade.* American Economic Review 72: PP 389-405.
33. FEHR, ERNST AND SIMON GAECHTER (1998). *Reciprocity and Economics: The Economic Implications of Homo Reciprocans.* European Economic Review 42: PP 845-859.
34. GOERKE, LASZLO (2002). *Taxes and Unemployment: Collective Bargaining and Efficiency Wage Models.* Kluwer Acadamic Publishers.
35. GRAVELLE, HUGH AND RAY REESE, (1992). *Microeconomics.* 2nd edition, Longman.

36. Grossman, Gene M. and Elhanan Helpman (1991). *Innovation and Growth in the Global Economy.* MIT Press.
37. Groot de, Henri-L. F. (1996). *The Struggle for Rents in a Schumpeterian Economy.* mimeo Tilburg University, Department of Economics and CentER.
38. Groot de, Henri-L. F. (2000). *Growth, Unemployment and Deindustrialization* . Edward Elgar.
39. Groot de, Henri-L. F. (2001). *Unemployment, Growth and Trade Unions.* Growth and Change 32: PP 69-91.
40. Grout, Paul A. (1984). *Investment and Wages in the Absence of Binding Wage Contracts: A Nash Bargaining Approach.* Econometrica 52: PP 449-460
41. Hamermesh, Daniel S. (1993). *Labor Demand.* Princeton University Press.
42. Harris, John R. and Michael P. Todaro (1970). *Migration, Unemployment and Development: A Two-Sector Analysis.* American Economic Review 60: PP 126-142.
43. Hayashi, Fumio (1982). *Tobin's Marginal q and Average q: A Neoclassical Interpretation.* Econometrica 50: PP 213-224.
44. Heijdra, Ben and Frederick van der Ploeg (2002). *Foundations of Modern Macroeconomics.* Oxford University Press.
45. Holmlund, Bertil (1997). *Macroeconomic Implications of Cash Limits in the Public Sector.* Economica 64: PP 49-62.
46. Jerger, Jürgen and Jochen Michaelis (1999). *Profit Sharing, Capital Formation and the NAIRU.* Scandinavian Journal of Economics 101: PP 257-275.
47. Jones, Larry E., Rudolfo E. Manuelli and Rossi Peter E. (1993). *Optimal Taxation in Models of Endogenous Growth* Journal of Political Economy 101: PP 485-517.
48. Jones, Charles I. (2002). *Introduction to Economic Growth.* 2nd edition, Norton.
49. Kamien, Morton I. and Nancy L. Schwartz (1991). *Dynamic Optimization.* 2nd edition, Elsevier.
50. Kim, Se-Jik (1998). *Growth Effect of Taxes in an Endogenous Growth Model: To What Extent Do Taxes Affect Economic Growth?.* Journal of Economic Dynamics and Control 23: PP 125-158.
51. Kemp, Murray C. and Ngo Van Long (1987). *Union Power in the Long Run.* Scandinavian Journal of Economics 89: PP 103-113.
52. Kemp, Murray C. and Ngo Van Long (1990). *Die langfristige Entwicklung der Gewerkschaftsmacht bei optimalem Sparen der Kapitaleigner.* Ifo-Studien: PP 229-244.
53. Kneller, Richard, Michael F. Bleany and Norman Gemmell (1999). *Fiscal Policy and Growth: Evidence from the OECD Countries.* Journal of Public Economics 74: PP 171-190.
54. Kolm, Ann-Sofie (1998).*Differentiated Payroll Taxes, Unemployment and Welfare.* Journal of Public Economics 70: PP 255-271.
55. Layard, Richard and Stephen Nickell (1990). *Is Unemployment Lower if Unions Bargain over Employment?.* Quarterly Journal of Economics 105: PP 773-787.

56. LAYARD, RICHARD, STEPHEN NICKELL AND RICHARD JACKMAN, (1991). *Unemployment - Macroeconomic Performance and the Labour Market.* Oxford University Press.
57. LINGENS, JÖRG (2003). *The Impact of A Unionised Labour Market in a Schumpeterian Growth Model.* Labour Economics 10: PP 91-104.
58. LINGENS, JÖRG (2002). *Growth and Employment Effects of Unions in a Simple Endogenous Growth Model.* Working Paper 34/02 of the University of Kassel.
59. LUCAS, ROBERT E. (1990). *Supply-Side Economics: An Analytical Review.* Oxford Economic Papers 42: PP 293-316.
60. MANZINI, PAOLA, (1998). *Game Theoretic Models of Wage Bargaining.* Journal of Economic Surveys 12: PP 1-49.
61. MENDOZA, ENRIQUE E., GIAN MARIA MILESI-FERETTI AND PATRICK ASEA (1997). *On the Ineffectiveness of Tax Policy in Altering Long-Run Growth: Harberger's Superneutrality Conjecture.* Journal of Public Economics 66: 99-126.
62. MUTHOO, ABHINAY (1999). *Bargaining Theory with Applications.* Cambrigde University Press.
63. NASH, JOHN (1950). *The Bargaining Problem.* Econometrica, 21: PP 155-162.
64. OECD, (2002). *OECD Economic Outlook.*
65. OSBORNE, MARTIN J. AND ARIEL RUBINSTEIN, (1994). *A Course in Game Theory.* The MIT Press.
66. OSWALD, ANDREW (1985). *The Economics of the Trade Union: An Introductory Survey.* Scandinavian Journal of Economics 87, PP 85-113.
67. PALOKANGAS, TAPIO (1989). *Union Power in the Long Run Reconsidered.* Scandinavian Journal of Economics 91: PP 625-635.
68. PALOKANGAS, TAPIO (1996). *Endogenous Growth and Collective Bargaining.* Journal of Economic Dynamics and Control 20: PP 925-944
69. PALOKANGAS, TAPIO (2000). *Labour Unions, Public Policy and Economic Growth.* Cambridge University Press.
70. PENCAVEL, JOHN (1994). *Labor Markets under Trade Unionism.* Blackwell.
71. THE PENN WORLD TABLES, MARK 5.6. http://www.nber.org/pub/pwt56/.
72. PHELPS, EDMUND S. (1968). *Money-Wage Dynamics and Labor Market Equilibrium.* Journal of Political Economy 76: 678-711.
73. PISSARIDES, CHRISTOPHER A. (2000). *Equilibrium Unemployment Theory.* MIT Press, second edition.
74. PLÜGER, MICHAEL (1997). *On the Employment Effects of Revenue Neutral Tax Reforms.* FinanzArchiv 54: 430-446.
75. PLOEG VAN DER, FREDERICK (1987). *Trade Unions, Investment, and Employment.* European Economic Review 31: PP 1465-1492.
76. QUANG, DOAN HONG AND NEIL VOUSDEN, (1999). *Unionisation, Unemployment and Economic Growth.* Mimeo.
77. ROMER, PAUL M. (1986). *Increasing Returns and Long Run Growth.* Journal of Political Economy 94: PP 1002-1037.
78. ROMER, PAUL M. (1990). *Endogenous Technological Change.* Journal of Political Economy 98: PP S71-S102.
79. RUBINSTEIN (1982). *Perfect Equilibrium in a Bargaining Model.* Econometrica 50: PP 97-109.

80. SAINT-PAUL GILLES (1996). *Dual Labor Markets.* MIT Press.
81. SALA-I-MARTIN, XAVIER (1991). *Internal and External Adjustment Costs in the Theory of Fixed Investment.* Yale University mimeo.
82. SCHUMPETER, JOSEPH (1911). *Theorie der wirtschaftlichen Entwicklung.* 9th edition, Duncker&Humblot.
83. SHAKED, AVNER AND JOHN SUTTON, (1984). *Involuntary Unemployment as a Perfect Equilibrium in a Bargaining Model.* Econometrica 52: PP 1351-1364.
84. SØRENSEN, PETER BIRCH (1997). *Public Finance Solution to European Unemployment.* Economic Policy 25: PP 221-251
85. SOLOW, ROBERT (1956). *A Contribution to the Theory of Economic Growth.* Quaterly Journal of Economics 70: PP 65-94.
86. MACDONALD, IAN AND ROBERT SOLOW (1985). *Wages and Employment in a Segmented Labor Market.* Quaterly Journal of Economics 100: PP 1115-1141.
87. STOCKEY, NANCY L. AND SERGIO REBELO (1995). *The Growth Effects of Flat-Rate Taxes.* Journal of Political Economy 103: PP 519-550.
88. TURNOVSKY, STEPHEN (2000). *Macroeconomic Dynamics.* MIT Press.
89. WALSH, CARL (1998). *Monetary Theory and Policy.* MIT Press.
90. WEISS, PIA (2001). *Unemployment in Open Economies.* Springer.
91. YOUNG, ALWYN (1995). *The Tyranny of Numbers: Confronting the Statistical Realities of the East Asian Growth Experience.* Quarterly Journal of Economics 110: PP 641-680.

Lecture Notes in Economics and Mathematical Systems

For information about Vols. 1–449
please contact your bookseller or Springer-Verlag

Vol. 450: P. M. Pardalos, D. W. Hearn, W. W. Hager, (Eds.), Network Optimization. VIII, 485 pages, 1997.

Vol. 451: M. Salge, Rational Bubbles. Theoretical Basis, Economic Relevance, and Empirical Evidence with a Special Emphasis on the German Stock Market.IX, 265 pages. 1997.

Vol. 452: P. Gritzmann, R. Horst, E. Sachs, R. Tichatschke (Eds.), Recent Advances in Optimization. VIII, 379 pages. 1997.

Vol. 453: A. S. Tangian, J. Gruber (Eds.), Constructing Scalar-Valued Objective Functions. VIII, 298 pages. 1997.

Vol. 454: H.-M. Krolzig, Markov-Switching Vector Autoregressions. XIV, 358 pages. 1997.

Vol. 455: R. Caballero, F. Ruiz, R. E. Steuer (Eds.), Advances in Multiple Objective and Goal Programming. VIII, 391 pages. 1997.

Vol. 456: R. Conte, R. Hegselmann, P. Terna (Eds.), Simulating Social Phenomena. VIII, 536 pages. 1997.

Vol. 457: C. Hsu, Volume and the Nonlinear Dynamics of Stock Returns. VIII, 133 pages. 1998.

Vol. 458: K. Marti, P. Kall (Eds.), Stochastic Programming Methods and Technical Applications. X, 437 pages. 1998.

Vol. 459: H. K. Ryu, D. J. Slottje, Measuring Trends in U.S. Income Inequality. XI, 195 pages. 1998.

Vol. 460: B. Fleischmann, J. A. E. E. van Nunen, M. G. Speranza, P. Stähly, Advances in Distribution Logistic. XI, 535 pages. 1998.

Vol. 461: U. Schmidt, Axiomatic Utility Theory under Risk. XV, 201 pages. 1998.

Vol. 462: L. von Auer, Dynamic Preferences, Choice Mechanisms, and Welfare. XII, 226 pages. 1998.

Vol. 463: G. Abraham-Frois (Ed.), Non-Linear Dynamics and Endogenous Cycles. VI, 204 pages. 1998.

Vol. 464: A. Aulin, The Impact of Science on Economic Growth and its Cycles. IX, 204 pages. 1998.

Vol. 465: T. J. Stewart, R. C. van den Honert (Eds.), Trends in Multicriteria Decision Making. X, 448 pages. 1998.

Vol. 466: A. Sadrieh, The Alternating Double Auction Market. VII, 350 pages. 1998.

Vol. 467: H. Hennig-Schmidt, Bargaining in a Video Experiment. Determinants of Boundedly Rational Behavior. XII, 221 pages. 1999.

Vol. 468: A. Ziegler, A Game Theory Analysis of Options. XIV, 145 pages. 1999.

Vol. 469: M. P. Vogel, Environmental Kuznets Curves. XIII, 197 pages. 1999.

Vol. 470: M. Ammann, Pricing Derivative Credit Risk. XII, 228 pages. 1999.

Vol. 471: N. H. M. Wilson (Ed.), Computer-Aided Transit Scheduling. XI, 444 pages. 1999.

Vol. 472: J.-R. Tyran, Money Illusion and Strategic Complementarity as Causes of Monetary Non-Neutrality. X, 228 pages. 1999.

Vol. 473: S. Helber, Performance Analysis of Flow Lines with Non-Linear Flow of Material. IX, 280 pages. 1999.

Vol. 474: U. Schwalbe, The Core of Economies with Asymmetric Information. IX, 141 pages. 1999.

Vol. 475: L. Kaas, Dynamic Macroeconomics with Imperfect Competition. XI, 155 pages. 1999.

Vol. 476: R. Demel, Fiscal Policy, Public Debt and the Term Structure of Interest Rates. X, 279 pages. 1999.

Vol. 477: M. Théra, R. Tichatschke (Eds.), Ill-posed Variational Problems and Regularization Techniques. VIII, 274 pages. 1999.

Vol. 478: S. Hartmann, Project Scheduling under Limited Resources. XII, 221 pages. 1999.

Vol. 479: L. v. Thadden, Money, Inflation, and Capital Formation. IX, 192 pages. 1999.

Vol. 480: M. Grazia Speranza, P. Stähly (Eds.), New Trends in Distribution Logistics. X, 336 pages. 1999.

Vol. 481: V. H. Nguyen, J. J. Strodiot, P. Tossings (Eds.). Optimation. IX, 498 pages. 2000.

Vol. 482: W. B. Zhang, A Theory of International Trade. XI, 192 pages. 2000.

Vol. 483: M. Königstein, Equity, Efficiency and Evolutionary Stability in Bargaining Games with Joint Production. XII, 197 pages. 2000.

Vol. 484: D. D. Gatti, M. Gallegati, A. Kirman, Interaction and Market Structure. VI, 298 pages. 2000.

Vol. 485: A. Garnaev, Search Games and Other Applications of Game Theory. VIII, 145 pages. 2000.

Vol. 486: M. Neugart, Nonlinear Labor Market Dynamics. X, 175 pages. 2000.

Vol. 487: Y. Y. Haimes, R. E. Steuer (Eds.), Research and Practice in Multiple Criteria Decision Making. XVII, 553 pages. 2000.

Vol. 488: B. Schmolck, Ommitted Variable Tests and Dynamic Specification. X, 144 pages. 2000.

Vol. 489: T. Steger, Transitional Dynamics and Economic Growth in Developing Countries. VIII, 151 pages. 2000.

Vol. 490: S. Minner, Strategic Safety Stocks in Supply Chains. XI, 214 pages. 2000.

Vol. 491: M. Ehrgott, Multicriteria Optimization. VIII, 242 pages. 2000.

Vol. 492: T. Phan Huy, Constraint Propagation in Flexible Manufacturing. IX, 258 pages. 2000.

Vol. 493: J. Zhu, Modular Pricing of Options. X, 170 pages. 2000.

Vol. 494: D. Franzen, Design of Master Agreements for OTC Derivatives. VIII, 175 pages. 2001.

Vol. 495: I Konnov, Combined Relaxation Methods for Variational Inequalities. XI, 181 pages. 2001.

Vol. 496: P. Weiß, Unemployment in Open Economies. XII, 226 pages. 2001.

Vol. 497: J. Inkmann, Conditional Moment Estimation of Nonlinear Equation Systems. VIII, 214 pages. 2001.

Vol. 498: M. Reutter, A Macroeconomic Model of West German Unemployment. X, 125 pages. 2001.

Vol. 499: A. Casajus, Focal Points in Framed Games. XI, 131 pages. 2001.

Vol. 500: F. Nardini, Technical Progress and Economic Growth. XVII, 191 pages. 2001.

Vol. 501: M. Fleischmann, Quantitative Models for Reverse Logistics. XI, 181 pages. 2001.

Vol. 502: N. Hadjisavvas, J. E. Martínez-Legaz, J.-P. Penot (Eds.), Generalized Convexity and Generalized Monotonicity. IX, 410 pages. 2001.

Vol. 503: A. Kirman, J.-B. Zimmermann (Eds.), Economics with Heterogenous Interacting Agents. VII, 343 pages. 2001.

Vol. 504: P.-Y. Moix (Ed.),The Measurement of Market Risk. XI, 272 pages. 2001.

Vol. 505: S. Voß, J. R. Daduna (Eds.), Computer-Aided Scheduling of Public Transport. XI, 466 pages. 2001.

Vol. 506: B. P. Kellerhals, Financial Pricing Models in Continuous Time and Kalman Filtering. XIV, 247 pages. 2001.

Vol. 507: M. Koksalan, S. Zionts, Multiple Criteria Decision Making in the New Millenium. XII, 481 pages. 2001.

Vol. 508: K. Neumann, C. Schwindt, J. Zimmermann, Project Scheduling with Time Windows and Scarce Resources. XI, 335 pages. 2002.

Vol. 509: D. Hornung, Investment, R&D, and Long-Run Growth. XVI, 194 pages. 2002.

Vol. 510: A. S. Tangian, Constructing and Applying Objective Functions. XII, 582 pages. 2002.

Vol. 511: M. Külpmann, Stock Market Overreaction and Fundamental Valuation. IX, 198 pages. 2002.

Vol. 512: W.-B. Zhang, An Economic Theory of Cities.XI, 220 pages. 2002.

Vol. 513: K. Marti, Stochastic Optimization Techniques. VIII, 364 pages. 2002.

Vol. 514: S. Wang, Y. Xia, Portfolio and Asset Pricing. XII, 200 pages. 2002.

Vol. 515: G. Heisig, Planning Stability in Material Requirements Planning System. XII, 264 pages. 2002.

Vol. 516: B. Schmid, Pricing Credit Linked Financial Instruments. X, 246 pages. 2002.

Vol. 517: H. I. Meinhardt, Cooperative Decision Making in Common Pool Situations. VIII, 205 pages. 2002.

Vol. 518: S. Napel, Bilateral Bargaining. VIII, 188 pages. 2002.

Vol. 519: A. Klose, G. Speranza, L. N. Van Wassenhove (Eds.), Quantitative Approaches to Distribution Logistics and Supply Chain Management. XIII, 421 pages. 2002.

Vol. 520: B. Glaser, Efficiency versus Sustainability in Dynamic Decision Making. IX, 252 pages. 2002.

Vol. 521: R. Cowan, N. Jonard (Eds.), Heterogenous Agents, Interactions and Economic Performance. XIV, 339 pages. 2003.

Vol. 522: C. Neff, Corporate Finance, Innovation, and Strategic Competition. IX, 218 pages. 2003.

Vol. 523: W.-B. Zhang, A Theory of Interregional Dynamics. XI, 231 pages. 2003.

Vol. 524: M. Frölich, Programme Evaluation and Treatment Choise. VIII, 191 pages. 2003.

Vol. 525:S. Spinler, Capacity Reservation for Capital-Intensive Technologies. XVI, 139 pages. 2003.

Vol. 526: C. F. Daganzo, A Theory of Supply Chains. VIII, 123 pages. 2003.

Vol. 527: C. E. Metz, Information Dissemination in Currency Crises. XI, 231 pages. 2003.

Vol. 528: R. Stolletz, Performance Analysis and Optimization of Inbound Call Centers. X, 219 pages. 2003.

Vol. 529: W. Krabs, S. W. Pickl, Analysis, Controllability and Optimization of Time-Discrete Systems and Dynamical Games. XII, 187 pages. 2003.

Vol. 530: R. Wapler, Unemployment, Market Structure and Growth. XXVII, 207 pages. 2003.

Vol. 531: M. Gallegati, A. Kirman, M. Marsili (Eds.), The Complex Dynamics of Economic Interaction. XV, 402 pages, 2004.

Vol. 532: K. Marti, Y. Ermoliev, G. Pflug (Eds.), Dynamic Stochastic Optimization. VIII, 336 pages. 2004.

Vol. 533: G. Dudek, Collaborative Planning in Supply Chains. X, 234 pages. 2004.

Vol. 534: M. Runkel, Environmental and Resource Policy for Consumer Durables. X, 197 pages. 2004.

Vol. 535: X. Gandibleux, M. Sevaux, K. Sörensen, V.T'kindt (Eds.), Metaheuristics for Multiobjective Optimisation. IX, 249 pages. 2004.

Vol. 536: R. Brüggemann, Model Reduction Methods for Vector Autoregressive Processes. X, 218 pages. 2004.

Vol. 537: A. Esser, Pricing in (In)Complete Markets. XI, 122 pages, 2004.

Vol. 538: S. Kokot, The Econometrics of Sequential Trade Models. XI, 193 pages. 2004.

Vol. 539: N. Hautsch, Modelling Irregularly Spaced Financial Data. XII, 291 pages. 2004.

Vol. 540: H. Kraft, Optimal Portfolios with Stochastic Interest Rates and Defaultable Assets. X, 173 pages. 2004.

Vol. 541:

Vol. 542: J. Lingens, Union Wage Bargaining and Economic Growth. XIII. 199 pages. 2004.